# CANDLE YOUTH BIBLE

Published by Candle Books
Part of the SPCK Group
Studio 101, The Record Hall
16-16A Baldwin's Gardens
London EC1N 7RJ

ISBN 978-1-78128-462-9

First edition 2023

1 3 5 7 9 10 8 6 4 2

**Acknowledgments**
Scripture quotations are taken from the *Holy Bible*, New Living Translation, copyright © 1996, 2004, 2015 by Tyndale House Foundation; Anglicized Text Version, © SPCK 2018. Used by permission of Tyndale House Publishers, Inc., Carol Stream, Illinois 60188, USA, and SPCK, London, UK. All rights reserved. New Living Translation, *NLT* and the New Living Translation logo are registered trademarks of Tyndale House Ministries.

A catalogue record for this book is available from the British Library

Produced on paper from sustainable sources
Printed and bound by Dream Colour (Hong Kong) Printing Ltd

Revd Ryan Carter & Revd Dr Don L. Davis

# CANDLE YOUTH BIBLE

Explore 90 passages
from the NLT Holy Bible
(Anglicized)

**CANDLE BOOKS**

# Table of Contents

## Prologue:

**From the Beginning to the Fullness of Time**

### Creation and the Fall

### The Promise and the Patriarchs

### Deliverance from Egypt

### From Egypt to Canaan

### The Promised Land

### The Exile

### The Remnant of Israel

# The Story of God in Christ:

## The Fullness of Time

# How to Use this Bible

God's story told in the Bible shapes our entire lives. Jesus Christ fulfils the story's true meaning for all people. Each story has a particular shape and elements that help us to discover that story's meaning.

As you read the Bible passages. this additional information will help guide you:

## Characters

Look out for the order and details of the actions, conversations, and events of the characters. Ask yourself, how are the characters shown in appearance, thoughts and attitudes, and their influence and effect on others? The characters may be tested and make choices. Look out for whether they grow or decline.

## Main Theme

The theme informs you about the key truths that can be drawn out of the story. Ask yourself, what's good and bad in the story, and what is of concern and importance? Reflect on how the truths of the story connect with the challenges, opportunities, threats, and issues of your life and in the world today.

## Setting

This information might tell you where the story takes place, what the place looked like, when it was set, and what was the culture and history of that time.

---

## 50 The Baptism of the Lord

**Main Theme**
Christ is the beloved Son of God the Father

**Characters**
John the Baptist, Jesus, and God the Father

**Setting**
The River Jordan

**Key Verse:**
**Matthew 3:16–17**
After his baptism, as Jesus came up out of the water, the heavens were opened and he saw the Spirit of God descending like a dove and settling on him. And a voice from heaven said, 'This is my dearly loved Son, who brings me great joy.'

John baptizes Jesus in the River Jordan.

## Key Verse

This helps to focus on the main theme.

## Key plot points

The key plot points inform you about the order and details of the events and actions, and how the story begins, develops, and ends. Ask yourself, why did the events happen as they did? Why did the characters respond as they did? And could they have done things differently? Look out for the conflicts with God, with others, or within the characters.

## Read the story Matthew 3:13–17

¹³ Then Jesus went from Galilee to the River Jordan to be baptized by John. ¹⁴ But John tried to talk him out of it. 'I am the one who needs to be baptized by you', he said, 'so why are you coming to me?'

¹⁵ But Jesus said, 'It should be done, for we must carry out all that God requires.' So John agreed to baptize him.

¹⁶ After his baptism, as Jesus came up out of the water, the heavens were opened and he saw the Spirit of God descending like a dove and settling on him. ¹⁷ And a voice from heaven said, 'This is my dearly loved Son, who brings me great joy.'

## Key plot points

**v.13** – Jesus comes down to the River Jordan to be baptized by John.

**v.14** – John objects saying that he needs to be baptized by Jesus.

**v.15** – Jesus convinces John to baptize him by saying that it is necessary to fulfill all righteousness.

**v.16** – As Jesus comes up from the water, the Spirit of God descends like a dove and rests on him.

### Where we end up

The voice of the Father comes from heaven and declares Jesus as his Son and beloved.

### Old Testament Foundation: Fully Human and Fully Divine

**Noah's Ark** (Genesis 6 – 9) – p. 26. As the Lord rescued Noah and his family through the waters, so too Christ enters the waters in order to fulfil all righteousness and bring about a great rescue from the coming destruction.

**The Red Sea** (Exodus 14 – 15) – p. 61. As Moses and the people passed through the Red Sea and then were led up into the wilderness to be tested, so too Christ passes through the waters and is led into the wilderness.

**David is Anointed** (1 Samuel 16:1–13) – p. 103. As Samuel anointed David to be king over Israel, so the Spirit of God anointed Jesus to be King of the universe.

### My Reflections

.......................................................................................

.......................................................................................

.......................................................................................

.......................................................................................

.......................................................................................

Epiphany: The Manifestation of Christ | 183

## Christ foreshadowed & Old Testament foundation

In the Old Testament, there are events that point to the person of Jesus Christ or the work he would fulfil in the New Testament. The connections between Old and New Testament stories are explained.

## My reflections

If you wish, use this space to record your thoughts about the setting, characters, theme, and plot points. Ask yourself, what influences you to sympathize, approve, or disapprove of the characters? Look out for phrases, themes, and issues that are repeated or what stands out for you in the story. Reflect on how the story connects with your specific life situation and the world today.

# About The Urban Ministry Institute (TUMI), a ministry of World Impact

The Urban Ministry Institute (TUMI) is a programme of World Impact that empowers churches and denominations to form church-based seminaries for Gospel ministry. World Impact's mission is to empower urban leaders and partner with local churches to enable them to reach their cities with the Gospel. Its vision is to see a healthy church in every community of poverty.

Since its start in 1995 in Wichita, Kansas, TUMI has helped hundreds of pastors and leaders learn Scripture and serve Christ effectively. Church-based seminaries host in-person and online classes in ministry venues, churches, and prisons that are biblical, affordable, and accessible. Over the years, TUMI has designed many discipleship and leadership development resources, such as World Impact's Evangel School of Urban Church Planting, which provides church plant teams with the tools to start new churches in at-risk communities where they live and serve.

World Impact's ministry programmes equip pastors and lay leaders who lead their neighbours to Christ and transform communities of poverty. For more than 25 years, TUMI has produced many excellent resources that have enabled pastors, lay ministers, and missionaries to do effective ministry for Christ in the US and around the globe.

# Prologue:
# From the Beginning to the Fullness of Time

Creation and the Fall

The Promise and the Patriarchs

Deliverance from Egypt

From Egypt to Canaan

The Promised Land

The Exile

The Remnant of Israel

# 0  Eternity Past

**Key Verse: 2 Timothy 1:8–10**

So never be ashamed to tell others about our Lord. And don't be ashamed of me, either, even though I'm in prison for him. With the strength God gives you, be ready to suffer with me for the sake of the Good News. For God saved us and called us to live a holy life. He did this, not because we deserved it, but because that was his plan from before the beginning of time – to show us his grace through Christ Jesus. And now he has made all of this plain to us by the appearing of Christ Jesus, our Saviour. He broke the power of death and illuminated the way to life and immortality through the Good News.

In eternity past, God determined to send his Son to save people from death.

# Read the story 1 Peter 1:18–21

**18** For you know that God paid a ransom to save you from the empty life you inherited from your ancestors. And it was not paid with mere gold or silver, which lose their value. **19** It was the precious blood of Christ, the sinless, spotless Lamb of God. **20** God chose him as your ransom long before the world began, but now in these last days he has been revealed for your sake. **21** Through Christ you have come to trust in God. And you have placed your faith and hope in God because he raised Christ from the dead and gave him great glory.

# Key plot points

**Introduction** – From everlasting to everlasting the Lord is God. The triune God, Father, Son, and Holy Spirit, has no beginning and no end.

**v.20** – Before the foundation of the world God determined to send his Son to draw out of the earth a people for himself.

**v.21** – In the fullness of time, God's Son was revealed for us and our salvation.

## My Reflections

# 1 Creation

**Main Theme**

The Lord is king over all his creation, and he gives human beings dominion over the earth.

**Setting**

The heavens and the earth

**Characters**

Yahweh (the Eternal God, the Lord) and the first human pair

**Key Verse: Genesis 1:26**

Then God said, 'Let us make human beings in our image, to be like us. They will reign over the fish in the sea, the birds in the sky, the livestock, all the wild animals on the earth, and the small animals that scurry along the ground.'

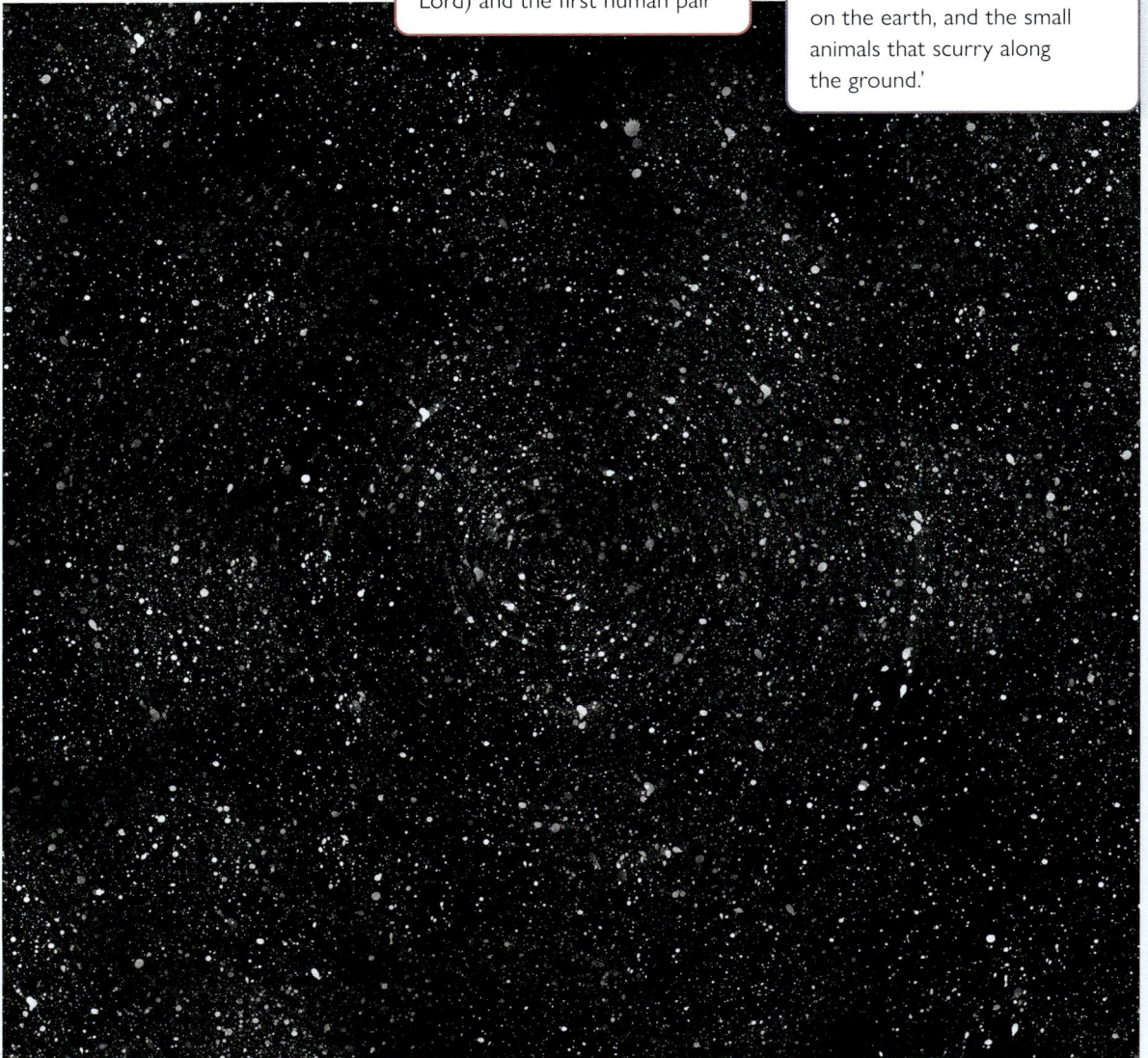

In the beginning God created the heavens and the earth.

# Read the story Genesis 1–2:4

**1** In the beginning God created the heavens and the earth. **²** The earth was formless and empty, and darkness covered the deep waters. And the Spirit of God was hovering over the surface of the waters. **³** Then God said, 'Let there be light,' and there was light. **⁴** And God saw that the light was good. Then he separated the light from the darkness. **⁵** God called the light 'day' and the darkness 'night.' And evening passed and morning came, marking the first day.

**⁶** Then God said, 'Let there be a space between the waters, to separate the waters of the heavens from the waters of the earth.' **⁷** And that is what happened. God made this space to separate the waters of the earth from the waters of the heavens. **⁸** God called the space 'sky.' And evening passed and morning came, marking the second day.

**⁹** Then God said, 'Let the waters beneath the sky flow together into one place, so dry ground may appear.' And that is what happened. **¹⁰** God called the dry ground 'land' and the waters 'seas.' And God saw that it was good. **¹¹** Then God said, 'Let the land sprout with vegetation – every sort of seed-bearing plant, and trees that grow seed-bearing fruit. These seeds will then produce the kinds of plants and trees from which they came.' And that is what happened. **¹²** The land produced vegetation – all sorts of seed-bearing plants, and trees with seed-bearing fruit. Their seeds produced plants and trees of the same kind. And God saw that it was good. **¹³** And evening passed and morning came, marking the third day.

**¹⁴** Then God said, 'Let lights appear in the sky to separate the day from the night. Let them be signs to mark the seasons, days, and years. **¹⁵** Let these lights in the sky shine down on the earth.' And that is what happened. **¹⁶** God made two great lights – the larger one to govern the day, and the smaller one to govern the night. He also made the stars. **¹⁷** God set these lights in the sky to light the earth, **¹⁸** to govern the day and night, and to separate the light from the darkness. And God saw that it was good. **¹⁹** And evening passed and morning came, marking the fourth day.

**²⁰** Then God said, 'Let the waters swarm with fish and other life. Let the skies be filled with birds of every kind.' **²¹** So God created great sea creatures and every living thing that moves and swarms in the water, and every sort of bird – each producing offspring of the same kind.

# Key plot points

**v.1** – In the beginning . . .

**v.3** – By his word, God speaks the heavens and the earth into existence.

**v.5–13** – In the first three days the Lord forms the formless heavens and earth, making the sky, the sea, and dry land.

**v.14–25** – In the second three days the Lord fills the void heavens and earth with the heavenly bodies, and creatures of all kinds.

And God saw that it was good. ²² Then God blessed them, saying, 'Be fruitful and multiply. Let the fish fill the seas, and let the birds multiply on the earth.' ²³ And evening passed and morning came, marking the fifth day.

²⁴ Then God said, 'Let the earth produce every sort of animal, each producing offspring of the same kind – livestock, small animals that move along the ground, and wild animals.' And that is what happened. ²⁵ God made all sorts of wild animals, livestock, and small animals, each able to produce offspring of the same kind. And God saw that it was good.

**v.26–28** – On the sixth day, the Lord creates human beings in the image of God to rule and care for the earth.

²⁶ Then God said, 'Let us make human beings in our image, to be like us. They will reign over the fish in the sea, the birds in the sky, the livestock, all the wild animals on the earth, and the small animals that move along the ground.'

²⁷ So God created human beings in his own image. In the image of God he created them; male and female he created them. ²⁸ Then God blessed them and said, 'Be fruitful and multiply. Fill the earth and govern it. Reign over the fish in the sea, the birds in the sky, and all the animals that move along the ground.'

²⁹ Then God said, 'Look! I have given you every seed-bearing plant throughout the earth and all the fruit trees for your food. ³⁰ And I have given every green plant as food for all the wild animals, the birds in the sky, and the small animals that move along the ground – everything that has life.' And that is what happened.

³¹ Then God looked over all he had made, and he saw that it was very good! And evening passed and morning came, marking the sixth day.

**v.1–3** – God rests on the seventh day as his work is finished.

2 So the creation of the heavens and the earth and everything in them was completed. ² On the seventh day God had finished his work of creation, so he rested from all his work. ³ And God blessed the seventh day and declared it holy, because it was the day when he rested from all his work of creation.

⁴ This is the account of the creation of the heavens and the earth.

## Where we end up

God sees all that has been created is very good.

# Adam and Eve in the Garden

**Main Theme**

The Lord, the Creator, is the giver of all life and ruler of all that lives.

**Setting**

The Garden of Eden

**Characters**

The Lord, the man, and the woman

**Key Verse: Genesis 2:7**

Then the LORD God formed the man from the dust of the ground. He breathed the breath of life into the man's nostrils, and the man became a living person.

The first human pair live in the Garden of Eden.

## Key plot points

**v.7** – The Lord forms the man out of the dirt of the earth and places him in the Garden of Eden.

**v.17** – The Lord forbids the man to eat from the tree of the knowledge of good and evil.

**v.18** – The Lord says that it is not good for the man to be alone.

**v.19** – God brings the animals in pairs and the man gives them names.

**v.20–21** – No match is found for him, so God causes a deep sleep to fall on the man.

**v.22** – God fashions woman out of the man's rib, as a suitable companion for him.

## Read the story Genesis 2:4–25

⁴ When the LORD God made the earth and the heavens, ⁵ neither wild plants nor grains were growing on the earth. For the LORD God had not yet sent rain to water the earth, and there were no people to cultivate the soil. ⁶ Instead, springs came up from the ground and watered all the land. ⁷ Then the LORD God formed the man from the dust of the ground. He breathed the breath of life into the man's nostrils, and the man became a living person.

⁸ Then the LORD God planted a garden in Eden in the east, and there he placed the man he had made. ⁹ The LORD God made all sorts of trees grow up from the ground – trees that were beautiful and that produced delicious fruit. In the middle of the garden he placed the tree of life and the tree of the knowledge of good and evil.

¹⁰ A river flowed from the land of Eden, watering the garden and then dividing into four branches. ¹¹ The first branch, called the Pishon, flowed around the entire land of Havilah, where gold is found. ¹² The gold of that land is exceptionally pure; aromatic resin and onyx stone are also found there. ¹³ The second branch, called the Gihon, flowed around the entire land of Cush. ¹⁴ The third branch, called the Tigris, flowed east of the land of Asshur. The fourth branch is called the Euphrates.

¹⁵ The LORD God placed the man in the Garden of Eden to tend and watch over it.

¹⁶ But the LORD God warned him, 'You may freely eat the fruit of every tree in the garden – ¹⁷ except the tree of the knowledge of good and evil. If you eat its fruit, you are sure to die.'

¹⁸ Then the LORD God said, 'It is not good for the man to be alone. I will make a helper who is just right for him.' ¹⁹ So the LORD God formed from the ground all the wild animals and all the birds of the sky. He brought them to the man to see what he would call them, and the man chose a name for each one. ²⁰ He gave names to all the livestock, all the birds of the sky, and all the wild animals. But still there was no helper just right for him.

²¹ So the LORD God caused the man to fall into a deep sleep. While the man slept, the LORD God took out one of the man's ribs and closed up the opening. ²² Then the LORD God made a woman from the rib, and he brought her to the man.

**23** 'At last!' the man exclaimed. 'This one is bone from my bone, and flesh from my flesh! She will be called "woman", because she was taken from "man."'

**24** This explains why a man leaves his father and mother and is joined to his wife, and the two are united into one.

**25** Now the man and his wife were both naked, but they felt no shame.

## Where we end up

The two human beings live in the Garden of Eden, working and tending it. They are only forbidden to eat of the tree of the knowledge of good and evil.

**Christ foreshadowed:** The Annunciation – p. 164

## My Reflections

# 3 The Serpent in the Garden

**Main Theme**

The first human beings join the rebellion of the serpent, Satan, against God's Kingdom reign.

**Setting**

The Garden of Eden

**Characters**

The serpent (Satan, the enemy of God), the woman, and the man

**Key Verse: Genesis 3:6**

The woman was convinced. She saw that the tree was beautiful and its fruit looked delicious, and she wanted the wisdom it would give her. So she took some of the fruit and ate it. Then she gave some to her husband, who was with her, and he ate it, too.

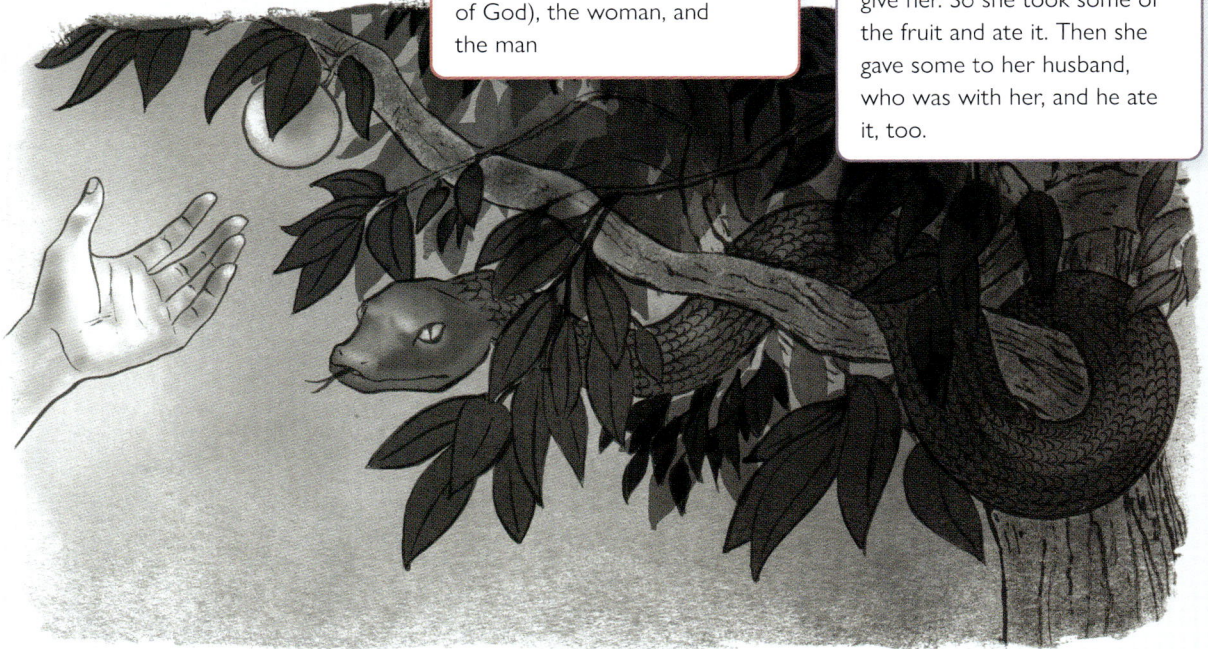

The serpent tempts the woman.

## Key plot points

**v.1–5** – The serpent, God's crafty enemy, tempts the woman with the fruit from the forbidden tree of the knowledge of good and evil.

## Read the story Genesis 3:1–7

**3** The serpent was the most crafty of all the wild animals the LORD God had made. One day he asked the woman, 'Did God really say you must not eat the fruit from any of the trees in the garden?'

² 'Of course we may eat fruit from the trees in the garden,' the woman replied. ³ 'It's only the fruit from the tree in the middle of the garden that we are not allowed to eat. God said, "You must not eat it or even touch it; if you do, you will die."'

⁴ 'You won't die!' the serpent replied to the woman. ⁵ 'God knows that your eyes will be opened as soon as you eat it, and you will be like God, knowing both good and evil.'

⁶ The woman was convinced. She saw that the tree was beautiful and its fruit looked delicious, and she wanted the wisdom it would give her. So she took some of the fruit and ate it. Then she gave some to her husband, who was with her, and he ate it, too. ⁷ At that moment their eyes were opened, and they suddenly felt shame at their nakedness. So they sewed fig leaves together to cover themselves.

**v.6** – In disobedience to God, the woman and the man listen to the serpent and eat.

**v.7** – Their eyes are opened, and they realize they are naked. They fashion garments for themselves out of fig leaves.

## Where we end up

The man and the woman have disobeyed God and now feel the shame of their actions. They try to hide and cover themselves up.

**Christ foreshadowed:** The Temptation of Our Lord – p. 184

## My Reflections

# 4  The Protoevangelium ("First Telling of the Gospel")

### Main Theme

The Lord will judge sin and rebellion against his Kingdom, but he promises to send a saviour who will destroy the devil and deliver humanity from sin and death.

### Setting

The Garden of Eden

### Characters

The Lord, the serpent, the woman, and the man

### Key Verse: Genesis 3:15

'And I will cause hostility between you and the woman, and between your offspring and her offspring. He will strike your head, and you will strike his heel.'

God promises a Saviour.

## Key plot points

**v.8** — After the disobedience of the first human pair, they hide themselves from God in fear and shame.

**v.11–13** — When the Lord comes to find them, he discovers that they have eaten the forbidden fruit.

**v.14** — The Lord pronounces a curse on the serpent, the woman, and the man.

## Read the story Genesis 3:8–21

⁸ When the cool evening breezes were blowing, the man and his wife heard the Lord God walking about in the garden. So they hid from the Lord God among the trees. ⁹ Then the Lord God called to the man, 'Where are you?'

¹⁰ He replied, 'I heard you walking in the garden, so I hid. I was afraid because I was naked.'

¹¹ 'Who told you that you were naked?' the Lord God asked. 'Have you eaten from the tree whose fruit I commanded you not to eat?'

¹² The man replied, 'It was the woman you gave me who gave me the fruit, and I ate it.'

¹³ Then the Lord God asked the woman, 'What have you done?'

"The serpent deceived me," she replied. "That's why I ate it."

¹⁴ Then the Lord God said to the serpent,

'Because you have done this, you are cursed
    more than all animals, domestic and wild.
You will crawl on your belly,
    grovelling in the dust as long as you live.

¹⁵ And I will cause hostility between you and the woman,
   and between your offspring and her offspring.
He will strike your head,
   and you will strike his heel.'

¹⁶ Then he said to the woman,

'I will sharpen the pain of your pregnancy,
   and in pain you will give birth.
And you will desire to control your husband,
   but he will rule over you.'

¹⁷ And to the man he said,

'Since you listened to your wife and ate from the tree
   whose fruit I commanded you not to eat,
the ground is cursed because of you.
   All your life you will struggle to scratch a living from it.
¹⁸ It will grow thorns and thistles for you,
   though you will eat of its grains.
¹⁹ By the sweat of your face
   will you have food to eat
until you return to the ground
   from which you were made.
For you were made from dust,
   and to dust you will return.'

²⁰ Then the man – Adam – named his wife Eve, because she would be the mother of all who live. ²¹ And the LORD God made clothing from animal skins for Adam and his wife.

**v.15** – Within his curse upon the serpent the Lord gives his first promise of redemption: the seed of the woman would come to crush the serpent's head, but the serpent would crush his heel.

**v.16–19** – The curse upon the woman multiplies her pain in childbirth, and the curse upon the man increases the futility and difficulty of his labour.

**v.20** – The man names his wife Eve, which means mother of all living.

**v.21** – The Lord graciously provides animal skins as clothing for the man and the woman.

## Where we end up

The promise of redemption means that God would send a saviour in the line of human beings who would defeat the devil and set humanity free, but who would suffer greatly in the process.

**Christ foreshadowed:** The Return of Christ – p. 273

# 5  The Fall

**Main Theme**

The great rebellion creates a rift between God and humanity, and subjects all things to death.

**Setting**

The Garden of Eden

**Characters**

The Lord, the man and the woman, and angels (guardians of the tree of life)

**Key Verse: Romans 5:17**

For the sin of this one man, Adam, caused death to rule over many. But even greater is God's wonderful grace and his gift of righteousness, for all who receive it will live in triumph over sin and death through this one man, Jesus Christ.

Adam and Eve are banished from the Garden.

# Read the story Genesis 3:22–24

²² Then the LORD God said, 'Look, the human beings have become like us, knowing both good and evil. What if they reach out, take fruit from the tree of life, and eat it? Then they will live for ever!' ²³ So the LORD God banished them from the Garden of Eden, and he sent Adam out to cultivate the ground from which he had been made. ²⁴ After sending them out, the LORD God stationed mighty cherubim to the east of the Garden of Eden. And he placed a flaming sword that flashed back and forth to guard the way to the tree of life.

# Key plot points

**v.22** – The Lord determines to prevent humankind from accessing the tree of life and living forever.

**v.23** – God banishes human beings from the Garden of Eden, sending them out of his presence, to the east.

**v.24** – He sets an angelic guard to prevent them from coming back.

## Where we end up

As the Lord warned, eating the fruit subjected the man and the woman, and all creation to death.

## My Reflections

# 6 Cain and Abel

### Main Theme

The Lord will judge sin and rebellion against his Kingdom, but he will show mercy to sinners.

### Setting

Fields near Adam and Eve's home

### Key Verse: Genesis 4:7

'You will be accepted if you do what is right. But if you refuse to do what is right, then watch out! Sin is crouching at the door, eager to control you. But you must subdue it and be its master.'

### Characters

Cain (Adam and Eve's first son), Abel (Cain's younger brother), and the Lord

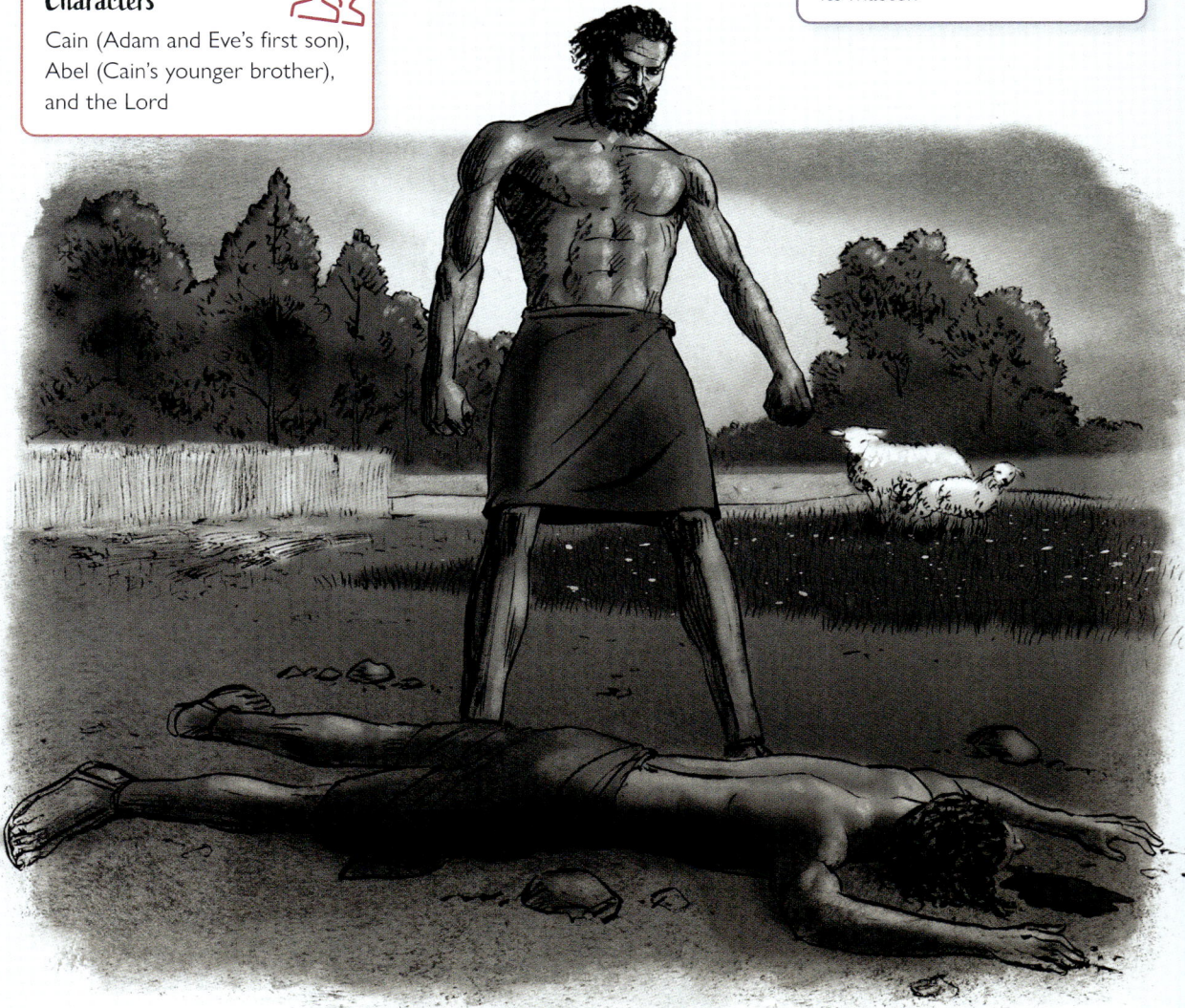

Cain kills his brother, Abel.

# Read the story Genesis 4:1–16

## Key plot points

¹ Now Adam had sexual relations with his wife, Eve, and she became pregnant. When she gave birth to Cain, she said, 'With the Lord's help, I have produced a man!' ² Later she gave birth to his brother and named him Abel.

When they grew up, Abel became a shepherd, while Cain cultivated the ground. ³ When it was time for the harvest, Cain presented some of his crops as a gift to the Lord. ⁴ Abel also brought a gift – the best portions of the first-born lambs from his flock. The Lord accepted Abel and his gift, ⁵ but he did not accept Cain and his gift. This made Cain very angry, and he looked dejected.

⁶ 'Why are you so angry?' the Lord asked Cain. 'Why do you look so dejected? ⁷ You will be accepted if you do what is right. But if you refuse to do what is right, then watch out! Sin is crouching at the door, eager to control you. But you must subdue it and be its master.'

⁸ One day Cain suggested to his brother, 'Let's go out into the fields.' And while they were in the field, Cain attacked his brother, Abel, and killed him.

⁹ Afterwards the Lord asked Cain, 'Where is your brother? Where is Abel?'

'I don't know,' Cain responded. 'Am I my brother's guardian?'

¹⁰ But the Lord said, 'What have you done? Listen! Your brother's blood cries out to me from the ground! ¹¹ Now you are cursed and banished from the ground, which has swallowed your brother's blood. ¹² No longer will the ground yield good crops for you, no matter how hard you work! From now on you will be a homeless wanderer on the earth.'

¹³ Cain replied to the Lord, 'My punishment is too great for me to bear! ¹⁴ You have banished me from the land and from your presence; you have made me a homeless wanderer. Anyone who finds me will kill me!'

¹⁵ The Lord replied, 'No, for I will give a sevenfold punishment to anyone who kills you.' Then the Lord put a mark on Cain to warn anyone who might try to kill him. ¹⁶ So Cain left the Lord's presence and settled in the land of Nod, east of Eden.

**v.2** – Cain is a farmer, while Abel raises livestock.

**v.3–5** – One time when they both bring an offering to the Lord, Abel's offering is accepted by God, while Cain's offering is rejected.

**v.8** – In retaliation, Cain decides to murder Abel. He invites his brother into a field and kills him.

**v.10** – The Lord confronts Cain and says that he hears Abel's blood crying out from the ground.

## Where we end up

The Lord banishes Cain to wander the earth but puts a mark on him so that no one will kill him.

# 7 The Flood

**Main Theme**

The Lord will judge sin and rebellion against his Kingdom, but by his grace, he will rescue a remnant of humankind.

**Setting**

The earth, the ark and Mount Ararat

**Characters**

The Lord, Noah, and Noah's family

**Key Verse: Genesis 8:21**

And the LORD was pleased with the aroma of the sacrifice and said to himself, 'I will never again curse the ground because of the human race, even though everything they think or imagine is bent toward evil from childhood. I will never again destroy all living things.'

The ark weathers the flood.

## Read the story Genesis 6 – 9

**6** <sup>5</sup> The LORD observed the extent of human wickedness on the earth, and he saw that everything they thought or imagined was consistently and totally evil. <sup>6</sup> So the LORD was sorry he had ever made them and put them on the earth. It broke his heart. <sup>7</sup> And the LORD said, 'I will wipe this human race I have created from the face of the earth. Yes, and I will destroy every living thing – all the people, the large animals, the small animals that move along the ground, and even the birds of the sky. I am sorry I ever made them.' <sup>8</sup> But Noah found favour with the LORD.

<sup>9</sup> This is the account of Noah and his family. Noah was a righteous man, the only blameless person living on earth at the time, and he walked in close fellow ship with God. <sup>10</sup> Noah was the father of three sons: Shem, Ham, and Japheth.

<sup>11</sup> Now God saw that the earth had become corrupt and was filled with violence. <sup>12</sup> God observed all this corruption in the world, for everyone on earth was corrupt. <sup>13</sup> So God said to Noah, 'I have decided to destroy all living creatures, for they have filled the earth with violence. Yes, I will wipe them all out along with the earth!

<sup>14</sup> 'Build a large boat from cypress wood and waterproof it with tar, inside and out. Then construct decks and stalls throughout its interior. <sup>15</sup> Make the boat 150 metres long, 25 metres wide, and 15 metres high. <sup>16</sup> Leave a 50-centimetre opening below the roof all the way around the boat. Put the door on the side, and build three decks inside the boat – lower, middle, and upper.

<sup>17</sup> 'Look! I am about to cover the earth with a flood that will destroy every living thing that breathes. Everything on earth will die. <sup>18</sup> But I will confirm my covenant with you. So enter the boat – you and your wife and your sons and their wives. <sup>19</sup> Bring a pair of every kind of animal – a male and a female – into the boat with you to keep them alive during the flood. <sup>20</sup> Pairs of every kind of bird, and every kind of animal, and every kind of small animal that moves along the ground, will come to you to be kept alive. <sup>21</sup> And be sure to take on board enough food for your family and for all the animals.'

<sup>22</sup> So Noah did everything exactly as God had commanded him.

…

## Key plot points

**v.5–6** – Human beings become so evil that God regrets that he made them.

**v.7** – He decides to flood the world and wipe it clean.

**v.9–10** – By grace, he chooses Noah and his family as the lone survivors.

**v.14, 18–19** – He commands Noah to build a boat (the ark) that will house his family along with two of every kind of animal.

**Genesis 7** – The Lord floods the world and every living thing dies except those in the ark.

Noah sends out a dove.

**v.8–18** – Once the rains stop, Noah sends out a dove to see if the ground is dry. When the dove brings back an olive branch, Noah unloads the ark.

**8** God remembered Noah and all the wild animals and livestock with him in the boat. He sent a wind to blow across the earth, and the flood waters began to recede. **2** The underground waters stopped flowing, and the torrential rains from the sky were stopped. **3** So the floodwaters gradually receded from the earth. After 150 days, **4** exactly five months from the time the flood began, the boat came to rest on the mountains of Ararat. **5** Two and a half months later, as the waters continued to go down, other mountain peaks became visible.

**6** After another forty days, Noah opened the window he had made in the boat **7** and released a raven. The bird flew back and forth until the flood waters on the earth had dried up. **8** He also released a dove to see if the water had receded and it could find dry ground. **9** But the dove could find no place to land because the water still covered the ground. So it returned to the boat, and Noah held out his hand and drew the dove back inside. **10** After waiting another seven days, Noah released the dove again. **11** This time the dove returned to him in the evening with a fresh olive leaf in its beak. Then Noah knew that the floodwaters were almost gone. **12** He waited another seven days and then released the dove again. This time it did not come back.

**13** Noah was now 601 years old. On the first day of the new year, ten and a half months after the flood began, the floodwaters had almost dried up from the earth. Noah lifted back the covering of the boat and saw that the surface of the ground was drying. **14** Two more months went by, and at last the earth was dry!

**15** Then God said to Noah, **16** 'Leave the boat, all of you – you and your wife, and your sons and their wives. **17** Release all the animals – the birds, the livestock, and the small animals that move along the ground – so they can be fruitful and multiply throughout the earth.'

**18** So Noah, his wife, and his sons and their wives left the boat. **19** And all of the large and small animals and birds came out of the boat, pair by pair.

**20** Then Noah built an altar to the LORD, and there he sacrificed as burnt offerings the animals and birds that had been approved for that purpose. **21** And the LORD was pleased with the aroma of the sacrifice and said to himself, 'I will never again curse the ground because of the human race, even though everything they think or imagine is bent towards evil from childhood. I will never again destroy all living things.

²² As long as the earth remains, there will be planting and harvest, cold and heat, summer and winter, day and night.'

…

**9** ¹² Then God said, 'I am giving you a sign of my covenant with you and with all living creatures, for all generations to come. ¹³ I have placed my rainbow in the clouds. It is the sign of my covenant with you and with all the earth. ¹⁴ When I send clouds over the earth, the rainbow will appear in the clouds, ¹⁵ and I will remember my covenant with you and with all living creatures. Never again will the floodwaters destroy all life. ¹⁶ When I see the rainbow in the clouds, I will remember the eternal covenant between God and every living creature on earth.' ¹⁷ Then God said to Noah, 'Yes, this rainbow is the sign of the covenant I am confirming with all the creatures on earth.'

## Where we end up

God puts his rainbow in the sky with a promise that he will never again destroy all life with a flood.

**Christ foreshadowed:** The Baptism of the Lord – p. 182

## My Reflections

# 8 Babel

**Main Theme**

The Lord will judge sin and rebellion against his Kingdom, but he will fulfill his Kingdom purposes in the world.

**Setting**

The plains of Shinar

**Key Verse: Genesis 11:9**

That is why the city was called Babel, because that is where the LORD confused the people with different languages. In this way he scattered them all over the world.

**Characters**

Human beings and the Lord

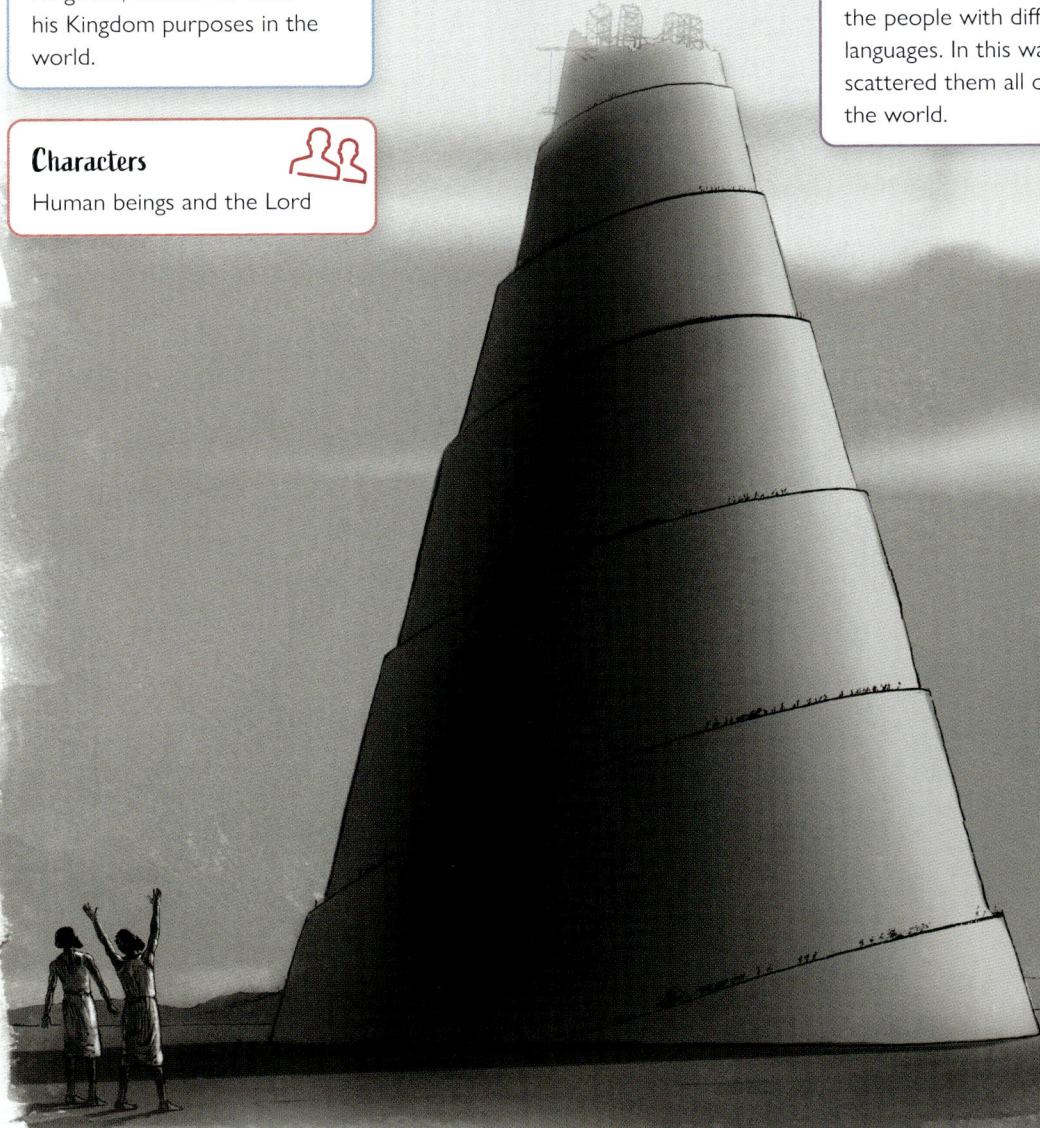

'Let's build a great city for ourselves with a tower that reaches the sky.'

# Read the story Genesis 11:1–9

## Key plot points

**1** At one time all the people of the world spoke the same language and used the same words. As the people migrated to the east, they found a plain in the land of Babylonia and settled there.

**v.1** – The whole earth has one language.

**3** They began saying to each other, 'Let's make bricks and harden them with fire.' (In this region bricks were used instead of stone, and tar was used for mortar.) **4** Then they said, 'Come, let's build a great city for ourselves with a tower that reaches into the sky. This will make us famous and keep us from being scattered all over the world.'

**v.4** – They come together to build a city with a tower reaching into the heavens.

**5** But the LORD came down to look at the city and the tower the people were building. **6** 'Look!' he said. 'The people are united, and they all speak the same language. After this, nothing they set out to do will be impossible for them! **7** Come, let's go down and confuse the people with different languages. Then they won't be able to understand each other.'

**v.5** – God looks down to see their tower.

**v.6–7** – God decides to confuse their speech to stop the building of the tower.

**8** In that way, the LORD scattered them all over the world, and they stopped building the city. **9** That is why the city was called Babel, because that is where the LORD confused the people with different languages. In this way he scattered them all over the world.

**v.8** – No longer able to communicate, the people stop building the tower.

### Where we end up

Human beings are scattered across the earth all speaking different languages. The place is named Babel.

## My Reflections

# 9  The Call of Abram

### Main Theme

The Lord makes a covenant promise to bring the blessing of his Kingdom to the whole earth through the seed of Abraham.

### Setting

Haran (the city where Abraham's family has settled) and Canaan (the land God promises to give Abraham)

### Characters

The Lord and Abraham (called Abram in these stories)

### Key Verse: Genesis 12:2–3, 15:6

'I will make you into a great nation. I will bless you and make you famous, and you will be a blessing to others. I will bless those who bless you and curse those who treat you with contempt. All the families on earth will be blessed through you.'

And Abram believed the LORD, and the LORD counted him as righteous because of his faith.

God makes a covenant with Abraham.

## Read the story Genesis 12, 15

**12** The LORD had said to Abram, 'Leave your native country, your relatives, and your father's family, and go to the land that I will show you. ² I will make you into a great nation. I will bless you and make you famous, and you will be a blessing to others. ³ I will bless those who bless you and curse those who treat you with contempt. All the families on earth will be blessed through you.'

⁴ So Abram departed as the LORD had instructed, and Lot went with him. Abram was seventy-five years old when he left Haran. ⁵ He took his wife, Sarai, his nephew Lot, and all his wealth – his livestock and all the people he had taken into his household at Haran – and headed for the land of Canaan. When they arrived in Canaan, ⁶ Abram travelled through the land as far as Shechem. There he set up camp beside the oak of Moreh. At that time, the area was inhabited by Canaanites.

⁷ Then the LORD appeared to Abram and said, 'I will give this land to your descendants.' And Abram built an altar there and dedicated it to the LORD, who had appeared to him. ⁸ After that, Abram travelled south and set up camp in the hill country, with Bethel to the west and Ai to the east. There he built another altar and dedicated it to the LORD, and he worshipped the LORD. ⁹ Then Abram continued travelling south by stages towards the Negev.

¹⁰ At that time a severe famine struck the land of Canaan, forcing Abram to go down to Egypt, where he lived as a foreigner. ¹¹ As he was approaching the border of Egypt, Abram said to his wife, Sarai, 'Look, you are a very beautiful woman. ¹² When the Egyptians see you, they will say, "This is his wife. Let's kill him; then we can have her!" ¹³ So please tell them you are my sister. Then they will spare my life and treat me well because of their interest in you.'

¹⁴ And sure enough, when Abram arrived in Egypt, everyone noticed Sarai's beauty. ¹⁵ When the palace officials saw her, they sang her praises to Pharaoh, their king, and Sarai was taken into his palace. ¹⁶ Then Pharaoh gave Abram many gifts because of her – sheep, goats, cattle, male and female donkeys, male and female servants, and camels.

¹⁷ But the LORD sent terrible plagues upon Pharaoh and his household because of Sarai, Abram's wife. ¹⁸ So Pharaoh summoned Abram and accused him sharply. 'What have you done to me?' he demanded. 'Why didn't you tell me she was your wife? ¹⁹ Why did you

## Key plot points

**v.1** – The Lord comes to Abram and calls him to leave his home and go to a new land.

**v.2–3** – He promises to make him into a great nation, to bless him, and through him to bless the whole world.

**v.4–5** – Abram obeys the Lord. He leaves Haran, with his wife Sarai and his nephew Lot, and journeys to Canaan.

say, "She is my sister," and allow me to take her as my wife? Now then, here is your wife. Take her and get out of here!' **20** Pharaoh ordered some of his men to escort them, and he sent Abram out of the country, along with his wife and all his possessions.

…

**15** Some time later, the Lord spoke to Abram in a vision and said to him, 'Do not be afraid, Abram, for I will protect you, and your reward will be great.'

**2** But Abram replied, 'O Sovereign Lord, what good are all your blessings when I don't even have a son? Since you've given me no children, Eliezer of Damascus, a servant in my household, will inherit all my wealth. **3** You have given me no descendants of my own, so one of my servants will be my heir.'

**4** Then the Lord said to him, 'No, your servant will not be your heir, for you will have a son of your own who will be your heir.' **5** Then the Lord took Abram outside and said to him, 'Look up into the sky and count the stars if you can. That's how many descendants you will have!'

**6** And Abram believed the Lord, and the Lord counted him as righteous because of his faith.

**7** Then the Lord told him, 'I am the Lord who brought you out of Ur of the Chaldeans to give you this land as your possession.'

**8** But Abram replied, 'O Sovereign Lord, how can I be sure that I will actually possess it?'

**9** The Lord told him, 'Bring me a three-year-old heifer, a three-year-old female goat, a three-year-old ram, a turtle-dove, and a young pigeon.' **10** So Abram presented all these to him and killed them. Then he cut each animal down the middle and laid the halves side by side; he did not, however, cut the birds in half. **11** Some vultures swooped down to eat the carcasses, but Abram chased them away.

**12** As the sun was going down, Abram fell into a deep sleep, and a terrifying darkness came down over him. **13** Then the Lord said to Abram, 'You can be sure that your descendants will be strangers in a foreign land, where they will be oppressed as slaves for 400 years. **14** But I will punish the nation that enslaves them, and in the end they will come away with great wealth. **15** (As for you, you will die in peace and be buried at a ripe old age.) **16** After four generations your descendants will return here to this land, for the sins of the Amorites do not yet warrant their destruction.'

**v.5** – The Lord confirms his promise to Abram, telling him his descendants will be as numerous as the stars in the sky.

**v.6** – Abram believes the Lord, and it is counted to him as righteousness.

God calls Abram to go to a new land.

**17** After the sun went down and darkness fell, Abram saw a smoking firepot and a flaming torch pass between the halves of the carcasses. **18** So the LORD made a covenant with Abram that day and said, 'I have given this land to your descendants, all the way from the border of Egypt to the great River Euphrates – **19** the land now occupied by the Kenites, Kenizzites, Kadmonites, **20** Hittites, Perizzites, Rephaites, **21** Amorites, Canaanites, Girgashites, and Jebusites.'

### Where we end up

The Lord makes a covenant with Abram to give the land of Canaan to his descendants.

**Christ foreshadowed:** The Annunciation – p. 164 and The Calling of the Disciples – p. 187

### My Reflections

# 10 Melchizedek

**Main Theme**

The Lord will appoint a king and priest to bless Abraham's descendants.

**Setting**

The King's Valley in Canaan

**Characters**

Abram and Melchizedek (king of Salem (Jerusalem) in the land of Canaan)

**Key Verse: Genesis 14:19–20**

Melchizedek blessed Abram with this blessing: 'Blessed be Abram by God Most High, Creator of heaven and earth. And blessed be God Most High, who has defeated your enemies for you.' Then Abram gave Melchizedek a tenth of all the goods he had recovered.

Melchizedek blesses Abram.

# Read the story Genesis 14:17–24

[17] After Abram returned from his victory over Kedorlaomer and all his allies, the king of Sodom went out to meet him in the valley of Shaveh (that is, the King's Valley). [18] And Melchizedek, the king of Salem and a priest of God Most High, brought Abram some bread and wine. [19] Melchizedek blessed Abram with this blessing:

'Blessed be Abram by God Most High,
    Creator of heaven and earth.
[20] And blessed be God Most High,
    who has defeated your enemies for you.'

Then Abram gave Melchizedek a tenth of all the goods he had recovered. [21] The king of Sodom said to Abram, 'Give back my people who were captured. But you may keep for yourself all the goods you have recovered.' [22] Abram replied to the king of Sodom, 'I solemnly swear to the LORD, God Most High, Creator of heaven and earth, [23] that I will not take so much as a single thread or sandal thong from what belongs to you. Otherwise you might say, "I am the one who made Abram rich." [24] I will accept only what my young warriors have already eaten, and I request that you give a fair share of the goods to my allies – Aner, Eshcol, and Mamre.'

## Key plot points

**v.17** – Abram has just led a military campaign to rescue Lot from a group of five kings who had conquered Sodom.

**v.18** – After the victory, Melchizedek, king of Salem and priest of God, brings provisions for Abram's forces.

**v.19** – Melchizedek blesses Abram in the name of God.

**v.20** – Abram gives Melchizedek one-tenth of all his goods.

## Where we end up

Abram does not keep any goods so his success can only be seen as provided by God.

**Christ foreshadowed:** The Ascension of Christ – p. 255

# 11 Sodom and Gomorrah

## Main Theme

The Lord will judge sin and rebellion against his Kingdom, but he will show his covenant faithfulness to deliver his people.

## Setting

Sodom and Gomorrah (two wicked cities) and Zoar (the city Lot flees to with his family)

## Characters

Two angels, Lot, Lot's wife and daughters, and the men of Sodom

## Key Verse: Genesis 19:15

At dawn the next morning the angels became insistent. 'Hurry,' they said to Lot. 'Take your wife and your two daughters who are here. Get out right now, or you will be swept away in the destruction of the city!'

Lot flees Sodom with his family.

# Read the story Genesis 19:1–29

¹ That evening the two angels came to the entrance of the city of Sodom. Lot was sitting there, and when he saw them, he stood up to meet them. Then he welcomed them and bowed with his face to the ground. ² 'My lords,' he said, 'come to my home to wash your feet, and be my guests for the night. You may then get up early in the morning and be on your way again.'

'Oh no,' they replied. 'We'll just spend the night out here in the city square.'

³ But Lot insisted, so at last they went home with him. Lot prepared a feast for them, complete with fresh bread made without yeast, and they ate. ⁴ But before they retired for the night, all the men of Sodom, young and old, came from all over the city and surrounded the house. ⁵ They shouted to Lot, 'Where are the men who came to spend the night with you? Bring them out to us so we can have sex with them!'

⁶ So Lot stepped outside to talk to them, shutting the door behind him. ⁷ 'Please, my brothers,' he begged, 'don't do such a wicked thing. ⁸ Look, I have two virgin daughters. Let me bring them out to you, and you can do with them as you wish. But please, leave these men alone, for they are my guests and are under my protection.'

⁹ 'Stand back!' they shouted. 'This fellow came to town as an outsider, and now he's acting like our judge! We'll treat you far worse than those other men!' And they lunged towards Lot to break down the door.

¹⁰ But the two angels reached out, pulled Lot into the house, and bolted the door. ¹¹ Then they blinded all the men, young and old, who were at the door of the house, so they gave up trying to get inside.

¹² Meanwhile, the angels questioned Lot. 'Do you have any other relatives here in the city?' they asked. 'Get them out of this place – your sons-in-law, sons, daughters, or anyone else. ¹³ For we are about to destroy this city completely. The outcry against this place is so great it has reached the LORD, and he has sent us to destroy it.'

¹⁴ So Lot rushed out to tell his daughters' fiancés, 'Quick, get out of the city! The LORD is about to destroy it.' But the young men thought he was only joking.

¹⁵ At dawn the next morning the angels became insistent. 'Hurry,' they said to Lot. 'Take your wife and your two daughters who are here.

**v.1** – The Lord sends two angels to investigate the evil of Sodom.

**v.2–3** – Lot invites the angels into his house to protect them from the wicked people of the city.

**v.12–13** – Because of God's love for Abraham, the angels warn Lot of the coming destruction and urge him to flee the city with his family.

**v.16** – Lot takes his wife and daughters and flees Sodom.

Get out right now, or you will be swept away in the destruction of the city!'

**16** When Lot still hesitated, the angels seized his hand and the hands of his wife and two daughters and rushed them to safety outside the city, for the LORD was merciful. **17** When they were safely out of the city, one of the angels ordered, 'Run for your lives! And don't look back or stop anywhere in the valley! Escape to the mountains, or you will be swept away!'

**18** 'Oh no, my lord!' Lot begged. **19** 'You have been so gracious to me and saved my life, and you have shown such great kindness. But I cannot go to the mountains. Disaster would catch up to me there, and I would soon die. **20** See, there is a small village nearby. Please let me go there instead; don't you see how small it is? Then my life will be saved.'

**21** 'All right,' the angel said, 'I will grant your request. I will not destroy the little village. **22** But hurry! Escape to it, for I can do nothing until you arrive there.' (This explains why that village was known as Zoar, which means 'little place.')

**23** Lot reached the village just as the sun was rising over the horizon.

**v.24–26** – As the angels are raining destruction on Sodom and Gomorrah, Lot's wife looks back and is turned into a pillar of salt.

**24** Then the LORD rained down fire and burning sulphur from the sky on Sodom and Gomorrah. **25** He utterly destroyed them, along with the other cities and villages of the plain, wiping out all the people and every bit of vegetation. **26** But Lot's wife looked back as she was following behind him, and she turned into a pillar of salt.

**27** Abraham got up early that morning and hurried out to the place where he had stood in the LORD's presence. **28** He looked across the plain towards Sodom and Gomorrah and watched as columns of smoke rose from the cities like smoke from a furnace.

**29** But God had listened to Abraham's request and kept Lot safe, removing him from the disaster that engulfed the cities on the plain.

## Where we end up

Sodom and Gomorrah are completely destroyed.

**Christ foreshadowed:** The Ministry of John the Baptist – p. 168

# God Tests Abraham

Abraham prepares to sacrifice Isaac.

**Main Theme**

The Lord will deliver his people and all peoples from sin and death by providing a sacrificial substitute.

**Setting**

The land of Moriah (and the road to Moriah)

**Characters**

The Lord, Abraham, Isaac, and the angel of the Lord

**Key Verse: Genesis 22:2**

'Take your son, your only son – yes, Isaac, whom you love so much – and go to the land of Moriah. Go and sacrifice him as a burnt offering on one of the mountains, which I will show you.'

## Key plot points

**v.2** – The Lord calls Abraham to sacrifice his promised son, Isaac.

**v.3** – Abraham loads all the supplies for the sacrifice and sets out with Isaac and two servants.

**v.6** – Abraham and Isaac leave the servants and journey to the mountain alone for the sacrifice.

**v.7** – As they walk, Isaac notices that they have not brought an animal for the sacrifice.

**v.9–10** – In obedience to the Lord, Abraham prepares to sacrifice Isaac, even taking the knife in his hand to kill the boy.

**v.11** – The angel of the Lord intervenes and tells Abraham not to kill Isaac.

## Read the story Genesis 22:1–19

¹ Some time later, God tested Abraham's faith. 'Abraham!' God called.

'Yes,' he replied. 'Here I am.'

² 'Take your son, your only son – yes, Isaac, whom you love so much – and go to the land of Moriah. Go and sacrifice him as a burnt offering on one of the mountains, which I will show you.'

³ The next morning Abraham got up early. He saddled his donkey and took two of his servants with him, along with his son, Isaac. Then he chopped wood for a fire for a burnt offering and set out for the place God had told him about. ⁴ On the third day of their journey, Abraham looked up and saw the place in the distance. ⁵ 'Stay here with the donkey,' Abraham told the servants. 'The boy and I will travel a little farther. We will worship there, and then we will come straight back.'

⁶ So Abraham placed the wood for the burnt offering on Isaac's shoulders, while he himself carried the fire and the knife. As the two of them walked on together, ⁷ Isaac turned to Abraham and said, 'Father?'

'Yes, my son?' Abraham replied.

'We have the fire and the wood,' the boy said, 'but where is the sheep for the burnt offering?'

⁸ 'God will provide a sheep for the burnt offering, my son,' Abraham answered. And they both walked on together.

⁹ When they arrived at the place where God had told him to go, Abraham built an altar and arranged the wood on it. Then he tied his son, Isaac, and laid him on the altar on top of the wood. ¹⁰ And Abraham picked up the knife to kill his son as a sacrifice. ¹¹ At that moment the angel of the LORD called to him from heaven, 'Abraham! Abraham!'

'Yes,' Abraham replied. 'Here I am!'

¹² 'Don't lay a hand on the boy!' the angel said. 'Do not hurt him in any way, for now I know that you truly fear God. You have not withheld from me even your son, your only son.'

¹³ Then Abraham looked up and saw a ram caught by its horns in a thicket. So he took the ram and sacrificed it as a burnt offering in place of his son. ¹⁴ Abraham named the place Yahweh-Yireh (which means 'the LORD will provide'). To this day, people still use that name as a proverb: 'On the mountain of the LORD it will be provided.'

**15** Then the angel of the LORD called again to Abraham from heaven. **16** 'This is what the LORD says: Because you have obeyed me and have not withheld even your son, your only son, I swear by my own name that **17** I will certainly bless you. I will multiply your descendants beyond number, like the stars in the sky and the sand on the seashore. Your descendants will conquer the cities of their enemies. **18** And through your descendants all the nations of the earth will be blessed – all because you have obeyed me.'

**19** Then they returned to the servants and travelled back to Beersheba, where Abraham continued to live.

## Where we end up

Because of Abraham's willingness to sacrifice his son, the Lord affirms that he will absolutely fulfill his promise to bless Abraham and make him a great nation.

**Christ foreshadowed:** The Crucifixion: Jesus Carries His Cross – p. 235

## My Reflections

# 13 Joseph

## Main Theme

The Lord will raise up a deliverer, who will be rejected by his people, but who will save them from death.

## Setting

The house of Jacob, a field near Shechem, and Egypt

## Characters

Joseph (favourite son of Jacob), Jacob (Joseph's father), the eleven other sons of Jacob by four different women (with a focus on Judah, Reuben, and Benjamin), Potiphar (Joseph's master in Egypt), and Pharaoh (king of Egypt)

## Key Verse: Genesis 50:20

'You intended to harm me, but God intended it all for good. He brought me to this position so I could save the lives of many people.'

Joseph's brothers throw him in a pit and sell him as a slave.

# Read the story Genesis 37, 45

**37** So Jacob settled again in the land of Canaan, where his father had lived as a foreigner.

² This is the account of Jacob and his family. When Joseph was seventeen years old, he often tended his father's flocks. He worked for his half-brothers, the sons of his father's wives Bilhah and Zilpah. But Joseph reported to his father some of the bad things his brothers were doing.

³ Jacob loved Joseph more than any of his other children because Joseph had been born to him in his old age. So one day Jacob had a special gift made for Joseph – a beautiful robe. ⁴ But his brothers hated Joseph because their father loved him more than the rest of them. They couldn't say a kind word to him.

**v.4, 8** – Jacob's favouritism and Joseph's dreams cause his brothers to hate Joseph.

⁵ One night Joseph had a dream, and when he told his brothers about it, they hated him more than ever. ⁶ 'Listen to this dream,' he said. ⁷ 'We were out in the field, tying up sheaves of grain. Suddenly my sheaf stood up, and your sheaves all gathered around and bowed low before mine!'

⁸ His brothers responded, 'So you think you will be our king, do you? Do you actually think you will reign over us?' And they hated him all the more because of his they hated him all the more because of his dreams and the way he talked about them.

⁹ Soon Joseph had another dream, and again he told his brothers about it. 'Listen, I have had another dream,' he said. 'The sun, moon, and eleven stars bowed low before me!'

¹⁰ This time he told the dream to his father as well as to his brothers, but his father scolded him. 'What kind of dream is that?' he asked. 'Will your mother and I and your brothers actually come and bow to the ground before you?' ¹¹ But while his brothers were jealous of Joseph, his father wondered what the dreams meant.

¹² Soon after this, Joseph's brothers went to pasture their father's flocks at Shechem. ¹³ When they had been gone for some time, Jacob said to Joseph, 'Your brothers are pasturing the sheep at Shechem. Get ready, and I will send you to them.'

'I'm ready to go,' Joseph replied.

¹⁴ 'Go and see how your brothers and the flocks are getting along,' Jacob said. 'Then come back and bring me a report.' So Jacob sent him

on his way, and Joseph travelled to Shechem from their home in the valley of Hebron.

¹⁵ When he arrived there, a man from the area noticed him wandering around the countryside. 'What are you looking for?' he asked.

¹⁶ 'I'm looking for my brothers,' Joseph replied. 'Do you know where they are pasturing their sheep?'

¹⁷ 'Yes,' the man told him. 'They have moved on from here, but I heard them say, "Let's go on to Dothan."' So Joseph followed his brothers to Dothan and found them there.

¹⁸ When Joseph's brothers saw him coming, they recognized him in the distance. As he approached, they made plans to kill him. ¹⁹ 'Here comes the dreamer!' they said. ²⁰ 'Come on, let's kill him and throw him into one of these cisterns. We can tell our father, "A wild animal has eaten him." Then we'll see what becomes of his dreams!'

²¹ But when Reuben heard of their scheme, he came to Joseph's rescue. 'Let's not kill him,' he said. ²² 'Why should we shed any blood? Let's just throw him into this empty cistern here in the wilderness. Then he'll die without our laying a hand on him.' Reuben was secretly planning to rescue Joseph and return him to his father.

²³ So when Joseph arrived, his brothers ripped off the beautiful robe he was wearing. ²⁴ Then they grabbed him and threw him into the cistern. Now the cistern was empty; there was no water in it. ²⁵ Then, just as they were sitting down to eat, they looked up and saw a caravan of camels in the distance coming towards them. It was a group of Ishmaelite traders taking a load of gum, balm, and aromatic resin from Gilead down to Egypt.

²⁶ Judah said to his brothers, 'What will we gain by killing our brother? We'd have to cover up the crime. ²⁷ Instead of hurting him, let's sell him to those Ishmaelite traders. After all, he is our brother – our own flesh and blood!' And his brothers agreed. ²⁸ So when the Ishmaelites, who were Midianite traders, came by, Joseph's brothers pulled him out of the cistern and sold him to them for twenty pieces of silver. And the traders took him to Egypt.

²⁹ Some time later, Reuben returned to get Joseph out of the cistern. When he discovered that Joseph was missing, he tore his clothes in grief. ³⁰ Then he went back to his brothers and lamented, 'The boy is gone! What will I do now?'

**v.28, 33** The brothers sell Joseph into slavery and convince Jacob he is dead.

**31** Then the brothers killed a young goat and dipped Joseph's robe in its blood. **32** They sent the beautiful robe to their father with this message: 'Look at what we found. Doesn't this robe belong to your son?'

**33** Their father recognized it immediately. 'Yes,' he said, 'it is my son's robe. A wild animal must have eaten him. Joseph has clearly been torn to pieces!' **34** Then Jacob tore his clothes and dressed himself in sackcloth. He mourned deeply for his son for a long time. **35** His family all tried to comfort him, but he refused to be comforted. 'I will go to my grave mourning for my son,' he would say, and then he would weep.

**36** Meanwhile, the Midianite traders arrived in Egypt, where they sold Joseph to Potiphar, an officer of Pharaoh, the king of Egypt. Potiphar was captain of the palace guard.

...

**45** Joseph could stand it no longer. There were many people in the room, and he said to his attendants, 'Out, all of you!' So he was alone with his brothers when he told them who he was. **2** Then he broke down and wept. He wept so loudly the Egyptians could hear him, and word of it quickly carried to Pharaoh's palace.

**3** 'I am Joseph!' he said to his brothers. 'Is my father still alive?' But his brothers were speechless! They were stunned to realize that Joseph was standing there in front of them. **4** 'Please, come closer,' he said to them. So they came closer. And he said again, 'I am Joseph, your brother, whom you sold into slavery in Egypt. **5** But don't be upset, and don't be angry with yourselves for selling me to this place. It was God who sent me here ahead of you to preserve your lives. **6** This famine that has ravaged the land for two years will last five more years, and there will be neither ploughing nor harvesting. **7** God has sent me ahead of you to keep you and your families alive and to preserve many survivors. **8** So it was God who sent me here, not you! And he is the one who made me an adviser to Pharaoh – the manager of his entire palace and the governor of all Egypt.

**9** 'Now hurry back to my father and tell him, "This is what your son Joseph says: God has made me master over all the land of Egypt. So come down to me immediately! **10** You can live in the region of Goshen, where you can be near me with all your children and grandchildren, your flocks and herds, and everything you own. **11** I will take care of you there, for there are still five years of famine ahead of us. Otherwise you, your household, and all your animals will starve."'

**v.36** – Joseph is sold in Egypt where he is put in charge of Potiphar's whole household. Potiphar's wife falsely accuses Joseph and he ends up in prison.

**Chapters 41 – 44** – Joseph ascends to great power in Egypt when, from prison, he interprets the dreams of Pharaoh. The dreams predict a great famine. When the famine comes, Joseph's brothers come to Egypt to buy grain from him. Joseph tests his brothers to see if they have changed.

**v.3** – Joseph reveals his identity to them and invites them to come to Egypt where he can provide for them.

Joseph reveals his identity to his brothers.

[12] Then Joseph added, 'Look! You can see for yourselves, and so can my brother Benjmin, that I really am Joseph! [13] Go tell my father of my honoured position here in Egypt. Describe for him everything you have seen, and then bring my father here quickly.' [14] Weeping with joy, he embraced Benjamin, and Benjamin did the same. [15] Then Joseph kissed each of his brothers and wept over them, and after that they began talking freely with him.

## Where we end up

Jacob and all his brothers and their households move to Egypt and are given land by Pharaoh.

**Christ foreshadowed:** The Passion: Prayer in the Garden — p. 228

## My Reflections

# The Birth of Moses

## Main Theme

The Lord will raise up a deliverer, who even as a baby will begin to save God's people from slavery and death.

## Characters

Pharaoh, Shiphrah and Puah (Hebrew midwives who save the baby boys from death), the Levite and his wife (Moses' parents), Miriam (Moses' sister), and Moses (the baby)

## Key Verse: Exodus 2:10

Later, when the boy was older, his mother brought him back to Pharaoh's daughter, who adopted him as her own son. The princess named him Moses, for she explained, 'I lifted him out of the water.'

## Setting

Egypt under the rule of a pharaoh who has forgotten about Joseph and the River Nile

Baby Moses is lifted from the River Nile.

## Key plot points

**v.8** – A pharaoh arises in Egypt who does not remember Joseph, and who oppresses and enslaves the Israelites.

**v.16** – He gives an order that all male Hebrew babies should be put to death as soon as they are born.

**v.17** – Shiphrah and Puah, who serve as midwives to the Hebrew women, conspire to let the boys live.

**v.2** – A Levite and his wife have a baby boy. Three months after his birth they set in him adrift in a basket on the River Nile.

## Read the story Exodus 1:8 – 2:10

**1** <sup>8</sup> Eventually, a new king came to power in Egypt who knew nothing about Joseph or what he had done. <sup>9</sup> He said to his people, 'Look, the people of Israel now outnumber us and are stronger than we are. <sup>10</sup> We must make a plan to keep them from growing even more. If we don't, and if war breaks out, they will join our enemies and fight against us. Then they will escape from the country.'

<sup>11</sup> So the Egyptians made the Israelites their slaves. They appointed brutal slave drivers over them, hoping to wear them down with crushing labour. They forced them to build the cities of Pithom and Rameses as supply centres for the king. <sup>12</sup> But the more the Egyptians oppressed them, the more the Israelites multiplied and spread, and the more alarmed the Egyptians became. <sup>13</sup> So the Egyptians worked the people of Israel without mercy. <sup>14</sup> They made their lives bitter, forcing them to mix mortar and make bricks and do all the work in the fields. They were ruthless in all their demands.

<sup>15</sup> Then Pharaoh, the king of Egypt, gave this order to the Hebrew midwives, Shiphrah and Puah: <sup>16</sup> 'When you help the Hebrew women as they give birth, watch as they deliver. If the baby is a boy, kill him; if it is a girl, let her live.' <sup>17</sup> But because the midwives feared God, they refused to obey the king's orders. They allowed the boys to live, too.

<sup>18</sup> So the king of Egypt called for the midwives. 'Why have you done this?' he demanded. 'Why have you allowed the boys to live?'

<sup>19</sup> 'The Hebrew women are not like the Egyptian women,' the midwives replied. 'They are more vigorous and have their babies so quickly that we cannot get there in time.'

<sup>20</sup> So God was good to the midwives, and the Israelites continued to multiply, growing more and more powerful. <sup>21</sup> And because the midwives feared God, he gave them families of their own.

<sup>22</sup> Then Pharaoh gave this order to all his people: 'Throw every newborn Hebrew boy into the River Nile. But you may let the girls live.'

**2** About this time, a man and woman from the tribe of Levi got married. <sup>2</sup> The woman became pregnant and gave birth to a son. She saw that he was a special baby and kept him hidden for three months. <sup>3</sup> But when she could no longer hide him, she got a basket made of papyrus reeds and waterproofed it with tar and pitch. She put the baby in the basket and laid it among the reeds along the bank of the River Nile. **⁴** The baby's sister then stood at a distance, watching to see what would happen to him.

**⁵** Soon Pharaoh's daughter came down to bathe in the river, and her attendants walked along the riverbank. When the princess saw the basket among the reeds, she sent her maid to get it for her. **⁶** When the princess opened it, she saw the baby. The little boy was crying, and she felt sorry for him. 'This must be one of the Hebrew children,' she said.

**⁷** Then the baby's sister approached the princess. 'Should I go and find one of the Hebrew women to nurse the baby for you?' she asked.

**⁸** 'Yes, do!' the princess replied. So the girl went and called the baby's mother.

**⁹** 'Take this baby and nurse him for me,' the princess told the baby's mother. 'I will pay you for your help.' So the woman took her baby home and nursed him.

**¹⁰** Later, when the boy was older, his mother brought him back to Pharaoh's daughter, who adopted him as her own son. The princess named him Moses, for she explained, 'I lifted him out of the water.'

**v.6** – Pharaoh's daughter finds the baby and takes pity on him. She draws him out of the water.

**v.9** – Pharaoh's daughter unknowingly gives the baby back to his mother to be weaned.

**v.10** – When he is weaned, the mother returns the baby to Pharaoh's daughter who names him Moses and raises him as her own.

### Where we end up
Moses grows up in the palace of Pharaoh, but he knows he is born a Hebrew.

## My Reflections

# 15  The Plagues of Egypt

## Main Theme

The Lord will fight his enemies to save his people from slavery and death.

## Setting

The land of Midian, in Egypt with the Israelites, and in Egypt with Pharaoh

## Characters

The Lord, Moses (God's deliverer for his people), Aaron (Moses' brother and spokesman), and Pharaoh (king of Egypt)

## Key Verse: Exodus 12:12

'On that night I will pass through the land of Egypt and strike down every first-born son and first-born male animal in the land of Egypt. I will execute judgment against all the gods of Egypt, for I am the LORD!'

Pharaoh holds his dead son.

# Read the story Exodus 3 – 11

**3** One day Moses was tending the flock of his father-in-law, Jethro, the priest of Midian. He led the flock far into the wilderness and came to Sinai, the mountain of God. ² There the angel of the LORD appeared to him in a blazing fire from the middle of a bush. Moses stared in amazement. Though the bush was engulfed in flames, it didn't burn up. ³ 'This is amazing,' Moses said to himself. 'Why isn't that bush burning up? I must go and see it.'

⁴ When the LORD saw Moses coming to take a closer look, God called to him from the middle of the bush, 'Moses! Moses!'

'Here I am!' Moses replied.

⁵ 'Do not come any closer,' the LORD warned. 'Take off your sandals, for you are standing on holy ground. ⁶ I am the God of your father – the God of Abraham, the God of Isaac, and the God of Jacob.' When Moses heard this, he covered his face because he was afraid to look at God.

⁷ Then the LORD told him, 'I have certainly seen the oppression of my people in Egypt. I have heard their cries of distress because of their harsh slave drivers. Yes, I am aware of their suffering. ⁸ So I have come down to rescue them from the power of the Egyptians and lead them out of Egypt into their own fertile and spacious land. It is a land flowing with milk and honey – the land where the Canaanites, Hittites, Amorites, Perizzites, Hivites, and Jebusites now live. ⁹ Look! The cry of the people of Israel has reached me, and I have seen how harshly the Egyptians abuse them. ¹⁰ Now go, for I am sending you to Pharaoh. You must lead my people Israel out of Egypt.'

¹¹ But Moses protested to God, 'Who am I to appear before Pharaoh? Who am I to lead the people of Israel out of Egypt?'

¹² God answered, 'I will be with you. And this is your sign that I am the one who has sent you: When you have brought the people out of Egypt, you will worship God at this very mountain.'

…

**4** ¹⁰ But Moses pleaded with the LORD, 'O LORD, I'm not very good with words. I never have been, and I'm not now, even though you have spoken to me. I get tongue-tied, and my words get tangled.'

¹¹ Then the LORD asked Moses, 'Who makes a person's mouth? Who decides whether people speak or do not speak, hear or do not hear, see

**v.7–10, 17** – When the Israelites cry out for deliverance, the Lord calls Moses to lead the people out of Egypt, and Aaron to be his spokesman.

or do not see? Is it not I, the LORD? <sup>12</sup> Now go! I will be with you as you speak, and I will instruct you in what to say.'

<sup>13</sup> But Moses again pleaded, 'LORD, please! Send anyone else.'

<sup>14</sup> Then the LORD became angry with Moses. 'All right,' he said. 'What about your brother, Aaron the Levite? I know he speaks well. And look! He is on his way to meet you now. He will be delighted to see you. <sup>15</sup> Talk to him, and put the words in his mouth. I will be with both of you as you speak, and I will instruct you both in what to do. <sup>16</sup> Aaron will be your spokesman to the people. He will be your mouthpiece, and you will stand in the place of God for him, telling him what to say. <sup>17</sup> And take your shepherd's staff with you, and use it to perform the miraculous signs I have shown you.'

…

**11** Then the LORD said to Moses, 'I will strike Pharaoh and the land of Egypt with one more blow. After that, Pharaoh will let you leave this country. In fact, he will be so eager to get rid of you that he will force you all to leave. <sup>2</sup> Tell all the Israelite men and women to ask their Egyptian neighbours for articles of silver and gold.' <sup>3</sup> (Now the LORD had caused the Egyptians to look favourably on the people of Israel. And Moses was considered a very great man in the land of Egypt, respected by Pharaoh's officials and the Egyptian people alike.)

<sup>4</sup> Moses had announced to Pharaoh, 'This is what the LORD says: At midnight tonight I will pass through the heart of Egypt. <sup>5</sup> All the first-born sons will die in every family in Egypt, from the oldest son of Pharaoh, who sits on his throne, to the oldest son of his lowliest servant girl who grinds the flour. Even the first-born of all the livestock will die. <sup>6</sup> Then a loud wail will rise throughout the land of Egypt, a wail like no one has heard before or will ever hear again. <sup>7</sup> But among the Israelites it will be so peaceful that not even a dog will bark. Then you will know that the LORD makes a distinction between the Egyptians and the Israelites. <sup>8</sup> All the officials of Egypt will run to me and fall to the ground before me. "Please leave!" they will beg. "Hurry! And take all your followers with you." Only then will I go!' Then, burning with anger, Moses left Pharaoh.

<sup>9</sup> Now the LORD had told Moses earlier, 'Pharaoh will not listen to you, but then I will do even more mighty miracles in the land of

---

**Chapter 5** – The Lord sends Moses to Pharaoh with a request to allow the people to leave Egypt and journey into the wilderness to celebrate a festival. Pharaoh refuses to let the people go.

**Chapters 7–10** – The Lord sends ten plagues on Egypt to demonstrate that he is God and to convince Pharaoh to let the Israelites go.

**v.5** – For the tenth plague, the Lord kills all of the first-born sons of Egypt including Pharaoh's own son.

Egypt.' [10] Moses and Aaron performed these miracles in Pharaoh's presence, but the LORD hardened Pharaoh's heart, and he wouldn't let the Israelites leave the country.

## Where we end up

Pharaoh's heart is hardened against letting Israel go.

## My Reflections

# 16 The Passover

**Main Theme**

The Lord will deliver his people from death through the blood of a sacrificial substitute.

**Setting**

Egypt on the night of the tenth plague

**Characters**

The Lord, Moses and Aaron, and Pharaoh

**Key Verse: Exodus 12:23**

'For the LORD will pass through the land to strike down the Egyptians. But when he sees the blood on the top and sides of the doorframe, the LORD will pass over your home. He will not permit his death angel to enter your house and strike you down.'

The blood of the lamb is marked on the doorpost.

# Read the story Exodus 12 – 13

**12** While the Israelites were still in the land of Egypt, the Lord gave the following instructions to Moses and Aaron: ² 'From now on, this month will be the first month of the year for you. ³ Announce to the whole community of Israel that on the tenth day of this month each family must choose a lamb or a young goat for a sacrifice, one animal for each household. ⁴ If a family is too small to eat a whole animal, let them share with another family in the neighbourhood. Divide the animal according to the size of each family and how much they can eat. ⁵ The animal you select must be a one-year-old male, either a sheep or a goat, with no defects.

⁶ 'Take special care of this chosen animal until the evening of the fourteenth day of this first month. Then the whole assembly of the community of Israel must slaughter their lamb or young goat at twilight. ⁷ They are to take some of the blood and smear it on the sides and top of the door-frames of the houses where they eat the animal. ⁸ That same night they must roast the meat over a fire and eat it along with bitter salad greens and bread made without yeast. ⁹ Do not eat any of the meat raw or boiled in water. The whole animal – including the head, legs, and internal organs – must be roasted over a fire. ¹⁰ Do not leave any of it until the next morning. Burn whatever is not eaten before morning.

¹¹ 'These are your instructions for eating this meal: Be fully dressed, wear your sandals, and carry your walking stick in your hand. Eat the meal with urgency, for this is the Lord's Passover. ¹² On that night I will pass through the land of Egypt and strike down every first-born son and first-born male animal in the land of Egypt. I will execute judgement against all the gods of Egypt, for I am the Lord! ¹³ But the blood on your doorposts will serve as a sign, marking the houses where you are staying. When I see the blood, I will pass over you. This plague of death will not touch you when I strike the land of Egypt.

¹⁴ 'This is a day to remember. Each year, from generation to generation, you must celebrate it as a special festival to the Lord. This is a law for all time. ¹⁵ For seven days the bread you eat must be made without yeast. On the first day of the festival, remove every trace of yeast from your homes. Anyone who eats bread made with yeast during the seven days of the festival will be cut off from the community of Israel. ¹⁶ On the first day of the festival and again on

# Key plot points

**Introduction** – On the night that he killed the first-born children of Egypt, the Lord passed over the children of Israel in the land.

**v.6–7** – Each family is to slaughter a pure lamb and spread its blood on their door-frames.

**v.13** – Wherever the Lord saw the blood, he would pass over that house.

the seventh day, all the people must observe an official day for holy assembly. No work of any kind may be done on these days except in the preparation of food.

**17** 'Celebrate this Festival of Unleavened Bread, for it will remind you that I brought your forces out of the land of Egypt on this very day. This festival will be a permanent law for you; celebrate this day from generation to generation…'

**28** So the people of Israel did just as the LORD had commanded through Moses and Aaron. **29** And that night at midnight, the LORD struck down all the first-born sons in the land of Egypt, from the first-born son of Pharaoh, who sat on his throne, to the first-born son of the prisoner in the dungeon. Even the first-born of their livestock were killed. **30** Pharaoh and all his officials and all the people of Egypt woke up during the night, and loud wailing was heard throughout the land of Egypt. There was not a single house where someone had not died.

**31** Pharaoh sent for Moses and Aaron during the night. 'Get out!' he ordered. 'Leave my people – and take the rest of the Israelites with you! Go and worship the LORD as you have requested. **32** Take your flocks and herds, as you said, and be gone. Go, but bless me as you leave.' **33** All the Egyptians urged the people of Israel to get out of the land as quickly as possible, for they thought, 'We will all die!'

**34** The Israelites took their bread dough before yeast was added. They wrapped their kneading boards in their cloaks and carried them on their shoulders. **35** And the people of Israel did as Moses had instructed; they asked the Egyptians for clothing and articles of silver and gold. **36** The LORD caused the Egyptians to look favourably on the Israelites, and they gave the Israelites whatever they asked for. So they stripped the Egyptians of their wealth!

**37** That night the people of Israel left Rameses and started for Succoth. There were about 600,000 men, plus all the women and children. **38** A rabble of non-Israelites went with them, along with great flocks and herds of livestock. **39** For bread they baked flat cakes from the dough without yeast they had brought from Egypt. It was made without yeast because the people were driven out of Egypt in such a hurry that they had no time to prepare the bread or other food.

**40** The people of Israel had lived in Egypt for 430 years. **41** In fact, it was on the last day of the 430th year that all the LORD's forces left the

**v.28** – Each Hebrew family smears the blood on their doors, eats the whole lamb and prepares to leave Egypt that night.

**v.29** – The Lord passes through and kills all of Egypt's first-born children.

**v.31** – Pharaoh summons Moses and Aaron and demands that they and all the Israelites leave Egypt.

land. **42** On this night the LORD kept his promise to bring his people out of the land of Egypt. So this night belongs to him, and it must be commemorated every year by all the Israelites, from generation to generation.

...

# 13

Then the LORD said to Moses, **2** 'Dedicate to me every first-born among the Israelites. The first offspring to be born, of both humans and animals, belongs to me.'

**3** So Moses said to the people, 'This is a day to remember for ever – the day you left Egypt, the place of your slavery. Today the LORD has brought you out by the power of his mighty hand. (Remember, eat no food containing yeast.) **4** On this day in early spring, in the month of Abib, you have been set free. **5** You must celebrate this event in this month each year after the LORD brings you into the land of the Canaanites, Hittites, Amorites, Hivites, and Jebusites. (He swore to your ancestors that he would give you this land – a land flowing with milk and honey.) **6** For seven days the bread you eat must be made without yeast. Then on the seventh day, celebrate a feast to the LORD. **7** Eat bread without yeast during those seven days. In fact, there must be no yeast bread or any yeast at all found within the borders of your land during this time.

**8** 'On the seventh day you must explain to your children, "I am celebrating what the LORD did for me when I left Egypt." **9** This annual festival will be a visible sign to you, like a mark branded on your hand or your forehead. Let it remind you always to recite this teaching of the LORD: "With a strong hand, the LORD rescued you from Egypt." **10** So observe the decree of this festival at the appointed time each year.

**11** 'This is what you must do when the LORD fulfils the promise he swore to you and to your ancestors. When he gives you the land where the Canaanites now live, **12** you must present all first-born sons and first-born male animals to the LORD, for they belong to him. **13** A first-born donkey may be bought back from the LORD by presenting a lamb or young goat in its place. But if you do not buy it back, you must break its neck. However, you must buy back every first-born son.

**14** 'And in the future, your children will ask you, "What does all this mean?" Then you will tell them, "With the power of his mighty hand, the LORD brought us out of Egypt, the place of our slavery. **15** Pharaoh

**v.1–16** – The Lord commands his people to celebrate this great event with a yearly festival called Passover, where they would reenact this meal to remember his great deliverance.

stubbornly refused to let us go, so the LORD killed all the first-born males throughout the land of Egypt, both people and animals. That is why I now sacrifice all the first-born males to the LORD – except that the first-born sons are always bought back." [16] This ceremony will be like a mark branded on your hand or your forehead. It is a reminder that the power of the LORD's mighty hand brought us out of Egypt.'

[17] When Pharaoh finally let the people go, God did not lead them along the main road that runs through Philistine territory, even though that was the shortest route to the Promised Land. God said, 'If the people are faced with a battle, they might change their minds and return to Egypt.' [18] So God led them in a roundabout way through the wilderness towards the Red Sea. Thus the Israelites left Egypt like an army ready for battle.

[19] Moses took the bones of Joseph with him, for Joseph had made the sons of Israel swear to do this. He said, 'God will certainly come to help you. When he does, you must take my bones with you from this place.'

[20] The Israelites left Succoth and camped at Etham on the edge of the wilderness. [21] The LORD went ahead of them. He guided them during the day with a pillar of cloud, and he provided light at night with a pillar of fire. This allowed them to travel by day or by night. [22] And the LORD did not remove the pillar of cloud or pillar of fire from its place in front of the people.

## Where we end up

God leads his people through the wilderness, guiding them with a pillar of cloud by day and a pillar of fire by night.

**Christ foreshadowed:** The Crucifixion: Jesus and the Two Criminals – p. 237

# The Red Sea

## 17

## Main Theme

The Lord will fight his enemies to save his people from slavery and death.

## Setting

The Red Sea

## Characters

The Lord, Moses, Pharaoh and the Egyptian army, and the Israelites

## Key Verse:
## Exodus 14:13–14

But Moses told the people, 'Don't be afraid. Just stand still and watch the LORD rescue you today. The Egyptians you see today will never be seen again. The LORD himself will fight for you. Just stay calm.'

Moses leads Israel through the Red Sea.

## Key plot points

**v.2** – The Lord leads the Israelites to the shore of the Red Sea.

**v.8** – Pharaoh regrets letting the people go and leads his army to recapture them in the wilderness. He catches up with them at the shore of the Red Sea.

**v.10, 15** – The Israelites are terrified of the army. Moses cries out to the Lord for help.

## Read the story Exodus 14 – 15

**14** Then the LORD gave these instructions to Moses: ² 'Order the Israelites to turn back and camp by Pi-hahiroth between Migdol and the sea. Camp there along the shore, across from Baal-zephon. ³ Then Pharaoh will think, "The Israelites are confused. They are trapped in the wilderness!" ⁴ And once again I will harden Pharaoh's heart, and he will chase after you. I have planned this in order to display my glory through Pharaoh and his whole army. After this the Egyptians will know that I am the LORD!' So the Israelites camped there as they were told.

⁵ When word reached the king of Egypt that the Israelites had fled, Pharaoh and his officials changed their minds. 'What have we done, letting all those Israelite slaves get away?' they asked. ⁶ So Pharaoh harnessed his chariot and called up his troops. ⁷ He took with him 600 of Egypt's best chariots, along with the rest of the chariots of Egypt, each with its commander. ⁸ The LORD hardened the heart of Pharaoh, the king of Egypt, so he chased after the people of Israel, who had left with fists raised in defiance. ⁹ The Egyptians chased after them with all the forces in Pharaoh's army – all his horses and chariots, his charioteers, and his troops. The Egyptians caught up with the people of Israel as they were camped beside the shore near Pi-hahiroth, across from Baal-zephon.

¹⁰ As Pharaoh approached, the people of Israel looked up and panicked when they saw the Egyptians overtaking them. They cried out to the LORD, ¹¹ and they said to Moses, 'Why did you bring us out here to die in the wilderness? Weren't there enough graves for us in Egypt? What have you done to us? Why did you make us leave Egypt? ¹² Didn't we tell you this would happen while we were still in Egypt? We said, "Leave us alone! Let us be slaves to the Egyptians. It's better to be a slave in Egypt than a corpse in the wilderness!"'

¹³ But Moses told the people, 'Don't be afraid. Just stand still and watch the LORD rescue you today. The Egyptians you see today will never be seen again. ¹⁴ The LORD himself will fight for you. Just stay calm.'

¹⁵ Then the LORD said to Moses, 'Why are you crying out to me? Tell the people to get moving! ¹⁶ Pick up your staff and raise your hand over the sea. Divide the water so the Israelites can walk through the middle of the sea on dry ground. ¹⁷ And I will harden the hearts of the

Egyptians, and they will charge in after the Israelites. My great glory will be displayed through Pharaoh and his troops, his chariots, and his charioteers. [18] When my glory is displayed through them, all Egypt will see my glory and know that I am the Lord!'

[19] Then the angel of God, who had been leading the people of Israel, moved to the rear of the camp. The pillar of cloud also moved from the front and stood behind moved from the front and stood behind them. [20] The cloud settled between the Egyptian and Israelite camps. As darkness fell, the cloud turned to fire, lighting up the night. But the Egyptians and Israelites did not approach each other all night.

[21] Then Moses raised his hand over the sea, and the Lord opened up a path through the water with a strong east wind. The wind blew all that night, turning the seabed into dry land. [22] So the people of Israel walked through the middle of the sea on dry ground, with walls of water on each side!

[23] Then the Egyptians – all of Pharaoh's horses, chariots, and charioteers – chased them into the middle of the sea. [24] But just before dawn the Lord looked down on the Egyptian army from the pillar of fire and cloud, and he threw their forces into total confusion. [25] He twisted their chariot wheels, making their chariots difficult to drive. 'Let's get out of here – away from these Israelites!' the Egyptians shouted. 'The Lord is fighting for them against Egypt!'

[26] When all the Israelites had reached the other side, the Lord said to Moses, 'Raise your hand over the sea again. Then the waters will rush back and cover the Egyptians and their chariots and charioteers.' [27] So as the sun began to rise, Moses raised his hand over the sea, and the water rushed back into its usual place. The Egyptians tried to escape, but the Lord swept them into the sea. [28] Then the waters returned and covered all the chariots and charioteers – the entire army of Pharaoh. Of all the Egyptians who had chased the Israelites into the sea, not a single one survived.

[29] But the people of Israel had walked through the middle of the sea on dry ground, as the water stood up like a wall on both sides. [30] That is how the Lord rescued Israel from the hand of the Egyptians that day. And the Israelites saw the bodies of the Egyptians washed up on the seashore. [31] When the people of Israel saw the mighty power that the Lord had unleashed against the Egyptians, they were filled with awe before him. They put their faith in the Lord and in his servant Moses.

**v.21–22** – The Lord split the sea so that the Israelites could escape. The water formed a wall on either side, but they walked through on dry ground.

**v.23, 28** – When Pharaoh pursues the Israelites into the sea, the Lord makes the water crash back in upon them and drowns the whole army.

...

**15** <sup>20</sup> Then Miriam the prophet, Aaron's sister, took a tambourine and led all the women as they played their tambourines and danced. <sup>21</sup> And Miriam sang this song:

> 'Sing to the LORD,
>> for he has triumphed gloriously;
> he has hurled both horse and rider
>> into the sea.'

## Where we end up

Moses and the Israelites praise God with a song proclaiming the Lord's victory.

**Christ foreshadowed:** The Baptism of the Lord – p. 182

## My Reflections

# The Tabernacle

## 18

**Main Theme**
The Lord will personally dwell among his people and lead them.

**Setting**
The camp of Israel in the wilderness

**Characters**
The Lord, Moses, Aaron and his sons

**Key Verse: Exodus 40:38**
The cloud of the Lord hovered over the Tabernacle during the day, and at night fire glowed inside the cloud so the whole family of Israel could see it. This continued throughout all their journeys.

The Tabernacle of the Lord is set up.

## Read the story Exodus 40

¹ Then the LORD said to Moses, ² 'Set up the Tabernacle on the first day of the new year. ³ Place the Ark of the Covenant inside, and install the inner curtain to enclose the Ark within the Most Holy Place. ⁴ Then bring in the table, and arrange the utensils on it. And bring in the lampstand, and set up the lamps.

⁵ 'Place the gold incense altar in front of the Ark of the Covenant. Then hang the curtain at the entrance of the Tabernacle. ⁶ Place the altar of burnt offering in front of the Tabernacle entrance. ⁷ Set the washbasin between the Tabernacle and the altar, and fill it with water. ⁸ Then set up the courtyard around the outside of the tent, and hang the curtain for the courtyard entrance.

## Key plot points

**Introduction:** After the great Exodus, the Lord met with his people to give them a Law. He told them how they should live, and that they should build a Tabernacle for his presence to be among them. The Tabernacle was a tent that could be set up and taken down easily as the Israelites journeyed through the wilderness.

**v.1–8** – The Lord gave specific requirements for the layout and design of the Tabernacle.

**v.12–15** – The Lord set apart Aaron and his sons to serve as the priests.

**v.16** – Moses ensured that the Tabernacle was completed exactly as the Lord has commanded.

⁹ 'Take the anointing oil and anoint the Tabernacle and all its furnishings to consecrate them and make them holy. ¹⁰ Anoint the altar of burnt offering and its utensils to consecrate them. Then the altar will become absolutely holy. ¹¹ Next anoint the washbasin and its stand to consecrate them.

¹² 'Present Aaron and his sons at the entrance of the Tabernacle, and wash them with water. ¹³ Dress Aaron with the sacred garments and anoint him, consecrating him to serve me as a priest. ¹⁴ Then present his sons and dress them in their tunics. ¹⁵ Anoint them as you did their father, so they may also serve me as priests. With their anointing, Aaron's descendants are set apart for the priesthood forever, from generation to generation.'

¹⁶ Moses proceeded to do everything just as the LORD had commanded him. ¹⁷ So the Tabernacle was set up on the first day of the first month of the second year. ¹⁸ Moses erected the Tabernacle by setting down its bases, inserting the frames, attaching the crossbars, and setting up the posts. ¹⁹ Then he spread the coverings over the Tabernacle framework and put on the protective layers, just as the LORD had commanded him.

²⁰ He took the stone tablets inscribed with the terms of the covenant and placed them inside the Ark. Then he attached the carrying poles to the Ark, and he set the Ark's cover – the place of atonement – on top of it. ²¹ Then he brought the Ark of the Covenant into the Tabernacle and hung the inner curtain to shield it from view, just as the LORD had commanded him.

²² Next Moses placed the table in the Tabernacle, along the north side of the Holy Place, just outside the inner curtain. ²³ And he arranged the Bread of the Presence on the table before the LORD, just as the LORD had commanded him.

²⁴ He set the lamp stand in the Tabernacle across from the table on the south side of the Holy Place. ²⁵ Then he lit the lamps in the LORD's presence, just as the LORD had commanded him. ²⁶ He also placed the gold incense altar in the Tabernacle, in the Holy Place in front of the inner curtain. ²⁷ On it he burned the fragrant incense, just as the LORD had commanded him.

²⁸ He hung the curtain at the entrance of the Tabernacle, ²⁹ and he placed the altar of burnt offering near the Tabernacle entrance. On it he offered a burnt offering and a grain offering, just as the LORD had commanded him.

**30** Next Moses placed the washbasin between the Tabernacle and the altar. He filled it with water so the priests could wash themselves. **31** Moses and Aaron and Aaron's sons used water from it to wash their hands and feet. **32** Whenever they approached the altar and entered the Tabernacle, they washed themselves, just as the Lord had commanded Moses.

**33** Then he hung the curtains forming the courtyard around the Tabernacle and the altar. And he set up the curtain at the entrance of the courtyard. So at last Moses finished the work.

**34** Then the cloud covered the Tabernacle, and the glory of the Lord filled the Tabernacle. **35** Moses could no longer enter the Tabernacle because the cloud had settled down over it, and the glory of the Lord filled the Tabernacle.

**36** Now whenever the cloud lifted from the Tabernacle, the people of Israel would set out on their journey, following it. **37** But if the cloud did not rise, they remained where they were until it lifted. **38** The cloud of the Lord hovered over the Tabernacle during the day, and at night fire glowed inside the cloud so the whole family of Israel could see it. This continued throughout all their journeys.

**v.38** — The pillar of cloud and fire descended on the completed Tabernacle.

## Where we end up

The Lord dwelt among his people and continued to lead them.

## My Reflections

# 19  The Twelve Spies

### Main Theme

The Lord will not give his victory and blessing to a faithless and disobedient people.

### Setting

Kadesh-Barnea (the location of the Israelites' camp on the southern edge of Canaan)

### Characters

The Lord, Moses, Joshua, Caleb, and the twelve spies

### Key Verse: Numbers 14:8–9

'And if the LORD is pleased with us, he will bring us safely into that land and give it to us. It is a rich land flowing with milk and honey. Do not rebel against the LORD, and don't be afraid of the people of the land. They are only helpless prey to us! They have no protection, but the LORD is with us! Don't be afraid of them!'

The spies return from Canaan.

# Read the story Numbers 13:1 – 14:10

**13** The LORD now said to Moses, ² 'Send out men to explore the land of Canaan, the land I am giving to the Israelites. Send one leader from each of the twelve ancestral tribes.' ³ So Moses did as the LORD commanded him. He sent out twelve men, all tribal leaders of Israel, from their camp in the wilderness of Paran. ⁴ These were the tribes and the names of their leaders:

| Tribe | Leader |
|---|---|
| Reuben | Shammua son of Zaccur |
| ⁵ Simeon | Shaphat son of Hori |
| ⁶ Judah | Caleb son of Jephunneh |
| ⁷ Issachar | Igal son of Joseph |
| ⁸ Ephraim | Hoshea son of Nun |
| ⁹ Benjamin | Palti son of Raphu |
| ¹⁰ Zebulun | Gaddiel son of Sodi |
| ¹¹ Manasseh son of Joseph | Gaddi son of Susi |
| ¹² Dan | Ammiel son of Gemalli |
| ¹³ Asher | Sethur son of Michael |
| ¹⁴ Naphtali | Nahbi son of Vophsi |
| ¹⁵ Gad | Geuel son of Maki |

¹⁶ These are the names of the men Moses sent out to explore the land. (Moses called Hoshea son of Nun by the name Joshua.)

¹⁷ Moses gave the men these instructions as he sent them out to explore the land: 'Go north through the Negev into the hill country. ¹⁸ See what the land is like, and find out whether the people living there are strong or weak, few or many. ¹⁹ See what kind of land they live in. Is it good or bad? Do their towns have walls, or are they unprotected like open camps? ²⁰ Is the soil fertile or poor? Are there many trees? Do your best to bring back samples of the crops you see.' (It happened to be the season for harvesting the first ripe grapes.)

²¹ So they went up and explored the land from the wilderness of Zin as far as Rehob, near Lebo-hamath. ²² Going north, they passed through the Negev and arrived at Hebron, where Ahiman, Sheshai, and Talmai – all descendants of Anak – lived. (The ancient town of Hebron was founded seven years before the Egyptian city of Zoan.) ²³ When

## Key plot points

**Introduction** – The Lord led h s people all the way to the border of Canaan, to an area called Kadesh-Barnea.

**v.2** – The Lord commands Moses to send a team of spies to see how good the land is, and what sort of people live in it.

they came to the valley of Eshcol, they cut down a branch with a single cluster of grapes so large that it took two of them to carry it on a pole between them! They also brought back samples of the pomegranates and figs. ²⁴ That place was called the valley of Eshcol (which means 'cluster'), because of the cluster of grapes the Israelite men cut there.

²⁵ After exploring the land for forty days, the men returned ²⁶ to Moses, Aaron, and the whole community of Israel at Kadesh in the wilderness of Paran. They reported to the whole community what they had seen and showed them the fruit they had taken from the land. ²⁷ This was their report to Moses: 'We entered the land you sent us to explore, and it is indeed a bountiful country – a land flowing with milk and honey. Here is the kind of fruit it produces. ²⁸ But the people living there are powerful, and their towns are large and fortified. We even saw giants there, the descendants of Anak! ²⁹ The Amalekites live in the Negev, and the Hittites, Jebusites, and Amorites live in the hill country. The Canaanites live along the coast of the Mediterranean Sea and along the Jordan Valley.'

³⁰ But Caleb tried to quiet the people as they stood before Moses. 'Let's go at once to take the land,' he said. 'We can certainly conquer it!'

³¹ But the other men who had explored the land with him disagreed. 'We can't go up against them! They are stronger than we are!' ³² So they spread this bad report about the land among the Israelites: 'The land we travelled through and explored will devour anyone who goes to live there. All the people we saw were huge. ³³ We even saw giants there, the descendants of Anak. Next to them we felt like grasshoppers, and that's what they thought, too!'

**14** Then the whole community began weeping aloud, and they cried all night. Their voices rose in a great chorus of protest against Moses and Aaron. 'If only we had died in Egypt, or even here in the wilderness!' they complained. ³ 'Why is the LORD taking us to this country only to have us die in battle? Our wives and our little ones will be carried off as plunder! Wouldn't it be better for us to return to Egypt?' ⁴ Then they plotted among themselves, 'Let's choose a new leader and go back to Egypt!'

⁵ Then Moses and Aaron fell face down on the ground before the whole community of Israel. ⁶ Two of the men who had explored the land, Joshua son of Nun and Caleb son of Jephunneh, tore their clothing. ⁷ They said to all the people of Israel, 'The land we travelled

**v.25** – The report on the quality of the land is very positive. The produce they bring back to the camp is amazing.

**v.28** – The spies also see numerous large and strong people. They fear that Israel will not be able to defeat them in battle.

**v.3** – The nation refuses to enter the land and take it.

**v.4** – They hatch a plan to choose a new leader and return to Egypt.

through and explored is a wonderful land! ⁸ And if the LORD is pleased with us, he will bring us safely into that land and give it to us. It is a rich land flowing with milk and honey. ⁹ Do not rebel against the LORD, and don't be afraid of the people of the land. They are only helpless prey to us! They have no protection, but the LORD is with us! Don't be afraid of them!'

¹⁰ But the whole community began to talk about stoning Joshua and Caleb.

**v.7–9** — Two of the spies, Caleb and Joshua, try to persuade the people to trust the Lord and to not be afraid.

## Where we end up

The whole community of the people threatens to kill Moses, Caleb, and Joshua.

## My Reflections

# 20 Wilderness Wanderings

### Main Theme

The Lord will judge sin and rebellion against his Kingdom, even among his covenant people.

### Setting

Kadesh-Barnea (an area at the south of the land of Canaan)

### Characters

The Lord, Moses, Aaron, Caleb and Joshua, the Israelites, and the inhabitants of Canaan

### Key Verse: Numbers 14:22–23

'Not one of these people will ever enter that land. They have all seen my glorious presence and the miraculous signs I performed both in Egypt and in the wilderness, but again and again they have tested me by refusing to listen to my voice. They will never even see the land I swore to give their ancestors. None of those who have treated me with contempt will ever see it.'

Israel wanders in the wilderness.

# Read the story Numbers 14:11–45

Then the glorious presence of the Lord appeared to all the Israelites at the Tabernacle. <sup>11</sup> And the Lord said to Moses, 'How long will these people treat me with contempt? Will they never believe me, even after all the miraculous signs I have done among them? <sup>12</sup> I will disown them and destroy them with a plague. Then I will make you into a nation greater and mightier than they are!'

<sup>13</sup> But Moses objected. 'What will the Egyptians think when they hear about it?' he asked the Lord. 'They know full well the power you displayed in rescuing your people from Egypt. <sup>14</sup> Now if you destroy them, the Egyptians will send a report to the inhabitants of this land, who have already heard that you live among your people. They know, Lord, that you have appeared to your people face to face and that your pillar of cloud hovers over them. They know that you go before them in the pillar of cloud by day and the pillar of fire by night. <sup>15</sup> Now if you slaughter all these people with a single blow, the nations that have heard of your fame will say, <sup>16</sup> "The Lord was not able to bring them into the land he swore to give them, so he killed them in the wilderness."

<sup>17</sup> 'Please, Lord, prove that your power is as great as you have claimed. For you said, <sup>18</sup> "The Lord is slow to anger and filled with unfailing love, forgiving every kind of sin and rebellion. But he does not excuse the guilty. He lays the sins of the parents upon their children; the entire family is affected – even children in the third and fourth generations." <sup>19</sup> In keeping with your magnificent, unfailing love, please pardon the sins of this people, just as you have forgiven them ever since they left Egypt.'

<sup>20</sup> Then the Lord said, 'I will pardon them as you have requested. <sup>21</sup> But as surely as I live, and as surely as the earth is filled with the Lord's glory, <sup>22</sup> not one of these people will ever enter that land. They have all seen my glorious presence and the miraculous signs I performed both in Egypt and in the wilderness, but again and again they have tested me by refusing to listen to my voice. <sup>23</sup> They will never even see the land I swore to give their ancestors. None of those who have treated me with contempt will ever see it. <sup>24</sup> But my servant Caleb has a different attitude from that of the others. He has remained loyal to me, so I will bring him into the land he explored. His descendants

# Key plot points

**v.11–12** – In response to the rebellion at Kadesh-Barnea, the Lord says that he is going to destroy the entire nation except for Moses, Joshua, Caleb, and Aaron.

**v.13–19** – Moses intercedes for the people and prays for the Lord to forgive them.

**v.20–23** – The Lord condemns the people to wander in the desert for forty years until every adult who refused to enter the land dies.

will possess their full share of that land. <sup>25</sup> Now turn around, and don't go on towards the land where the Amalekites and Canaanites live. Tomorrow you must set out for the wilderness in the direction of the Red Sea.'

. . .

**v.39** – Once the people hear this, they change their mind and decide to attack the Canaanites.

<sup>39</sup> When Moses reported the Lord's words to all the Israelites, the people were filled with grief. <sup>40</sup> Then they got up early the next morning and went to the top of the range of hills. 'Let's go,' they said. 'We realize that we have sinned, but now we are ready to enter the land the Lord has promised us.'

<sup>41</sup> But Moses said, 'Why are you now disobeying the Lord's orders to return to the wilderness? It won't work. <sup>42</sup> Do not go up into the land now. You will only be crushed by your enemies because the Lord is not with you. <sup>43</sup> When you face the Amalekites and Canaanites in battle, you will be slaughtered. The Lord will abandon you because you have abandoned the Lord.'

<sup>44</sup> But the people defiantly pushed ahead towards the hill country, even though neither Moses nor the Ark of the Lord's Covenant left the camp. <sup>45</sup> Then the Amalekites and the Canaanites who lived in those hills came down and attacked them and chased them back as far as Hormah.

**v.45** – The Canaanites defeat them easily.

## Where we end up

For the next forty years, the pillar of cloud and fire leads the people all around the wilderness.

**Christ foreshadowed:** The Temptation of Our Lord – p. 184

# Crossing the Jordan

## 21

### Main Theme

The Lord's people will remember and reenact his mighty saving deeds.

### Setting

The River Jordan (the eastern edge of the land of Canaan)

### Characters

The Lord, Joshua, the priests (carriers of the Ark of the Covenant), and the Israelites (a new generation after forty years in the wilderness)

### Key Verse: Joshua 3:7

The LORD told Joshua, 'Today I will begin to make you a great leader in the eyes of all the Israelites. They will know that I am with you, just as I was with Moses.'

The priests carry the Ark into the River Jordan.

## Key plot points

**Introduction** – After forty years wandering in the wilderness, the Lord anoints Joshua to lead a new generation into the land of Canaan.

**v.1** – They come to the east side of Canaan and encounter the River Jordan.

**v.7** – The Lord tells Joshua that just as the Israelites followed Moses through the Red Sea, so they would follow him through the River Jordan.

**v.15** – The priests carrying the Ark of the Covenant step foot in the river and the water stops flowing.

**v.16** – With the waters piling up in a heap, the Israelites cross the river on dry land.

## Read the story Joshua 3 – 4

**3** Early the next morning Joshua and all the Israelites left Acacia Grove and arrived at the banks of the River Jordan, where they camped before crossing. ² Three days later the Israelite officers went through the camp, ³ giving these instructions to the people: 'When you see the Levitical priests carrying the Ark of the Covenant of the Lord your God, move out from your positions and follow them. ⁴ Since you have never travelled this way before, they will guide you. Stay about a kilometre behind them, keeping a clear distance between you and the Ark. Make sure you don't come any closer.'

⁵ Then Joshua told the people, 'Purify yourselves, for tomorrow the Lord will do great wonders among you.'

⁶ In the morning Joshua said to the priests, 'Lift up the Ark of the Covenant and lead the people across the river.' And so they started out and went ahead of the people.

⁷ The Lord told Joshua, 'Today I will begin to make you a great leader in the eyes of all the Israelites. They will know that I am with you, just as I was with Moses. ⁸ Give this command to the priests who carry the Ark of the Covenant: "When you reach the banks of the River Jordan, take a few steps into the river and stop there."'

⁹ So Joshua told the Israelites, 'Come and listen to what the Lord your God says. ¹⁰ Today you will know that the living God is among you. He will surely drive out the Canaanites, Hittites, Hivites, Perizzites, Girgashites, Amorites, and Jebusites ahead of you. ¹¹ Look, the Ark of the Covenant, which belongs to the Lord of the whole earth, will lead you across the River Jordan! ¹² Now choose twelve men from the tribes of Israel, one from each tribe. ¹³ The priests will carry the Ark of the Lord, the Lord of all the earth. As soon as their feet touch the water, the flow of water will be cut off upstream, and the river will stand up like a wall.'

¹⁴ So the people left their camp to cross the Jordan, and the priests who were carrying the Ark of the Covenant went ahead of them. ¹⁵ It was the harvest season, and the Jordan was overflowing its banks. But as soon as the feet of the priests who were carrying the Ark touched the water at the river's edge, ¹⁶ the water above that point began backing up a great distance away at a town called Adam, which is near Zarethan. And the water below that point flowed on to the Dead Sea

until the river bed was dry. Then all the people crossed over near the town of Jericho.

**17** Meanwhile, the priests who were carrying the Ark of the Lord's Covenant stood on dry ground in the middle of the river bed as the people passed by. They waited there until the whole nation of Israel had crossed the Jordan on dry ground.

**4** When all the people had crossed the Jordan, the Lord said to Joshua, **2** 'Now choose twelve men, one from each tribe. **3** Tell them, "Take twelve stones from the very place where the priests are standing in the middle of the Jordan. Carry them out and pile them up at the place where you will camp tonight."'

**4** So Joshua called together the twelve men he had chosen – one from each of the tribes of Israel. **5** He told them, 'Go into the middle of the Jordan, in front of the Ark of the Lord your God. Each of you must pick up one stone and carry it out on your shoulder – twelve stones in all, one for each of the twelve tribes of Israel. **6** We will use these stones to build a memorial. In the future your children will ask you, "What do these stones mean?" **7** Then you can tell them, "They remind us that the River Jordan stopped flowing when the Ark of the Lord's Covenant went across." These stones will stand as a memorial among the people of Israel for ever.'

**8** So the men did as Joshua had commanded them. They took twelve stones from the middle of the River Jordan, one for each tribe, just as the Lord had told Joshua. They carried them to the place where they camped for the night and constructed the memorial there.

**9** Joshua also set up another pile of twelve stones in the middle of the Jordan, at the place where the priests who carried the Ark of the Covenant were standing. And they are there to this day.

**10** The priests who were carrying the Ark stood in the middle of the river until all of the Lord's commands that Moses had given to Joshua were carried out. Meanwhile, the people hurried across the river bed. **11** And when everyone was safely on the other side, the priests crossed over with the Ark of the Lord as the people watched.

**12** The armed warriors from the tribes of Reuben, Gad, and the half-tribe of Manasseh led the Israelites across the Jordan, just as Moses had directed. **13** These armed men – about 40,000 strong – were ready for battle, and the Lord was with them as they crossed over to the plains of Jericho.

**Chapter 4** – They set up two monuments of twelve stones to remember this great event. One they set up in the river itself where the priests stood. For the second monument they took twelve stones from the dry riverbed and set them up at their camp in Gilgal.

[14] That day the Lord made Joshua a great leader in the eyes of all the Israelites, and for the rest of his life they revered him as much as they had revered Moses.

[15] The Lord had said to Joshua, [16] 'Command the priests carrying the Ark of the Covenant to come up out of the river bed.' [17] So Joshua gave the command. [18] As soon as the priests carrying the Ark of the Lord's Covenant came up out of the river bed and their feet were on high ground, the water of the Jordan returned and overflowed its banks as before.

[19] The people crossed the Jordan on the tenth day of the first month. Then they camped at Gilgal, just east of Jericho. [20] It was there at Gilgal that Joshua piled up the twelve stones taken from the River Jordan.

[21] Then Joshua said to the Israelites, 'In the future your children will ask, "What do these stones mean?" [22] Then you can tell them, "This is where the Israelites crossed the Jordan on dry ground." [23] For the Lord your God dried up the river right before your eyes, and he kept it dry until you were all across, just as he did at the Red Sea when he dried it up until we had all crossed over. [24] He did this so all the nations of the earth might know that the Lord's hand is powerful, and so you might fear the Lord your God for ever.'

## Where we end up

The stones were there to help the people remember the deeds of the Lord and tell the story to their children.

## My Reflections

# Winning Canaan

## 22

## Main Theme

The Lord will give victory through the faith and obedience of his people.

## Setting

Jericho (a major city in the eastern part of Canaan)

## Characters

The Lord, Joshua, and the Israelite army

## Key Verse: Joshua 6:20

When the people heard the sound of the rams' horns, they shouted as loud as they could. Suddenly, the walls of Jericho collapsed, and the Israelites charged straight into the town and captured it.

Joshua leads the victory over Jericho.

# Read the story Joshua 5:13 – 6:27

**Introduction** – Israel camps near Jericho and prepares to attack it.

**v.13–14** – The commander of the Lord's army meets with Joshua to reassure him that God is indeed with his people.

**v.1** – Jericho is protected by stone walls that were high and thick. It would be very difficult for an invading army to take such a city.

¹³ When Joshua was near the town of Jericho, he looked up and saw a man standing in front of him with sword in hand. Joshua went up to him and demanded, 'Are you friend or foe?'

¹⁴ 'Neither,' he replied. 'I am the commander of the LORD's army.'

At this, Joshua fell with his face to the ground in reverence. 'I am at your command,' Joshua said. 'What do you want your servant to do?'

¹⁵ The commander of the LORD's army replied, 'Take off your sandals, for the place where you are standing is holy.' And Joshua did as he was told.

**6** Now the gates of Jericho were tightly shut because the people were afraid of the Israelites. No one was allowed to go out or in. ² But the LORD said to Joshua, 'I have given you Jericho, its king, and all its strong warriors. ³ You and your fighting men should march around the town once a day for six days. ⁴ Seven priests will walk ahead of

Joshua meets the commander of the Lord's army.

the Ark, each carrying a ram's horn. On the seventh day you are to march around the town seven times, with the priests blowing the horns.⁵ When you hear the priests give one long blast on the rams' horns, have all the people shout as loud as they can. Then the walls of the town will collapse, and the people can charge straight into the town.'

⁶ So Joshua called together the priests and said, 'Take up the Ark of the LORD's Covenant, and assign seven priests to walk in front of it, each carrying a ram's horn.' ⁷ Then he gave orders to the people: 'March around the town, and the armed men will lead the way in front of the Ark of the LORD.'

⁸ After Joshua spoke to the people, the seven priests with the rams' horns started marching in the presence of the LORD, blowing the horns as they marched. And the Ark of the LORD's Covenant followed behind them. ⁹ Some of the armed men marched in front of the priests with the horns and some behind the Ark, with the priests continually blowing the horns. ¹⁰ 'Do not shout; do not even talk,' Joshua commanded. 'Not a single word from any of you until I tell you to shout. Then shout!' ¹¹ So the Ark of the LORD was carried around the town once that day, and then everyone returned to spend the night in the camp.

¹² Joshua got up early the next morning, and the priests again carried the Ark of the LORD. ¹³ The seven priests with the rams' horns marched in front of the Ark of the LORD, blowing their horns. Again the armed men marched both in front of the priests with the horns and behind the Ark of the LORD. All this time the priests were blowing their horns. ¹⁴ On the second day they again marched around the town once and returned to the camp. They followed this pattern for six days.

¹⁵ On the seventh day the Israelites got up at dawn and marched around the town as they had done before. But this time they went around the town seven times. ¹⁶ The seventh time around, as the priests sounded the long blast on their horns, Joshua commanded the people, 'Shout! For the LORD has given you the town! ¹⁷ Jericho and everything in it must be completely destroyed as an offering to the LORD. Only Rahab the prostitute and the others in her house will be spared, for she protected our spies.

¹⁸ 'Do not take any of the things set apart for destruction, or you yourselves will be completely destroyed, and you will bring trouble on

**v.2–5** – The Lord tells the people to march around the city for seven days.

**v.20** – Israel obeys the plan laid out by the Lord and, on the seventh day, the great walls of Jericho come crashing down.

the camp of Israel. [19] Everything made from silver, gold, bronze, or iron is sacred to the LORD and must be brought into his treasury.'

[20] When the people heard the sound of the rams' horns, they shouted as loud as they could. Suddenly, the walls of Jericho collapsed, and the Israelites charged straight into the town and captured it. [21] They completely destroyed everything in it with their swords – men and women, young and old, cattle, sheep, goats, and donkeys.

[22] Meanwhile, Joshua said to the two spies, 'Keep your promise. Go to the prostitute's house and bring her out, along with all her family.'

[23] The men who had been spies went in and brought out Rahab, her father, mother, brothers, and all the other relatives who were with her. They moved her whole family to a safe place near the camp of Israel.

[24] Then the Israelites burned the town and everything in it. Only the things made from silver, gold, bronze, or iron were kept for the treasury of the LORD's house. [25] So Joshua spared Rahab the prostitute and her relatives who were with her in the house, because she had hidden the spies Joshua sent to Jericho. And she lives among the Israelites to this day.

[26] At that time Joshua invoked this curse:

'May the curse of the LORD fall on anyone
    who tries to rebuild the town of Jericho.
At the cost of his first-born son,
    he will lay its foundation.
At the cost of his youngest son,
    he will set up its gates.'

[27] So the LORD was with Joshua, and his reputation spread throughout the land.

## Where we end up

Jericho is destroyed completely. The Lord also commands that Rahab the prostitute be spared from the destruction of the city because of her help for the spies Joshua had sent (see Joshua 2 for this story).

**Christ foreshadowed:** The Gerasene Demoniac – p. 191

# Gideon

## 23

**Main Theme**

The Lord will deliver not by the might of armies and the courage of leaders, but by the victory of faith.

**Setting**

Gideon's winepress, Gideon's hometown, and Gideon's army camp

**Characters**

The Lord, Gideon, and Gideon's army

**Key Verse: Judges 6:14**

Then the LORD turned to him and said, 'Go with the strength you have, and rescue Israel from the Midianites. I am sending you!'

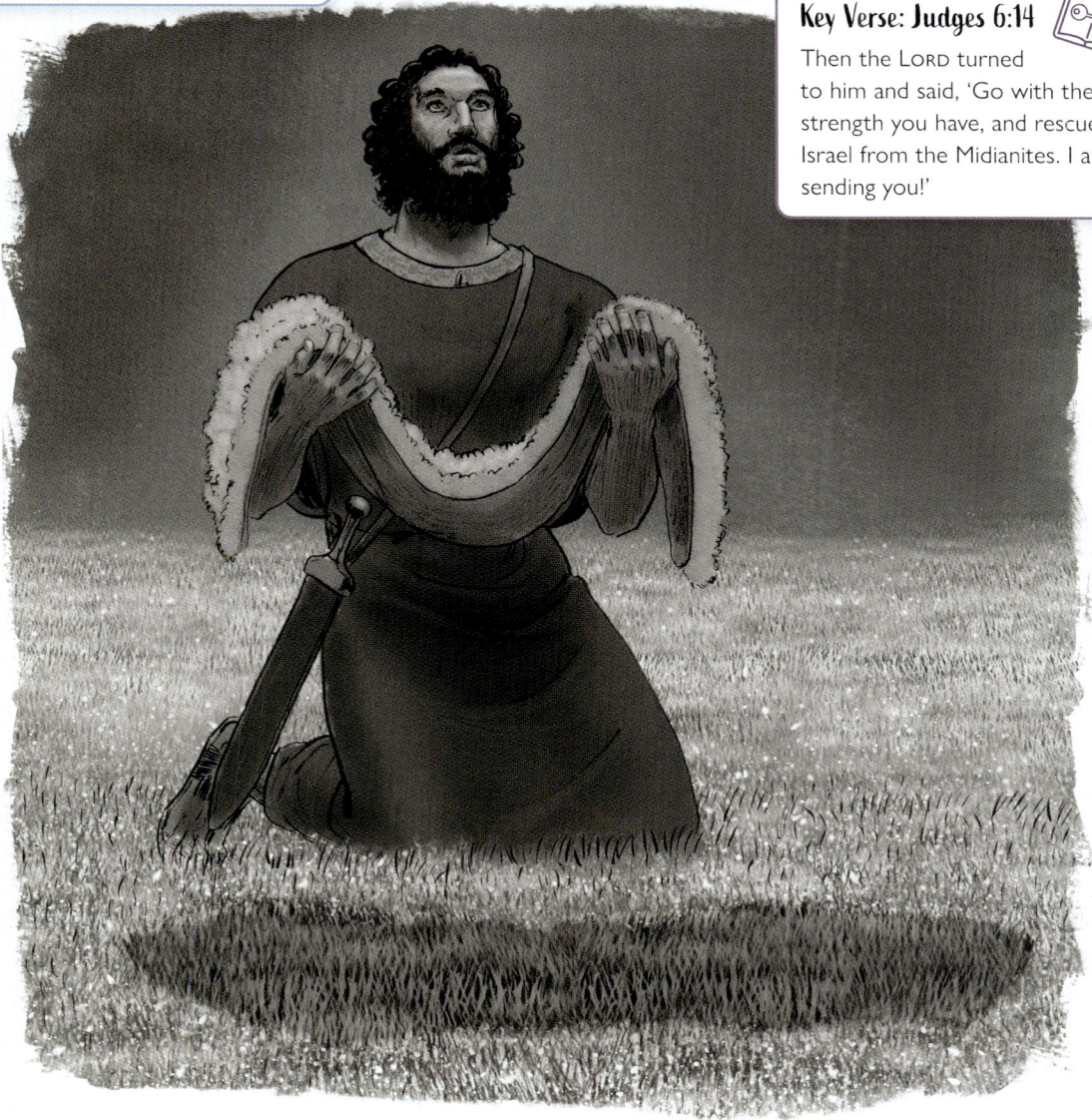

Gideon asks the Lord for a sign.

## Key plot points

**v.1–10** – After the Israelites enter the land, they do not stay faithful to the Lord. The Lord allows their enemies to defeat them, but he raises up judges to deliver them.

**v.11** – When the Midianites defeat Israel, the Lord calls Gideon, who is treading out grain in his winepress.

## Read the story Judges 6 – 7

6 The Israelites did evil in the Lord's sight. So the Lord handed them over to the Midianites for seven years. ² The Midianites were so cruel that the Israelites made hiding places for themselves in the mountains, caves, and strongholds. ³ Whenever the Israelites planted their crops, marauders from Midian, Amalek, and the people of the east would attack Israel, ⁴ camping in the land and destroying crops as far away as Gaza. They left the Israelites with nothing to eat, taking all the sheep, goats, cattle, and donkeys. ⁵ These enemy hordes, coming with their livestock and tents, were as thick as locusts; they arrived on droves of camels too numerous to count. And they stayed until the land was stripped bare. ⁶ So Israel was reduced to starvation by the Midianites. Then the Israelites cried out to the Lord for help.

⁷ When they cried out to the Lord because of Midian, ⁸ the Lord sent a prophet to the Israelites. He said, 'This is what the Lord, the God of Israel, says: I brought you up out of slavery in Egypt. ⁹ I rescued you from the Egyptians and from all who oppressed you. I drove out your enemies and gave you their land. ¹⁰ I told you, "I am the Lord your God. You must not worship the gods of the Amorites, in whose land you now live." But you have not listened to me.'

¹¹ Then the angel of the Lord came and sat beneath the great tree at Ophrah, which belonged to Joash of the clan of Abiezer. Gideon son of Joash was threshing wheat at the bottom of a winepress to hide the grain from the Midianites. ¹² The angel of the Lord appeared to him and said, 'Mighty hero, the Lord is with you!'

¹³ 'Sir,' Gideon replied, 'if the Lord is with us, why has all this happened to us? And where are all the miracles our ancestors told us about? Didn't they say, "The Lord brought us up out of Egypt"? But now the Lord has abandoned us and handed us over to the Midianites.'

¹⁴ Then the Lord turned to him and said, 'Go with the strength you have, and rescue Israel from the Midianites. I am sending you!'

¹⁵ 'But Lord,' Gideon replied, 'how can I rescue Israel? My clan is the weakest in the whole tribe of Manasseh, and I am the least in my entire family!'

¹⁶ The Lord said to him, 'I will be with you. And you will destroy the Midianites as if you were fighting against one man.'

**17** Gideon replied, 'If you are truly going to help me, show me a sign to prove that it is really the Lord speaking to me. **18** Don't go away until I come back and bring my offering to you.'

He answered, 'I will stay here until you return.'

**19** Gideon hurried home. He cooked a young goat, and with a basket of flour he baked some bread without yeast. Then, carrying the meat in a basket and the broth in a pot, he brought them out and presented them to the angel, who was under the great tree.

**20** The angel of God said to him, 'Place the meat and the unleavened bread on this rock, and pour the broth over it.' And Gideon did as he was told. **21** Then the angel of the Lord touched the meat and bread with the tip of the staff in his hand, and fire flamed up from the rock and consumed all he had brought. And the angel of the Lord disappeared.

**22** When Gideon realized that it was the angel of the Lord, he cried out, 'Oh, Sovereign Lord, I'm doomed! I have seen the angel of the Lord face to face!'

**23** 'It is all right,' the Lord replied. 'Do not be afraid. You will not die.' **24** And Gideon built an altar to the Lord there and named it Yahweh-Shalom (which means 'the Lord is peace'). The altar remains in Ophrah in the land of the clan of Abiezer to this day.

**25** That night the Lord said to Gideon, 'Take the second bull from your father's herd, the one that is seven years old. Pull down your father's altar to Baal, and cut down the Asherah pole standing beside it. **26** Then build an altar to the Lord your God here on this hilltop sanctuary, laying the stones carefully. Sacrifice the bull as a burnt offering on the altar, using as fuel the wood of the Asherah pole you cut down.'

**27** So Gideon took ten of his servants and did as the Lord had commanded. But he did it at night because he was afraid of the did it at night because he was afraid of the other members of his father's household and the people of the town.

**28** Early the next morning, as the people of the town began to stir, someone discovered that the altar of Baal had been broken down and that the Asherah pole beside it had been cut down. In their place a new altar had been built, and on it were the remains of the bull that had been sacrificed. **29** The people said to each other, 'Who did this?' And after asking around and making a careful search, they learned that it was Gideon, the son of Joash.

**v.17** – Gideon repeatedly asks the Lord for signs to confirm the word of the Lord.

**v.25** – The Lord calls Gideon to destroy the altar of Baal in his hometown.

³⁰ 'Bring out your son,' the men of the town demanded of Joash. 'He must die for destroying the altar of Baal and for cutting down the Asherah pole.'

³¹ But Joash shouted to the mob that confronted him, 'Why are you defending Baal? Will you argue his case? Whoever pleads his case will be put to death by morning! If Baal truly is a god, let him defend himself and destroy the one who broke down his altar!' ³² From then on Gideon was called Jerub-baal, which means 'Let Baal defend himself', because he broke down Baal's altar.

³³ Soon afterwards the armies of Midian, Amalek, and the people of the east formed an alliance against Israel and crossed the Jordan, camping in the valley of Jezreel. ³⁴ Then the Spirit of the LORD clothed Gideon with power. He blew a ram's horn as a call to arms, and the men of the clan of Abiezer came to him. ³⁵ He also sent messengers throughout Manasseh, Asher, Zebulun, and Naphtali, summoning their warriors, and all of them responded.

³⁶ Then Gideon said to God, 'If you are truly going to use me to rescue Israel as you promised, ³⁷ prove it to me in this way. I will put a wool fleece on the threshing floor tonight. If the fleece is wet with dew in the morning but the ground is dry, then I will know that you are going to help me rescue Israel as you promised.' ³⁸ And that is just what happened. When Gideon got up early the next morning, he squeezed the fleece and wrung out a whole bowlful of water.

³⁹ Then Gideon said to God, 'Please don't be angry with me, but let me make one more request. Let me use the fleece for one more test. This time let the fleece remain dry while the ground around it is wet with dew.' ⁴⁰ So that night God did as Gideon asked. The fleece was dry in the morning, but the ground was covered with dew.

**7** So Jerub-baal (that is, Gideon) and his army got up early and went as far as the spring of Harod. The armies of Midian were camped north of them in the valley near the hill of Moreh. ² The LORD said to Gideon, 'You have too many warriors with you. If I let all of you fight the Midianites, the Israelites will boast to me that they saved themselves by their own strength. ³ Therefore, tell the people, "Whoever is timid or afraid may leave this mountain and go home."' So 22,000 of them went home, leaving only 10,000 who were willing to fight.

⁴ But the LORD told Gideon, 'There are still too many! Bring them down to the spring, and I will test them to determine who will go with

**v.36–40** – Before he leads the army out to fight the Midianites, Gideon twice asks the Lord to confirm his word through a sign with a fleece. The Lord confirms his word.

**v.1–8** – He pares Gideon's army down from 32,000 to 300.

you and who will not.' **5** When Gideon took his warriors down to the water, the LORD told him, 'Divide the men into two groups. In one group put all those who cup water in their hands and lap it up with their tongues like dogs. In the other group put all those who kneel down and drink with their mouths in the stream.' **6** Only 300 of the men drank from their hands. All the others got down on their knees and drank with their mouths in the stream.

**7** The LORD told Gideon, 'With these 300 men I will rescue you and give you victory over the Midianites. Send all the others home.' **8** So Gideon collected the provisions and rams' horns of the other warriors and sent them home. But he kept the 300 men with him.

The Midianite camp was in the valley just below Gideon. **9** That night the LORD said, 'Get up! Go down into the Midianite camp, for I have given you victory over them! **10** But if you are afraid to attack, go down to the camp with your servant Purah.

**11** Listen to what the Midianites are saying, and you will be greatly encouraged. Then you will be eager to attack.'

So Gideon took Purah and went down to the edge of the enemy camp. **12** The armies of Midian, Amalek, and the people of the east had settled in the valley like a swarm of locusts. Their camels were like grains of sand on the seashore – too many to count! **13** Gideon crept up just as a man was telling his companion about a dream. The man said, 'I had this dream, and in my dream a loaf of barley bread came tumbling down into the Midianite camp. It hit a tent, turned it over, and knocked it flat!'

**14** His companion answered, 'Your dream can mean only one thing – God has given Gideon son of Joash, the Israelite, victory over Midian and all its allies!'

**15** When Gideon heard the dream and its interpretation, he bowed in worship before the LORD. Then he returned to the Israelite camp and shouted, 'Get up! For the LORD has given you victory over the Midianite hordes!' **16** He divided the 300 men into three groups and gave each man a ram's horn and a clay jar with a torch in it.

**17** Then he said to them, 'Keep your eyes on me. When I come to the edge of the camp, do just as I do. **18** As soon as I and those with me blow the rams' horns, blow your horns, too, all around the entire camp, and shout, "For the LORD and for Gideon!"'

**19** It was just after midnight, after the changing of the guard, when Gideon and the 100 men with him reached the edge of the Midianite camp. Suddenly, they blew the rams' horns and broke their clay jars. [20] Then all three groups blew their horns and broke their jars. They held the blazing torches in their left hands and the horns in their right hands, and they all shouted, 'A sword for the LORD and for Gideon!'

[21] Each man stood at his position around the camp and watched as all the Midianites rushed around in a panic, shouting as they ran to escape. [22] When the 300 Israelites blew their rams' horns, the LORD caused the warriors in the camp to fight against each other with their swords. Those who were not killed fled to places as far away as Beth-shittah near Zererah and to the border of Abel-meholah near Tabbath.

[23] Then Gideon sent for the warriors of Naphtali, Asher, and Manasseh, who joined in chasing the army of Midian. [24] Gideon also sent messengers throughout the hill country of Ephraim, saying, 'Come down to attack the Midianites. Cut them off at the shallow crossings of the River Jordan at Beth-barah.'

So all the men of Ephraim did as they were told. [25] They captured Oreb and Zeeb, the two Midianite commanders, killing Oreb at the rock of Oreb, and Zeeb at the winepress of Zeeb. And they continued to chase the Midianites. Afterwards the Israelites brought the heads of Oreb and Zeeb to Gideon, who was by the River Jordan.

## Where we end up

With the 300, the Lord delivers Israel from Midian.

## My Reflections

# Samson

## 24

**Main Theme**

The Lord will be faithful to his promise, even when his people are faithless.

**Setting**

The Valley of Sorek (home of Delilah) and Gaza (a major Philistine city)

**Characters**

Samson, Delilah, and the Philistines

**Key Verse: Judges 16:28**

Then Samson prayed to the LORD, 'Sovereign LORD, remember me again. O God, please strengthen me just one more time. With one blow let me pay back the Philistines for the loss of my two eyes.'

Samson brings down the walls on the Philistines.

## Key plot points

**Introduction** – Samson is a Nazirite from birth. He has amazing strength as long as he keeps his vows (one of which is not cutting his hair).

**v.4–5** – He falls in love with Delilah, and the Philistine lords pressure her to find out the secret of Samson's great strength.

## Read the story Judges 16

¹ One day Samson went to the Philistine town of Gaza and spent the night with a prostitute. ² Word soon spread that Samson was there, so the men of Gaza gathered together and waited all night at the town gates. They kept quiet during the night, saying to themselves, 'When the light of morning comes, we will kill him.'

³ But Samson stayed in bed only until midnight. Then he got up, took hold of the doors of the town gate, including the two posts, and lifted them up, bar and all. He put them on his shoulders and carried them all the way to the top of the hill across from Hebron.

⁴ Some time later Samson fell in love with a woman named Delilah, who lived in the valley of Sorek. ⁵ The rulers of the Philistines went to her and said, 'Entice Samson to tell you what makes him so strong and how he can be overpowered and tied up securely. Then each of us will give you 1,100 pieces of silver.'

⁶ So Delilah said to Samson, 'Please tell me what makes you so strong and what it would take to tie you up securely.'

⁷ Samson replied, 'If I were tied up with seven new bowstrings that have not yet been dried, I would become as weak as anyone else.'

⁸ So the Philistine rulers brought Delilah seven new bowstrings, and she tied Samson up with them. ⁹ She had hidden some men in one of the inner rooms of her house, and she cried out, 'Samson! The Philistines have come to capture you!' But Samson snapped the bowstrings as a piece of string snaps when it is burned by a fire. So the secret of his strength was not discovered.

¹⁰ Afterwards Delilah said to him, 'You've been making fun of me and telling me lies! Now please tell me how you can be tied up securely.'

¹¹ Samson replied, 'If I were tied up with brand-new ropes that had never been used, I would become as weak as anyone else.'

¹² So Delilah took new ropes and tied him up with them. The men were hiding in the inner room as before, and again Delilah cried out, 'Samson! The Philistines have come to capture you!' But again Samson snapped the ropes from his arms as if they were thread.

¹³ Then Delilah said, 'You've been making fun of me and telling me lies! Now tell me how you can be tied up securely.'

Samson replied, 'If you were to weave the seven braids of my hair into the fabric on your loom and tighten it with the loom shuttle, I would become as weak as anyone else.'

So while he slept, Delilah wove the seven braids of his hair into the fabric. **14** Then she tightened it with the loom shuttle. Again she cried out, 'Samson! The Philistines have come to capture you!' But Samson woke up, pulled back the loom shuttle, and yanked his hair away from the loom and the fabric.

**15** Then Delilah pouted, 'How can you tell me, "I love you," when you don't share your secrets with me? You've made fun of me three times now, and you still haven't told me what makes you so strong!' **16** She tormented him with her nagging day after day until he was sick to death of it.

**17** Finally, Samson shared his secret with her. 'My hair has never been cut,' he confessed, 'for I was dedicated to God as a Nazirite from birth. If my head were shaved, my strength would leave me, and I would become as weak as anyone else.'

**v.17** — Samson eventually tells Delilah that he will lose his strength if his hair is cut.

**18** Delilah realized he had finally told her the truth, so she sent for the Philistine rulers. 'Come back one more time,' she said, 'for he has finally told me his secret.' So the Philistine rulers returned with the money in their hands. **19** Delilah lulled Samson to sleep with his head in her lap, and then she called in a man to shave off the seven locks of his hair. In this way she began to bring him down, and his strength left him.

**v.19** — She cuts his hair and binds him for the Philistines to capture him.

**20** Then she cried out, 'Samson! The Philistines have come to capture you!'

When he woke up, he thought, 'I will do as before and shake myself free.' But he didn't realize the LORD had left him.

**21** So the Philistines captured him and gouged out his eyes. They took him to Gaza, where he was bound with bronze chains and forced to grind grain in the prison.

**v.21** — The Philistines gouge out Samson's eyes and imprison him.

**22** But before long, his hair began to grow back.

**23** The Philistine rulers held a great festival, offering sacrifices and praising their god, Dagon. They said, 'Our god has given us victory over our enemy Samson!'

**24** When the people saw him, they praised their god, saying, 'Our god has delivered our enemy to us! The one who killed so many of us is now in our power!'

**25** Half drunk by now, the people demanded, 'Bring out Samson so he can amuse us!' So he was brought from the prison to amuse them, and they had him stand between the pillars supporting the roof.

**v.25** — At a great gathering, the Philistines bring out Samson to entertain the crowd.

**26** Samson said to the young servant who was leading him by the hand, 'Place my hands against the pillars that hold up the temple. I want to rest against them.' **27** Now the temple was completely filled with people. All the Philistine rulers were there, and there were about 3,000 men and women on the roof who were watching as Samson amused them.

**28** Then Samson prayed to the LORD, 'Sovereign LORD, remember me again. O God, please strengthen me just one more time. With one blow let me pay back the Philistines for the loss of my two eyes.' **29** Then Samson put his hands on the two central pillars that held up the temple. Pushing against them with both hands, **30** he prayed, 'Let me die with the Philistines.' And the temple crashed down on the Philistine rulers and all the people. So he killed more people when he died than he had during his entire lifetime.

**31** Later his brothers and other relatives went down to get his body. They took him back home and buried him between Zorah and Eshtaol, where his father, Manoah, was buried. Samson had judged Israel for twenty years.

## Where we end up

Samson asks the Lord for one last act of great strength. He pushes down the pillars of the building and all of the Philistines present are killed in the collapse.

**My Reflections**

# Saul

## 25

**Main Theme**

The Lord will anoint a human king to rule his people.

**Setting**

The Land of Zuph, Gibeah, and Mizpah

**Characters**

The Lord, Samuel (prophet of the Lord), Saul (son of Kish, a Benjamite) and the Israelites

**Key Verse:**
**1 Samuel 10:19**

'But though I have rescued you from your misery and distress, you have rejected your God today and have said, 'No, we want a king instead!' Now, therefore, present yourselves before the LORD by tribes and clans.'

Samuel proclaims Saul king.

## Read the story 1 Samuel 8 – 10:24

**8** As Samuel grew old, he appointed his sons to be judges over Israel. ² Joel and Abijah, his oldest sons, held court in Beersheba. ³ But they were not like their father, for they were greedy for money. They accepted bribes and perverted justice.

⁴ Finally, all the elders of Israel met at Ramah to discuss the matter with Samuel. ⁵ 'Look,' they told him, 'you are now old, and your sons are not like you. Give us a king to judge us like all the other nations have.'

## Key plot points

**v.5** – The Israelites demand a king like the other nations around them.

⁶ Samuel was displeased with their request and went to the Lord for guidance. ⁷ 'Do everything they say to you,' the Lord replied, 'for they are rejecting me, not you. They don't want me to be their king any longer. ⁸ Ever since I brought them from Egypt they have continually abandoned me and followed other gods. And now they are giving you the same treatment. ⁹ Do as they ask, but solemnly warn them about the way a king will reign over them.'

¹⁰ So Samuel passed on the Lord's warning to the people who were asking him for a king. ¹¹ 'This is how a king will reign over you,' Samuel said. 'The king will draft your sons and assign them to his chariots and his charioteers, making them run before his chariots. ¹² Some will be generals and captains in his army, some will be forced to plough in his fields and harvest his crops, and some will make his weapons and chariot equipment. ¹³ The king will take your daughters from you and force them to cook and bake and make perfumes for him. ¹⁴ He will take away the best of your fields and vineyards and olive groves and give them to his own officials. ¹⁵ He will take a tenth of your grain and your grape harvest and distribute it among his officers and attendants. ¹⁶ He will take your male and female slaves and demand the finest of your cattle and donkeys for his own use. ¹⁷ He will demand a tenth of your flocks, and you will be his slaves. ¹⁸ When that day comes, you will beg for relief from this king you are demanding, but then the Lord will not help you.'

¹⁹ But the people refused to listen to Samuel's warning. 'Even so, we still want a king,' they said. ²⁰ 'We want to be like the nations around us. Our king will judge us and lead us into battle.'

²¹ So Samuel repeated to the Lord what the people had said, ²² and the Lord replied, 'Do as they say, and give them a king.' Then Samuel agreed and sent the people home.

**9** There was a wealthy, influential man named Kish from the tribe of Benjamin. He was the son of Abiel, son of Zeror, son of Becorath, son of Aphiah, of the tribe of Benjamin. ² His son Saul was the most handsome man in Israel – head and shoulders taller than anyone else in the land.

³ One day Kish's donkeys strayed away, and he told Saul, 'Take a servant with you, and go to look for the donkeys.' ⁴ So Saul took one of the servants and travelled through the hill country of Ephraim, the land of Shalishah, the Shaalim area, and the entire land of Benjamin, but they couldn't find the donkeys anywhere.

**v.22** – The Lord warns the people through Samuel but grants their request.

**v.2** – Saul, the son of Kish from the tribe of Benjamin, is a head taller than anyone else in Israel.

**v.4** – Saul is out looking for his father's lost donkeys.

⁵ Finally, they entered the region of Zuph, and Saul said to his servant, 'Let's go home. By now my father will be more worried about us than about the donkeys!'

⁶ But the servant said, 'I've just thought of something! There is a man of God who lives here in this town. He is held in high honour by all the people because everything he says comes true. Let's go and find him. Perhaps he can tell us which way to go.'

⁷ 'But we don't have anything to offer him,' Saul replied. 'Even our food is gone, and we don't have a thing to give him.'

⁸ 'Well,' the servant said, 'I have one small silver piece. We can at least offer it to the man of God and see what happens!' ⁹ (In those days if people wanted a message from God, they would say, 'Let's go and ask the seer,' for prophets used to be called seers.)

¹⁰ 'All right,' Saul agreed, 'let's try it!' So they started into the town where the man of God lived.

¹¹ As they were climbing the hill to the town, they met some young women coming out to draw water. So Saul and his servant asked, 'Is the seer here today?'

¹² 'Yes,' they replied. 'Stay right on this road. He is at the town gates. He has just arrived to take part in a public sacrifice up at the place of worship. ¹³ Hurry and catch him before he goes up there to eat. The guests won't begin eating until he arrives to bless the food.'

¹⁴ So they entered the town, and as they passed through the gates, Samuel was coming out towards them to go up to the place of worship.

¹⁵ Now the LORD had told Samuel the previous day, ¹⁶ 'About this time tomorrow I will send you a man from the land of Benjamin. Anoint him to be the leader of my people, Israel. He will rescue them from the Philistines, for I have looked down on my people in mercy and have heard their cry.'

**v.15–16** — The Lord sends Samuel to anoint Saul.

¹⁷ When Samuel saw Saul, the LORD said, 'That's the man I told you about! He will rule my people.'

**v.17** — The Lord directs Samuel to anoint his king.

¹⁸ Just then Saul approached Samuel at the gateway and asked, 'Can you please tell me where the seer's house is?'

¹⁹ 'I am the seer!' Samuel replied. 'Go up to the place of worship ahead of me. We will eat there together, and in the morning I'll tell you what you want to know and send you on your way. ²⁰ And don't worry about those donkeys that were lost three days ago, for they have been

found. And I am here to tell you that you and your family are the focus of all Israel's hopes.'

²¹ Saul replied, 'But I'm only from the tribe of Benjamin, the smallest tribe in Israel, and my family is the least important of all the families of that tribe! Why are you talking like this to me?'

²² Then Samuel brought Saul and his servant into the hall and placed them at the head of the table, honouring them above the thirty special guests. ²³ Samuel then instructed the cook to bring Saul the finest cut of meat, the piece that had been set aside for the guest of honour. ²⁴ So the cook brought in the meat and placed it before Saul. 'Go ahead and eat it,' Samuel said. 'I was saving it for you even before I invited these others!' So Saul ate with Samuel that day.

²⁵ When they came down from the place of worship and returned to town, Samuel took Saul up to the roof of the house and prepared a bed for him there. ²⁶ At daybreak the next morning, Samuel called to Saul, 'Get up! It's time you were on your way.' So Saul got ready, and he and Samuel left the house together. ²⁷ When they reached the edge of town, Samuel told Saul to send his servant on ahead. After the servant was gone, Samuel said, 'Stay here, for I have received a special message for you from God.'

**v.1** – Samuel first anoints Saul secretly in the land of Zuph.

**10** Then Samuel took a flask of olive oil and poured it over Saul's head. He kissed Saul and said, 'I am doing this because the LORD has appointed you to be the ruler over Israel, his special possession. ² When you leave me today, you will see two men beside Rachel's tomb at Zelzah, on the border of Benjamin. They will tell you that the donkeys have been found and that your father has stopped worrying about them and is now worried about you. He is asking, "Have you seen my son?"

³ 'When you get to the oak of Tabor, you will see three men coming towards you who are on their way to worship God at Bethel. One will be bringing three young goats, another will have three loaves of bread, and the third will be carrying a wineskin full of wine. ⁴ They will greet you and offer you two of the loaves, which you are to accept.

⁵ 'When you arrive at Gibeah of God, where the garrison of the Philistines is located, you will meet a band of prophets coming down from the place of worship. They will be playing a harp, a tambourine, a flute, and a lyre, and they will be prophesying. ⁶ At that time the Spirit

of the Lord will come powerfully upon you, and you will prophesy with them. You will be changed into a different person. [7] After these signs take place, do what must be done, for God is with you. [8] Then go down to Gilgal ahead of me. I will join you there to sacrifice burnt offerings and peace offerings. You must wait for seven days until I arrive and give you further instructions.'

[9] As Saul turned and started to leave, God gave him a new heart, and all Samuel's signs were fulfilled that day. [10] When Saul and his servant arrived at Gibeah, they saw a group of prophets coming towards them. Then the Spirit of God came powerfully upon Saul, and he, too, began to prophesy. [11] When those who knew Saul heard about it, they exclaimed, 'What? Is even Saul a prophet? How did the son of Kish become a prophet?'

**v.10** – On his return trip, Saul meets a group of prophets in Gibeah. The Spirit of God possesses him and he begins to prophesy with them.

[12] And one of those standing there said, 'Can anyone become a prophet, no matter who his father is?' So that is the origin of the saying 'Is even Saul a prophet?'

[13] When Saul had finished prophesying, he went up to the place of worship. [14] 'Where have you been?' Saul's uncle asked him and his servant.

'We were looking for the donkeys,' Saul replied, 'but we couldn't find them. So we went to Samuel to ask him where they were.'

[15] 'Oh? And what did he say?' his uncle asked.

[16] 'He told us that the donkeys had already been found,' Saul replied. But Saul didn't tell his uncle what Samuel said about the kingdom.

[17] Later Samuel called all the people of Israel to meet before the Lord at Mizpah. [18] And he said, 'This is what the Lord, the God of Israel, has declared: I brought you from Egypt and rescued you from the Egyptians and from all of the nations that were oppressing you. [19] But though I have rescued you from your misery and distress, you have rejected your God today and have said, "No, we want a king instead!" Now, therefore, present yourselves before the Lord by tribes and clans.'

**v.17** – At Mizpah, Samuel calls all Israel to come before him so that a king can be chosen.

[20] So Samuel brought all the tribes of Israel before the Lord, and the tribe of Benjamin was chosen by lot. [21] Then he brought each family of the tribe of Benjamin before the Lord, and the family of the Matrites was chosen. And finally Saul son of Kish was chosen from among them. But when they looked for him, he had disappeared! [22] So they asked the Lord, 'Where is he?'

**v.20–24** – Saul's family is chosen by lot, but Saul is hiding among the baggage. When he is found, Samuel presents him to the people as their king.

And the LORD replied, 'He is hiding among the baggage.' **23** So they found him and brought him out, and he stood head and shoulders above anyone else.

**24** Then Samuel said to all the people, 'This is the man the LORD has chosen as your king. No one in all Israel is like him!'

And all the people shouted, 'Long live the king!'

## Where we end up

Saul is anointed by Samuel as the first king of Israel.

## My Reflections

# Tearing Samuel's Robe

## 26

**Main Theme**

The Lord's king will be completely faithful and obedient.

**Setting**

Mount Carmel

**Characters**

The Lord, Samuel, and Saul

**Key Verse:**
**1 Samuel 15:22**

But Samuel replied, 'What is more pleasing to the LORD: your burnt offerings and sacrifices or your obedience to his voice? Listen! Obedience is better than sacrifice, and submission is better than offering the fat of rams.'

The kingdom is ripped away from Saul.

## Key plot points

**v.1–3** – Samuel explains to Saul that he is to attack and completely destroy the Amalekites, not taking any spoils for himself.

**v.7–9** – Saul attacks and defeats the Amalekites, but takes the best of the spoils, and allows King Agag to live.

**v.10–11** – The Lord tells Samuel what is happening. He says that he regrets making Saul king, and then he will give the kingdom to another.

**v.14** – Samuel confronts Saul at Carmel, on the way to Gilgal.

**v.15** – Saul tries to explain that he was keeping the spoils as a sacrifice for the Lord.

## Read the story 1 Samuel 15

¹ One day Samuel said to Saul, 'It was the LORD who told me to anoint you as king of his people, Israel. Now listen to this message from the LORD! ² This is what the LORD of Heaven's Armies has declared: I have decided to settle accounts with the nation of Amalek for opposing Israel when they came from Egypt. ³ Now go and completely destroy the entire Amalekite nation – men, women, children, babies, cattle, sheep, goats, camels, and donkeys.'

⁴ So Saul mobilized his army at Telaim. There were 200,000 soldiers from Israel and 10,000 men from Judah. ⁵ Then Saul and his army went to a town of the Amalekites and lay in wait in the valley. ⁶ Saul sent this warning to the Kenites: 'Move away from where the Amalekites live, or you will die with them. For you showed kindness to all the people of Israel when they came up from Egypt.' So the Kenites packed up and left.

⁷ Then Saul slaughtered the Amalekites from Havilah all the way to Shur, east of Egypt. ⁸ He captured Agag, the Amalekite king, but completely destroyed everyone else. ⁹ Saul and his men spared Agag's life and kept the best of the sheep and goats, the cattle, the fat calves, and the lambs – everything, in fact, that appealed to them. They destroyed only what was worthless or of poor quality.

¹⁰ Then the LORD said to Samuel, ¹¹ 'I am sorry that I ever made Saul king, for he has not been loyal to me and has refused to obey my command.' Samuel was so deeply moved when he heard this that he cried out to the LORD all night.

¹² Early the next morning Samuel went to find Saul. Someone told him, 'Saul went to the town of Carmel to set up a monument to himself; then he went on to Gilgal.'

¹³ When Samuel finally found him, Saul greeted him cheerfully. 'May the LORD bless you,' he said. 'I have carried out the LORD's command!'

¹⁴ 'Then what is all the bleating of sheep and goats and the lowing of cattle I hear?' Samuel demanded.

¹⁵ 'It's true that the army spared the best of the sheep, goats, and cattle,' Saul admitted. 'But they are going to sacrifice them to the LORD your God. We have destroyed everything else.'

¹⁶ Then Samuel said to Saul, 'Stop! Listen to what the LORD told me last night!'

'What did he tell you?' Saul asked.

[17] And Samuel told him, 'Although you may think little of yourself, are you not the leader of the tribes of Israel? The LORD has anointed you king of Israel. [18] And the LORD sent you on a mission and told you, "Go and completely destroy the sinners, the Amalekites, until they are all dead." [19] Why haven't you obeyed the LORD? Why did you rush for the plunder and do what was evil in the LORD's sight?'

[20] 'But I did obey the LORD,' Saul insisted. 'I carried out the mission he gave me. I brought back King Agag, but I destroyed everyone else. [21] Then my troops brought in the best of the sheep, goats, cattle, and plunder to sacrifice to the LORD your God in Gilgal.'

[22] But Samuel replied,

**v.22** – Samuel says the Lord desires obedience rather than sacrifice.

"What is more pleasing to the LORD:
your burnt offerings and sacrifices
or your obedience to his voice?
Listen! Obedience is better than sacrifice,
and submission is better than offering the fat of rams.
[23] Rebellion is as sinful as witchcraft,
and stubbornness as bad as worshipping idols.
So because you have rejected the command of the LORD,
he has rejected you as king."

[24] Then Saul admitted to Samuel, 'Yes, I have sinned. I have disobeyed your instructions and the LORD's command, for I was afraid of the people and did what they demanded. [25] But now, please forgive my sin and come back with me so that I may worship the LORD.'

[26] But Samuel replied, 'I will not go back with you! Since you have rejected the LORD's command, he has rejected you as king of Israel.'

[27] As Samuel turned to go, Saul tried to hold him back and tore the hem of his robe. [28] And Samuel said to him, 'The LORD has torn the kingdom of Israel from you today and has given it to someone else – one who is better than you. [29] And he who is the Glory of Israel will not lie, nor will he change his mind, for he is not human that he should change his mind!'

[30] Then Saul pleaded again, 'I know I have sinned. But please, at least honour me before the elders of my people and before Israel by coming back with me so that I may worship the LORD your God.' [31] So Samuel finally agreed and went back with him, and Saul worshipped the LORD.

**v.27–28** – As Samuel turns to leave, Saul grabs his robe and it rips. Samuel says that in the same way, the Lord will rip the kingdom from Saul's hand.

**v.33** — Samuel then kills Agag himself.

³² Then Samuel said, 'Bring King Agag to me.' Agag arrived full of hope, for he thought, 'Surely the worst is over, and I have been spared!' ³³ But Samuel said, 'As your sword has killed the sons of many mothers, now your mother will be childless.' And Samuel cut Agag to pieces before the LORD at Gilgal.

³⁴ Then Samuel went home to Ramah, and Saul returned to his house at Gibeah of Saul. ³⁵ Samuel never went to meet with Saul again, but he mourned constantly for him. And the LORD was sorry he had ever made Saul king of Israel.

## Where we end up

Samuel never meets with Saul again and the Lord regrets ever making Saul king of Israel.

## My Reflections

# David is Anointed

## 27

## Main Theme

The Lord's anointed king will be chosen not for his appearance but for his heart.

## Setting

Bethlehem (the hometown of David)

## Characters

The Lord, Samuel, Jesse, Eliab, and David

## Key Verse: 1 Samuel 16:7

But the LORD said to Samuel, 'Don't judge by his appearance or height, for I have rejected him. The LORD doesn't see things the way you see them. People judge by outward appearance, but the LORD looks at the heart.'

Samuel anoints David as the new king.

## Key plot points

**v.1** – The Lord sends Samuel to the house of Jesse, the Bethlehemite, to anoint a new king in place of Saul.

**v.5** – Samuel invites Jesse's whole family to a sacrifice.

**v.6** – Samuel is impressed by Jesse's first son, Eliab, and believes that surely he is the one to be the next king.

**v.7** – The Lord tells Samuel that he is not looking at the man's appearance but his heart.

**v.8–10** – Jesse made seven of his sons pass before Samuel, but the Lord did not choose any of them.

**v.11** – When Samuel hears that there is another son out keeping the sheep, he tells them to bring him.

## Read the story 1 Samuel 16:1–13

[1] Now the LORD said to Samuel, 'You have mourned long enough for Saul. I have rejected him as king of Israel, so fill your flask with olive oil and go to Bethlehem. Find a man named Jesse who lives there, for I have selected one of his sons to be my king.'

[2] But Samuel asked, 'How can I do that? If Saul hears about it, he will kill me.'

'Take a heifer with you,' the LORD replied, 'and say that you have come to make a sacrifice to the LORD. [3] Invite Jesse to the sacrifice, and I will show you which of his sons to anoint for me.'

[4] So Samuel did as the LORD instructed. When he arrived at Bethlehem, the elders of the town came trembling to meet him. 'What's wrong?' they asked. 'Do you come in peace?'

[5] 'Yes,' Samuel replied. 'I have come to sacrifice to the LORD. Purify yourselves and come with me to the sacrifice.' Then Samuel performed the purification rite for Jesse and his sons and invited them to the sacrifice, too.

[6] When they arrived, Samuel took one look at Eliab and thought, 'Surely this is the LORD's anointed!'

[7] But the LORD said to Samuel, 'Don't judge by his appearance or height, for I have rejected him. The LORD doesn't see things the way you see them. People judge by outward appearance, but the LORD looks at the heart.'

[8] Then Jesse told his son Abinadab to step forward and walk in front of Samuel. But Samuel said, 'This is not the one the LORD has chosen.' [9] Next Jesse summoned Shimea, but Samuel said, 'Neither is this the one the LORD has chosen.' [10] In the same way all seven of Jesse's sons were presented to Samuel. But Samuel said to Jesse, 'The LORD has not chosen any of these.' [11] Then Samuel asked, 'Are these all the sons you have?'

'There is still the youngest,' Jesse replied. 'But he's out in the fields watching the sheep and goats.'

'Send for him at once,' Samuel said. 'We will not sit down to eat until he arrives.'

[12] So Jesse sent for him. He was dark and handsome, with beautiful eyes.

And the LORD said, 'This is the one; anoint him.'

**13** So as David stood there among his brothers, Samuel took the flask of olive oil he had brought and anointed David with the oil. And the Spirit of the LORD came powerfully upon David from that day on. Then Samuel returned to Ramah.

### Where we end up

Samuel anoints David, the youngest son of Jesse, as the next king of Israel.

**Christ foreshadowed:** The Baptism of the Lord – p. 182

### My Reflections

# 28 David and Goliath

## Main Theme

The Lord's anointed king will defeat the enemy and deliver God's people from slavery, not by physical might but by faith in the Lord.

## Setting

Socoh (a field of battle between the Philistines and Israelites)

## Characters

Goliath, Saul, David, and the Israelite army

## Key Verse: 1 Samuel 17:46–47

'Today the LORD will conquer you, and I will kill you and cut off your head. And then I will give the dead bodies of your men to the birds and wild animals, and the whole world will know that there is a God in Israel! And everyone assembled here will know that the LORD rescues his people, but not with sword and spear. This is the LORD's battle, and he will give you to us!'

David fights the giant Goliath.

# Read the story 1 Samuel 17

1 The Philistines now mustered their army for battle and camped between Socoh in Judah and Azekah at Ephes-dammim. 2 Saul countered by gathering his Israelite troops near the valley of Elah. 3 So the Philistines and Israelites faced each other on opposite hills, with the valley between them.

4 Then Goliath, a Philistine champion from Gath, came out of the Philistine ranks to face the forces of Israel. He was over three metres tall! 5 He wore a bronze helmet, and his bronze coat of mail weighed 57 kilograms. 6 He also wore bronze leg armour, and he carried a bronze javelin on his shoulder. 7 The shaft of his spear was as heavy and thick as a weaver's beam, tipped with an iron spearhead that weighed nearly 7 kilograms. His armour bearer walked ahead of him carrying a shield.

8 Goliath stood and shouted a taunt across to the Israelites. 'Why are you all coming out to fight?' he called. 'I am the Philistine champion, but you are only the servants of Saul. Choose one man to come down here and fight me! 9 If he kills me, then we will be your slaves. But if I kill him, you will be our slaves! 10 I defy the armies of Israel today! Send me a man who will fight me!' 11 When Saul and the Israelites heard this, they were terrified and deeply shaken.

**v.8** – Goliath, the gigantic Philistine champion, challenges Israel to send forth a man for individual combat.

12 Now David was the son of a man named Jesse, an Ephrathite from Bethlehem in the land of Judah. Jesse was an old man at that time, and he had eight sons. 13 Jesse's three oldest sons – Eliab, Abinadab, and Shimea – had already joined Saul's army to fight the Philistines. 14 David was the youngest son. David's three oldest brothers stayed with Saul's army, 15 but David went back and forth so he could help his father with the sheep in Bethlehem.

**v.11** – Saul, along with the whole army of Israel, is terrified of Goliath.

16 For forty days, every morning and evening, the Philistine champion strutted in front of the Israelite army.

17 One day Jesse said to David, 'Take this basket of roasted grain and these ten loaves of bread, and carry them quickly to your brothers. 18 And give these ten cuts of cheese to their captain. See how your brothers are getting along, and bring back a report on how they are doing.' 19 David's brothers were with Saul and the Israelite army at the valley of Elah, fighting against the Philistines.

20 So David left the sheep with another shepherd and set out early

**v.20** – David arrives with provisions for his brothers who are in the army.

the next morning with the gifts, as Jesse had directed him. He arrived at the camp just as the Israelite army was leaving for the battlefield with shouts and battle cries. [21] Soon the Israelite and Philistine forces stood facing each other, army against army. [22] David left his things with the keeper of supplies and hurried out to the ranks to greet his brothers. [23] As he was talking with them, Goliath, the Philistine champion from Gath, came out from the Philistine ranks. Then David heard him shout his usual taunt to the army of Israel.

[24] As soon as the Israelite army saw him, they began to run away in fright. [25] 'Have you seen the giant?' the men asked. 'He comes out each day to defy Israel. The king has offered a huge reward to anyone who kills him. He will give that man one of his daughters for a wife, and the man's entire family will be exempted from paying taxes!'

**v.26** – When he hears the challenge of Goliath, David is ready to fight him.

[26] David asked the soldiers standing nearby, 'What will a man get for killing this Philistine and ending his defiance of Israel? Who is this pagan Philistine anyway, that he is allowed to defy the armies of the living God?'

[27] And these men gave David the same reply. They said, 'Yes, that is the reward for killing him.'

[28] But when David's oldest brother, Eliab, heard David talking to the men, he was angry. 'What are you doing around here anyway?' he demanded. 'What about those few sheep you're supposed to be looking after? I know about your pride and deceit. You just want to see the battle!'

[29] 'What have I done now?' David replied. 'I was only asking a question!' [30] He walked over to some others and asked them the same thing and received the same answer. [31] Then David's question was reported to King Saul, and the king sent for him.

[32] 'Don't worry about this Philistine,' David told Saul. 'I'll go and fight him!'

[33] 'Don't be ridiculous!' Saul replied. 'There's no way you can fight this Philistine and possibly win! You're only a boy, and he's been a man of war since his youth.'

[34] But David persisted. 'I have been looking after my father's sheep and goats,' he said. 'When a lion or a bear comes to steal a lamb from the flock, [35] I go after it with a club and rescue the lamb from its mouth. If the animal turns on me, I catch it by the jaw and club it to death. [36] I have done this to both lions and bears, and I'll do it to this

pagan Philistine, too, for he has defied the armies of the living God! 37 The Lord who rescued me from the claws of the lion and the bear will rescue me from this Philistine!'

Saul finally consented. 'All right, go ahead,' he said. 'And may the Lord be with you!'

38 Then Saul gave David his own armour – a bronze helmet and a coat of mail. 39 David put it on, strapped the sword over it, and took a step or two to see what it was like, for he had never worn such things before.

'I can't go in these,' he protested to Saul. 'I'm not used to them.' So David took them off again. 40 He picked up five smooth stones from a stream and put them into his shepherd's bag. Then, armed only with his shepherd's staff and sling, he started across the valley to fight the Philistine.

**v.38–40** — Saul tries to outfit David with his armour, but David takes only five smooth stones and a slingshot to fight the giant.

41 Goliath walked out towards David with his shield bearer ahead of him, 42 sneering in contempt at this ruddy-faced boy. 43 'Am I a dog,' he roared at David, 'that you come at me with a stick?' And he cursed David by the names of his gods. 44 'Come over here, and I'll give your flesh to the birds and wild animals!' Goliath yelled.

45 David replied to the Philistine, 'You come to me with sword, spear, and javelin, but I come to you in the name of the Lord of Heaven's Armies – the God of the armies of Israel, whom you have defied. 46 Today the Lord will conquer you, and I will kill you and cut off your head. And then I will give the dead bodies of your men to the birds and wild animals, and the whole world will know that there is a God in Israel! 47 And everyone assembled here will know that the Lord rescues his people, but not with sword and spear. This is the Lord's battle, and he will give you to us!'

**v.45–51** — After declaring that the battle belongs to the Lord, David kills Goliath.

48 As Goliath moved closer to attack, David quickly ran out to meet him. 49 Reaching into his shepherd's bag and taking out a stone, he hurled it with his sling and hit the Philistine in the forehead. The stone sank in, and Goliath stumbled and fell face down on the ground.

50 So David triumphed over the Philistine with only a sling and a stone, for he had no sword. 51 Then David ran over and pulled Goliath's sword from its sheath. David used it to kill him and cut off his head.

When the Philistines saw that their champion was dead, they turned and ran away. 52 Then the men of Israel and Judah gave a great shout of triumph and rushed after the Philistines, chasing them as far as Gath and the gates of Ekron. The bodies of the dead and wounded Philistines were strewn all along the road from Shaaraim, as far as Gath and Ekron. [53] Then the Israelite army returned and plundered the deserted Philistine camp. [54] (David took the Philistine's head to Jerusalem, but he stored the man's armour in his own tent.)

[55] As Saul watched David go out to fight the Philistine, he asked Abner, the commander of his army, 'Abner, whose son is this young man?'

'I really don't know,' Abner declared.

[56] 'Well, find out who he is!' the king told him.

[57] As soon as David returned from killing Goliath, Abner brought him to Saul with the Philistine's head still in his hand. [58] 'Tell me about your father, young man,' Saul said.

And David replied, 'His name is Jesse, and we live in Bethlehem.'

## Where we end up

David then leads Israel in a rout of the Philistines.

## My Reflections

# Solomon

### Main Theme

The Lord's king will reign with God's wisdom, ruling in righteousness and dispensing justice.

### Setting

Gibeon, where Solomon went to offer a sacrifice, and Jerusalem

### Key Verse: Kings 3:12

'I will give you what you asked for! I will give you a wise and understanding heart such as no one else has had or ever will have!'

### Characters

The Lord, Solomon, and the two mothers

Solomon gives a wise judgement.

## Key plot points

**v.5** – The Lord comes to Solomon and offers to give him whatever he asks.

**v.9** – Solomon asks for the wisdom to rule God's people well.

**v.10–14** – The Lord grants Solomon's request by making him wiser than any other person, and also grants him power, wealth, and victory.

## Read the story 1 Kings 3

¹ Solomon made an alliance with Pharaoh, the king of Egypt, and married one of his daughters. He brought her to live in the City of David until he could finish building his palace and the Temple of the LORD and the wall around the city. ² At that time the people of Israel sacrificed their offerings at local places of worship, for a temple honouring the name of the LORD had not yet been built.

³ Solomon loved the LORD and followed all the decrees of his father, David, except that Solomon, too, offered sacrifices and burned incense at the local places of worship. ⁴ The most important of these places of worship was at Gibeon, so the king went there and sacrificed 1,000 burnt offerings. ⁵ That night the LORD appeared to Solomon in a dream, and God said, 'What do you want? Ask, and I will give it to you!'

⁶ Solomon replied, 'You showed great and faithful love to your servant my father, David, because he was honest and true and faithful to you. And you have continued to show this great and faithful love to him today by giving him a son to sit on his throne.

⁷ 'Now, O LORD my God, you have made me king instead of my father, David, but I am like a little child who doesn't know his way around. ⁸ And here I am in the midst of your own chosen people, a nation so great and numerous they cannot be counted! ⁹ Give me an understanding heart so that I can govern your people well and know the difference between right and wrong. For who by himself is able to govern this great people of yours?'

¹⁰ The LORD was pleased that Solomon had asked for wisdom. ¹¹ So God replied, 'Because you have asked for wisdom in governing my people with justice and have not asked for a long life or wealth or the death of your enemies – ¹² I will give you what you asked for! I will give you a wise and understanding heart such as no one else has had or ever will have! ¹³ And I will also give you what you did not ask for – riches and fame! No other king in all the world will be compared to you for the rest of your life! ¹⁴ And if you follow me and obey my decrees and my commands as your father, David, did, I will give you a long life.'

¹⁵ Then Solomon woke up and realized it had been a dream. He returned to Jerusalem and stood before the Ark of the LORD's Covenant, where he sacrificed burnt offerings and peace offerings. Then he invited all his officials to a great banquet.

**16** Some time later two prostitutes came to the king to have an argument settled. **17** 'Please, my lord,' one of them began, 'this woman and I live in the same house. I gave birth to a baby while she was with me in the house. **18** Three days later this woman also had a baby. We were alone; there were only two of us in the house.

**19** 'But her baby died during the night when she rolled over on it. **20** Then she got up in the night and took my son from beside me while I was asleep. She laid her dead child in my arms and took mine to sleep beside her. **21** And in the morning when I tried to nurse my son, he was dead! But when I looked more closely in the morning light, I saw that it wasn't my son at all.'

**22** Then the other woman interrupted, 'It certainly was your son, and the living child is mine.'

'No,' the first woman said, 'the living child is mine, and the dead one is yours.' And so they argued back and forth before the king.

**23** Then the king said, 'Let's get the facts straight. Both of you claim the living child is yours, and each says that the dead one belongs to the other. **24** All right, bring me a sword.' So a sword was brought to the king.

**25** Then he said, 'Cut the living child in two, and give half to one woman and half to the other!'

**26** Then the woman who was the real mother of the living child, and who loved him very much, cried out, 'Oh no, my lord! Give her the child – please do not kill him!'

But the other woman said, 'All right, he will be neither yours nor mine; divide him between us!'

**27** Then the king said, 'Do not kill the child, but give him to the woman who wants him to live, for she is his mother!'

**28** When all Israel heard the king's decision, the people were in awe of the king, for they saw the wisdom God had given him for rendering justice.

**v.16** – Solomon demonstrates this great wisdom in deciding a tough case between two mothers.

**v.19–21** – One mother accuses the other of switching their babies in the night after her own has died.

**v.25–27** – Solomon says that the baby should be cut in two and half given to each woman. One woman accepts the decision, but the child's true mother begs for the boy to live.

## Where we end up

Solomon's wise decision revealed the truth of the matter.

# 30 Solomon's Temple

## Main Theme

The Lord will be present with his people in a temple, through the sacrifice of a priest.

## Setting

Jerusalem (the site of the Temple)

## Characters

The Lord, Solomon, and the elders and priests of Israel

## Key Verse: 1 Kings 8:30

'May you hear the humble and earnest requests from me and your people Israel when we pray toward this place. Yes, hear us from heaven where you live, and when you hear, forgive.'

Solomon's Temple for the Lord is built in Jerusalem.

# Read the story 1 Kings 8

¹ Solomon then summoned to Jerusalem the elders of Israel and all the heads of the tribes – the leaders of the ancestral families of the Israelites. They were to bring the Ark of the LORD's Covenant to the Temple from its location in the City of David, also known as Zion. ² So all the men of Israel assembled before King Solomon at the annual Festival of Shelters, which is held in early autumn in the month of Ethanim.

³ When all the elders of Israel arrived, the priests picked up the Ark. ⁴ The priests and Levites brought up the Ark of the LORD along with the special tent and all the sacred items that had been in it. ⁵ There, before the Ark, King Solomon and the entire community of Israel sacrificed so many sheep, goats, and cattle that no one could keep count!

⁶ Then the priests carried the Ark of the LORD's Covenant into the inner sanctuary of the Temple – the Most Holy Place – and placed it beneath the wings of the cherubim. ⁷ The cherubim spread their wings over the Ark, forming a canopy over the Ark and its carrying poles. ⁸ These poles were so long that their ends could be seen from the Holy Place, which is in front of the Most Holy Place, but not from the outside. They are still there to this day. ⁹ Nothing was in the Ark except the two stone tablets that Moses had placed in it at Mount Sinai, where the LORD made a covenant with the people of Israel when they left the land of Egypt.

¹⁰ When the priests came out of the Holy Place, a thick cloud filled the Temple of the LORD. ¹¹ The priests could not continue their service because of the cloud, for the glorious presence of the LORD filled the Temple of the LORD.

¹² Then Solomon prayed, 'O LORD, you have said that you would live in a thick cloud of darkness. ¹³ Now I have built a glorious Temple for you, a place where you can live for ever!'

¹⁴ Then the king turned around to the entire community of Israel standing before him and gave this blessing: ¹⁵ 'Praise the LORD, the God of Israel, who has kept the promise he made to my father, David. For he told my father, ¹⁶ "From the day I brought my people Israel out of Egypt, I have never chosen a city among any of the tribes of Israel as the place where a Temple should be built to honour my name. But I have chosen David to be king over my people Israel."'

## Key plot points

**v.1** – Solomon builds a temple for the Lord and brings the Ark of the Covenant into the Most Holy Place.

**v.10–11** – Just as he did for Moses and the Tabernacle, the Lord shows his presence by a thick cloud that will not allow anyone to enter the Temple for a time.

**17** Then Solomon said, 'My father, David, wanted to build this Temple to honour the name of the LORD, the God of Israel. **18** But the LORD told him, "You wanted to build the Temple to honour my name. Your intention is good, **19** but you are not the one to do it. One of your own sons will build the Temple to honour me."

**20** 'And now the LORD has fulfilled the promise he made, for I have become king in my father's place, and now I sit on the throne of Israel, just as the LORD promised. I have built this Temple to honour the name of the LORD, the God of Israel. **21** And I have prepared a place there for the Ark, which contains the covenant that the LORD made with our ancestors when he brought them out of Egypt.'

**22** Then Solomon stood before the altar of the LORD in front of the entire community of Israel. He lifted his hands towards heaven, **23** and he prayed,

**v.23–30** – Solomon offers a prayer of dedication for the Temple.

'O LORD, God of Israel, there is no God like you in all of heaven above or on the earth below. You keep your covenant and show unfailing love to all who walk before you in wholehearted devotion. **24** You have kept your promise to your servant David, my father. You made that promise with your own mouth, and with your own hands you have fulfilled it today.'

…

**54** When Solomon finished making these prayers and petitions to the LORD, he stood up in front of the altar of the LORD, where he had been kneeling with his hands raised towards heaven. **55** He stood and in a loud voice blessed the entire congregation of Israel:

**v.56–61** – Then he blesses the assembly and charges them to keep the law of the Lord.

**56** 'Praise the LORD who has given rest to his people Israel, just as he promised. Not one word has failed of all the wonderful promises he gave through his servant Moses. **57** May the LORD our God be with us as he was with our ancestors; may he never leave us or abandon us. **58** May he give us the desire to do his will in everything and to obey all the commands, decrees, and regulations that he gave our ancestors. **59** And may these words that I have prayed in the presence of the LORD be before him constantly, day and night, so that the LORD our God may give justice to me and to his people Israel, according to each day's needs. **60** Then people all over the earth will know that the LORD alone is God and there is no other. **61** And may you be completely faithful to the LORD our God. May you always obey his decrees and commands, just as you are doing today.'

**62** Then the king and all Israel with him offered sacrifices to the LORD. **63** Solomon offered to the LORD a peace offering of 22,000 cattle and 120,000 sheep and goats. And so the king and all the people of Israel dedicated the Temple of the LORD.

**64** That same day the king consecrated the central area of the courtyard in front of the LORD's Temple. He offered burnt offerings, grain offerings, and the fat of peace offerings there, because the bronze altar in the LORD's presence was too small to hold all the burnt offerings, grain offerings, and the fat of the peace offerings.

**65** Then Solomon and all Israel celebrated the Festival of Shelters in the presence of the LORD our God. A large congregation had gathered from as far away as Lebo-hamath in the north and the Brook of Egypt in the south. The celebration went on for fourteen days in all – seven days for the dedication of the altar and seven days for the Festival of Shelters. **66** After the festival was over, Solomon sent the people home. They blessed the king and went to their homes joyful and glad because the LORD had been good to his servant David and to his people Israel.

**v.62–63** – He offers thousands and thousands of sacrifices to dedicate the Temple.

**v.65** – Israel held a great festival to celebrate the building and dedication of the Temple.

## Where we end up

Solomon dismisses the people to go home in the joy of the Lord.

## My Reflections

# 31 Elijah

## Main Theme
The Lord is the only true and living God, and his people will worship him alone.

## Setting
Mount Carmel

## Characters
Elijah (the prophet of the Lord), Obadiah (a godly palace attendant), Ahab (wicked king of Israel), and 450 prophets of Baal

## Key Verse: 1 Kings 18:38–39
Immediately the fire of the LORD flashed down from heaven and burned up the young bull, the wood, the stones, and the dust. It even licked up all the water in the trench! And when all the people saw it, they fell face down on the ground and cried out, 'The LORD – he is God! Yes, the LORD is God!'

Elijah calls down fire from heaven.

# Read the story 1 Kings 18:1–40

[1] Later on, in the third year of the drought, the LORD said to Elijah, 'Go and present yourself to King Ahab. Tell him that I will soon send rain!' [2] So Elijah went to appear before Ahab.

Meanwhile, the famine had become very severe in Samaria. [3] So Ahab summoned Obadiah, who was in charge of the palace. (Obadiah was a devoted follower of the LORD. [4] Once when Jezebel had tried to kill all the LORD's prophets, Obadiah had hidden 100 of them in two caves. He put fifty prophets in each cave and supplied them with food and water.) [5] Ahab said to Obadiah, 'We must check every spring and valley in the land to see if we can find enough grass to save at least some of my horses and mules.' [6] So they divided the land between them. Ahab went one way by himself, and Obadiah went another way by himself.

[7] As Obadiah was walking along, he suddenly saw Elijah coming towards him. Obadiah recognized him at once and bowed low to the ground before him. 'Is it really you, my lord Elijah?' he asked.

[8] 'Yes, it is,' Elijah replied. 'Now go and tell your master, "Elijah is here."'

[9] 'Oh, sir,' Obadiah protested, 'what harm have I done to you that you are sending me to my death at the hands of Ahab? [10] For I swear by the LORD your God that the king has searched every nation and kingdom on earth from end to end to find you. And each time he was told, "Elijah isn't here," King Ahab forced the king of that nation to swear to the truth of his claim. [11] And now you say, "Go and tell your master, 'Elijah is here.'" [12] But as soon as I leave you, the Spirit of the LORD will carry you away to who knows where. When Ahab comes and cannot find you, he will kill me. Yet I have been a true servant of the LORD all my life. [13] Has no one told you, my lord, about the time when Jezebel was trying to kill the LORD's prophets? I hid 100 of them in two caves and supplied them with food and water. [14] And now you say, "Go and tell your master, 'Elijah is here.'" Sir, if I do that, Ahab will certainly kill me.'

[15] But Elijah said, 'I swear by the LORD Almighty, in whose presence I stand, that I will present myself to Ahab this very day.'

[16] So Obadiah went to tell Ahab that Elijah had come, and Ahab went out to meet Elijah. [17] When Ahab saw him, he exclaimed, 'So, is it really you, you troublemaker of Israel?'

## Key plot points

**v.1** – Three years into a drought, the Lord calls Elijah to return to Israel and confront Ahab.

**v.7–8** – Obadiah, who is faithful to the Lord, meets Elijah and goes to tell Ahab where he is.

**v.18–19** — Elijah confronts Ahab and sets up a contest. He asks that the prophets of Baal and Asherah meet him on Mount Carmel.

<sup>18</sup> 'I have made no trouble for Israel,' Elijah replied. 'You and your family are the troublemakers, for you have refused to obey the commands of the LORD and have worshipped the images of Baal instead. <sup>19</sup> Now summon all Israel to join me at Mount Carmel, along with the 450 prophets of Baal and the 400 prophets of Asherah who are supported by Jezebel.'

<sup>20</sup> So Ahab summoned all the people of Israel and the prophets to Mount Carmel. <sup>21</sup> Then Elijah stood in front of them and said, 'How much longer will you waver, hobbling between two opinions? If the LORD is God, follow him! But if Baal is God, then follow him!' But the people were completely silent.

<sup>22</sup> Then Elijah said to them, 'I am the only prophet of the LORD who is left, but Baal has 450 prophets. <sup>23</sup> Now bring two bulls. The prophets of Baal may choose whichever one they wish and cut it into pieces and lay it on the wood of their altar, but without setting fire to it. I will prepare the other bull and lay it on the wood on the altar, but not set fire to it. <sup>24</sup> Then call on the name of your god, and I will call on the name of the LORD. The god who answers by setting fire to the wood is the true God!' And all the people agreed.

**v.24** — The contest is to see whose God will answer when called.

<sup>25</sup> Then Elijah said to the prophets of Baal, 'You go first, for there are many of you. Choose one of the bulls, and prepare it and call on the name of your god. But do not set fire to the wood.'

<sup>26</sup> So they prepared one of the bulls and placed it on the altar. Then they called on the name of Baal from morning until noontime, shouting, 'O Baal, answer us!' But there was no reply of any kind. Then they danced, hobbling around the altar they had made.

<sup>27</sup> About midday Elijah began mocking them. 'You'll have to shout louder,' he scoffed, 'for surely he is a god! Perhaps he is daydreaming, or is relieving himself. Or maybe he is away on a trip, or is asleep and needs to be wakened!'

<sup>28</sup> So they shouted louder, and following their normal custom, they cut themselves with knives and swords until the blood gushed out. <sup>29</sup> They raved all afternoon until the time of the evening sacrifice, but still there was no sound, no reply, no response.

**v.29** — The prophets of Baal and Asherah call on their gods for several hours, but nothing happens.

<sup>30</sup> Then Elijah called to the people, 'Come over here!' They all crowded around him as he repaired the altar of the LORD that had been torn down. <sup>31</sup> He took twelve stones, one to represent each of the tribes of Israel, <sup>32</sup> and he used the stones to rebuild the altar in the

name of the LORD. Then he dug a trench around the altar large enough to hold about fourteen litres. ³³ He piled wood on the altar, cut the bull into pieces, and laid the pieces on the wood. Then he said, 'Fill four large jars with water, and pour the water over the offering and the wood.'

³⁴ After they had done this, he said, 'Do the same thing again!' And when they were finished, he said, 'Now do it a third time!' So they did as he said, ³⁵ and the water ran around the altar and even filled the trench.

³⁶ At the usual time for offering the evening sacrifice, Elijah the prophet walked up to the altar and prayed, 'O LORD, God of Abraham, Isaac, and Jacob, prove today that you are God in Israel and that I am your servant. Prove that I have done all this at your command. ³⁷ O LORD, answer me! Answer me so these people will know that you, O LORD, are God and that you have brought them back to yourself.'

³⁸ Immediately the fire of the LORD flashed down from heaven and burned up the young bull, the wood, the stones, and the dust. It even licked up all the water in the trench! ³⁹ And when all the people saw it, they fell face down on the ground and cried out, 'The LORD – he is God! Yes, the LORD is God!'

⁴⁰ Then Elijah commanded, 'Seize all the prophets of Baal. Don't let a single one escape!' So the people seized them all, and Elijah took them down to the Kishon Valley and killed them there.

**v.33** – Then Elijah sets up his sacrifice. He calls for several gallons of water to be poured over the offering.

**v.38** – The Lord answers in spectacular fashion by consuming not only the sacrifice, but all the water that Elijah had poured over it as well.

## Where we end up

The people respond with repentance, declaring that the Lord is the true God. Elijah then commands that the prophets of the false gods be put to death.

# 32  Elisha

### Main Theme

The Lord of heaven's armies will fight for his servants and conquer his enemies.

### Setting

Aram, Dothan (home of Elisha), and Samaria (home of the king of Israel)

### Characters

The king of Aram, Elisha, Elisha's servant, and the king of Israel

### Key Verse: 2 Kings 6:16–17

'Don't be afraid!' Elisha told him. 'For there are more on our side than on theirs!' Then Elisha prayed, 'O LORD, open his eyes and let him see!' The LORD opened the young man's eyes, and when he looked up, he saw that the hillside around Elisha was filled with horses and chariots of fire.

The Lord opens the eyes of Elisha's servant.

# Read the story 2 Kings 6:8–23

## Key plot points

[8] When the king of Aram was at war with Israel, he would confer with his officers and say, 'We will mobilize our forces at such and such a place.'

[9] But immediately Elisha, the man of God, would warn the king of Israel, 'Do not go near that place, for the Arameans are planning to mobilize their troops there.' [10] So the king of Israel would send word to the place indicated by the man of God. Time and again Elisha warned the king, so that he would be on the alert there.

[11] The king of Aram became very upset over this. He called his officers together and demanded, 'Which of you is the traitor? Who has been informing the king of Israel of my plans?'

[12] 'It's not us, my lord the king,' one of the officers replied. 'Elisha, the prophet in Israel, tells the king of Israel even the words you speak in the privacy of your bedroom!'

[13] 'Go and find out where he is,' the king commanded, 'so I can send troops to seize him.'

And the report came back: 'Elisha is at Dothan.' [14] So one night the king of Aram sent a great army with many chariots and horses to surround the city.

[15] When the servant of the man of God got up early the next morning and went outside, there were troops, horses, and chariots everywhere. 'Oh, sir, what will we do now?' the young man cried to Elisha.

[16] 'Don't be afraid!' Elisha told him. 'For there are more on our side than on theirs!' [17] Then Elisha prayed, 'O Lord, open his eyes and let him see!' The Lord opened the young man's eyes, and when he looked up, he saw that the hillside around Elisha was filled with horses and chariots of fire.

[18] As the Aramean army advanced towards him, Elisha prayed, 'O Lord, please make them blind.' So the Lord struck them with blindness as Elisha had asked.

[19] Then Elisha went out and told them, 'You have come the wrong way! This isn't the right city! Follow me, and I will take you to the man you are looking for.' And he led them to the city of Samaria.

[20] As soon as they had entered Samaria, Elisha prayed, 'O Lord, now open their eyes and let them see.' So the Lord opened their eyes, and they discovered that they were in the middle of Samaria.

**v.12–13** – When the king of Aram finds out that Elisha has been thwarting his plans by revealing them to the king of Israel, he sends his army to Dothan to seize Elisha.

**v.15** – Elisha's servant is terrified when he wakes up in the morning to find the Aramean army around the city.

**v.17** – Elisha prays that the Lord would open his servant's eyes. He then sees that the hills are full of angelic armies all around.

**v.18** – Elisha prays that the Aramean army would be struck blind.

**v.19–20** – Elisha leads the blinded army to Samaria where he prays again to restore their vision.

**v.21–22** – The king of Israel wants to kill them, but Elisha says they should be treated well.

²¹ When the king of Israel saw them, he shouted to Elisha, 'My father, should I kill them? Should I kill them?'

²² 'Of course not!' Elisha replied. 'Do we kill prisoners of war? Give them food and drink and send them home again to their master.'

²³ So the king made a great feast for them and then sent them home to their master. After that, the Aramean raiders stayed away from the land of Israel.

## Where we end up

After feeding the army, the king of Israel sent them back to Aram. The Arameans no longer raided or attacked Israel.

## My Reflections

# Jonah

### Main Theme

The Lord will accept anyone who repents and turns to him in faith; he desires that none should perish.

### Setting

Joppa, a ship to Tarshish, and Nineveh

### Characters

The Lord, Jonah, the sailors, and the Ninevites

### Key Verse: Jonah 3:10

When God saw what they had done and how they had put a stop to their evil ways, he changed his mind and did not carry out the destruction he had threatened.

Jonah is thrown overboard.

## Key plot points

**v.1–3** – The Lord calls Jonah to go and preach to Nineveh, but Jonah flees in the opposite direction. In the port of Joppa, he boards a ship for Tarshish.

**v.4** – The ship is caught up in a terrible storm.

**v.7** – The sailors cast lots and find that Jonah is the cause of the storm.

**v.15** – The sailors throw Jonah into the sea and the storm stops.

## Read the story Jonah 1 – 4

**1** The LORD gave this message to Jonah son of Amittai: **2** 'Get up and go to the great city of Nineveh. Announce my judgement against it because I have seen how wicked its people are.'

**3** But Jonah got up and went in the opposite direction to get away from the LORD. He went down to the port of Joppa, where he found a ship leaving for Tarshish. He bought a ticket and went on board, hoping to escape from the LORD by sailing to Tarshish.

**4** But the LORD hurled a powerful wind over the sea, causing a violent storm that threatened to break the ship apart. **5** Fearing for their lives, the desperate sailors shouted to their gods for help and threw the cargo overboard to lighten the ship.

But all this time Jonah was sound asleep down in the hold. **6** So the captain went down after him. 'How can you sleep at a time like this?' he shouted. 'Get up and pray to your god! Maybe he will pay attention to us and spare our lives.'

**7** Then the crew cast lots to see which of them had offended the gods and caused the terrible storm. When they did this, the lots identified Jonah as the culprit. **8** 'Why has this awful storm come down on us?' they demanded. 'Who are you? What is your line of work? What country are you from? What is your nationality?'

**9** Jonah answered, 'I am a Hebrew, and I worship the LORD, the God of heaven, who made the sea and the land.'

**10** The sailors were terrified when they heard this, for he had already told them he was running away from the LORD. 'Oh, why did you do it?' they groaned. **11** And since the storm was getting worse all the time, they asked him, 'What should we do to you to stop this storm?'

**12** 'Throw me into the sea,' Jonah said, 'and it will become calm again. I know that this terrible storm is all my fault.'

**13** Instead, the sailors rowed even harder to get the ship to the land. But the stormy sea was too violent for them, and they couldn't make it. **14** Then they cried out to the LORD, Jonah's God. 'O LORD,' they pleaded, 'don't make us die for this man's sin. And don't hold us responsible for his death. O LORD, you have sent this storm upon him for your own good reasons.'

**15** Then the sailors picked Jonah up and threw him into the raging sea, and the storm stopped at once! **16** The sailors were awestruck by the Lord's great power, and they offered him a sacrifice and vowed to serve him.

¹⁷ Now the Lord had arranged for a great fish to swallow Jonah. And Jonah was inside the fish for three days and three nights.

**2** Then Jonah prayed to the Lord his God from inside the fish. ² He said,

'I cried out to the Lord in my great trouble,
    and he answered me.
I called to you from the land of the dead,
    and Lord, you heard me!
³ You threw me into the ocean depths,
    and I sank down to the heart of the sea.
The mighty waters engulfed me;
    I was buried beneath your wild and stormy waves.
⁴ Then I said, "O Lord, you have driven me from your presence.
    Yet I will look once more towards your holy Temple."

⁵ 'I sank beneath the waves,
    and the waters closed over me.
    Seaweed wrapped itself around my head.
⁶ I sank down to the very roots of the mountains.
    I was imprisoned in the earth,
    whose gates lock shut for ever.
But you, O Lord my God,
    snatched me from the jaws of death!
⁷ As my life was slipping away,
    I remembered the Lord.
And my earnest prayer went out to you
    in your holy Temple.
⁸ Those who worship false gods
    turn their backs on all God's mercies.
⁹ But I will offer sacrifices to you with songs of praise,
    and I will fulfil all my vows.
    For my salvation comes from the Lord alone.'

¹⁰ Then the Lord ordered the fish to spit Jonah out on to the beach.

**v.17** – The Lord appoints a big fish to swallow Jonah.

**Chapter 2** – From the fish's belly Jonah cries out for mercy.

**v.10** – After three days, the Lord causes the fish to spit Jonah out on the shore.

**v.1–4** — The Lord calls Jonah to Nineveh a second time and Jonah obeys. He goes and preaches to the Ninevites.

**3** Then the LORD spoke to Jonah a second time: **2** 'Get up and go to the great city of Nineveh, and deliver the message I have given you.'

**3** This time Jonah obeyed the LORD's command and went to Nineveh, a city so large that it took three days to see it all. **4** On the day Jonah entered the city, he shouted to the crowds: 'Forty days from now Nineveh will be destroyed!' **5** The people of Nineveh believed God's message, and from the greatest to the least, they declared a fast and put on sackcloth to show their sorrow.

**v.6–9** — Jonah's preaching inspires a great repentance in Nineveh.

**6** When the king of Nineveh heard what Jonah was saying, he stepped down from his throne and took off his royal robes. He dressed himself in sackcloth and sat on a heap of ashes. **7** Then the king and his nobles sent this decree throughout the city:

'No one, not even the animals from your herds and flocks, may eat or drink anything at all. **8** People and animals alike must wear garments of mourning, and everyone must pray earnestly to God. They must turn from their evil ways and stop all their violence. **9** Who can tell? Perhaps even yet God will change his mind and hold back his fierce anger from destroying us.'

**v.10** — The Lord relents from the destruction he had planned.

**10** When God saw what they had done and how they had put a stop to their evil ways, he changed his mind and did not carry out the destruction he had threatened.

**v.1** — Jonah is angry that the Lord spares Nineveh.

**4** This change of plans greatly upset Jonah, and he became very angry. **2** So he complained to the LORD about it: 'Didn't I say before I left home that you would do this, LORD? That is why I ran away to Tarshish! I knew that you are a merciful and compassionate God, slow to get angry and filled with unfailing love. You are eager to turn back from destroying people. **3** Just kill me now, LORD! I'd rather be dead than alive if what I predicted will not happen.'

**4** The LORD replied, 'Is it right for you to be angry about this?'

**5** Then Jonah went out to the east side of the city and made a shelter to sit under as he waited to see what would happen to the city. **6** And the LORD God arranged for a leafy plant to grow there, and soon it spread its broad leaves over Jonah's head, shading him from the sun. This eased his discomfort, and Jonah was very grateful for the plant.

**7** But God also arranged for a worm! The next morning at dawn the worm ate through the stem of the plant so that it withered away. **8** And as the sun grew hot, God arranged for a scorching east wind to blow on Jonah. The sun beat down on his head until he grew faint and wished to die. 'Death is certainly better than living like this!' he exclaimed.

⁹ Then God said to Jonah, 'Is it right for you to be angry because the plant died?'

'Yes,' Jonah retorted, 'even angry enough to die!'

¹⁰ Then the LORD said, 'You feel sorry about the plant, though you did nothing to put it there. It came quickly and died quickly. ¹¹ But Nineveh has more than 120,000 people living in spiritual darkness, not to mention all the animals. Shouldn't I feel sorry for such a great city?'

## Where we end up

The Lord gives Jonah an object lesson with a plant and tells him that he cares for Nineveh.

**Christ foreshadowed:** The Guards at the Tomb – p. 243

## My Reflections

# 34    The Captivity

### Main Theme

The Lord will judge the sin and rebellion of his people, but he will not forsake his covenant promise.

### Setting

Jerusalem, Babylon, and Persia

### Characters

The Lord, the final kings of Judah, Nebuchadnezzar (king of Babylon), Jeremiah, and Cyrus (king of Persia)

### Key Verse: 2 Chronicles 36:15–16

The LORD, the God of their ancestors, repeatedly sent his prophets to warn them, for he had compassion on his people and his Temple. But the people mocked these messengers of God and despised their words. They scoffed at the prophets until the LORD's anger could no longer be restrained and nothing could be done.

God's people are taken into captivity.

# Read the story 2 Chronicles 36

**1** Then the people of the land took Josiah's son Jehoahaz and made him the next king in Jerusalem. **2** Jehoahaz was twenty-three years old when he became king, and he reigned in Jerusalem for three months. **3** Then he was deposed by the king of Egypt, who demanded that Judah pay 3,400 kilograms of silver and 34 kilograms of gold as tribute.

**4** The king of Egypt then installed Eliakim, the brother of Jehoahaz, as the next king of Judah and Jerusalem, and he changed Eliakim's name to Jehoiakim. Then Neco took Jehoahaz to Egypt as a prisoner.

**5** Jehoiakim was twenty-five years old when he became king, and he reigned in Jerusalem for eleven years. He did what was evil in the sight of the LORD his God.

**6** Then King Nebuchadnezzar of Babylon came to Jerusalem and captured it, and he bound Jehoiakim in bronze chains and led him away to Babylon. **7** Nebuchadnezzar also took some of the treasures from the Temple of the LORD, and he placed them in his palace in Babylon.

**8** The rest of the events in Jehoiakim's reign, including all the evil things he did and everything found against him, are recorded in The Book of the Kings of Israel and Judah. Then his son Jehoiachin became the next king.

**9** Jehoiachin was eighteen years old when he became king, and he reigned in Jerusalem for three months and ten days. Jehoiachin did what was evil in the LORD's sight.

**10** In the spring of the year King Nebuchadnezzar took Jehoiachin to Babylon. Many treasures from the Temple of the LORD were also taken to Babylon at that time. And Nebuchadnezzar installed Jehoiachin's uncle, Zedekiah, as the next king in Judah and Jerusalem.

**11** Zedekiah was twenty-one years old when he became king, and he reigned in Jerusalem for eleven years. **12** But Zedekiah did what was evil in the sight of the LORD his God, and he refused to humble himself when the prophet Jeremiah spoke to him directly from the LORD. **13** He also rebelled against King Nebuchadnezzar, even though he had taken an oath of loyalty in God's name. Zedekiah was a hard and stubborn man, refusing to turn to the LORD, the God of Israel.

**14** Likewise, all the leaders of the priests and the people became more and more unfaithful. They followed all the pagan practices of the surrounding nations, desecrating the Temple of the LORD that had been consecrated in Jerusalem.

# Key plot points

**v.1–5** — The final kings of Israel are all evil. The sin of Judah becomes so great that the Lord brings his wrath against them.

**v.6** — The Lord allows Nebuchadnezzar the Chaldean, king of Babylon to conquer them and take them into exile.

**15** The LORD, the God of their ancestors, repeatedly sent his prophets to warn them, for he had compassion on his people and his Temple. **16** But the people mocked these messengers of God and despised their words. They scoffed at the prophets until the LORD's anger could no longer be restrained and nothing could be done.

**17** So the LORD brought the king of Babylon against them. The Babylonians killed Judah's young men, even chasing after them into the Temple. They had no pity on the people, killing both young men and young women, the old and the infirm. God handed all of them over to Nebuchadnezzar. **18** The king took home to Babylon all the articles, large and small, used in the Temple of God, and the treasures from both the LORD's Temple and from the palace of the king and his officials. **19** Then his army burned the Temple of God, tore down the walls of Jerusalem, burned all the palaces, and completely destroyed everything of value. **20** The few who survived were taken as exiles to Babylon, and they became servants to the king and his sons until the kingdom of Persia came to power.

**21** So the message of the LORD spoken through Jeremiah was fulfilled. The land finally enjoyed its Sabbath rest, lying desolate until the seventy years were fulfilled, just as the prophet had said.

**22** In the first year of King Cyrus of Persia, the LORD fulfilled the prophecy he had given through Jeremiah. He stirred the heart of Cyrus to put this proclamation in writing and to send it throughout his kingdom:

**23** 'This is what King Cyrus of Persia says:

'The LORD, the God of heaven, has given me all the kingdoms of the earth. He has appointed me to build him a Temple at Jerusalem, which is in Judah. Any of you who are his people may go there for this task. And may the LORD your God be with you!'

**v.19–20** – The capital city of Jerusalem and the Temple are completely destroyed. The people are either killed in the battle or taken into exile in Babylon hundreds of miles away.

**v.21** – The prophet Jeremiah is the Lord's messenger sent during this time to interpret the events of the exile for the people.

## Where we end up

Through Jeremiah, the Lord had promised that his people would return to their land. Under the rule of King Cyrus of Persia, the exiles are allowed to return to Judah.

**Christ foreshadowed:** The Guards at the Tomb – p. 243

# The Valley of Dry Bones

## 35

### Main Theme

The Lord will send his Spirit to bring new life to his people who are dead in sin.

### Setting

A prophetic vision (during the Exile)

### Key Verse: Ezekiel 37:14

'I will put my Spirit in you, and you will live again and return home to your own land. Then you will know that I, the LORD, have spoken, and I have done what I said. Yes, the LORD has spoken!'

### Characters

The Lord, Ezekiel, and the dry bones

Ezekiel had a vision of the valley of dry bones.

## Read the story Ezekiel 37:1–14

[1] The LORD took hold of me, and I was carried away by the Spirit of the LORD to a valley filled with bones. [2] He led me all around among the bones that covered the valley floor. They were scattered everywhere across the ground and were completely dried out. [3] Then he asked me, 'Son of man, can these bones become living people again?'

## Key plot points

**v.1** – The Lord shows Ezekiel a vision of a valley full of dry bones.

**v.3** – He asks Ezekiel if they can live.

**v.4–5** – The Lord then calls Ezekiel to prophesy life to the bones.

**v.7–8** – As Ezekiel speaks, the bones begin to join together, and muscles, and flesh return to them

**v.9** – The Lord then calls Ezekiel to prophesy to the breath, telling it to come and make them live again.

**v.10** – As Ezekiel spoke, the people in the valley came to life and stood as a great multitude.

'O Sovereign Lord,' I replied, 'you alone know the answer to that.'

[4] Then he said to me, 'Speak a prophetic message to these bones and say, "Dry bones, listen to the word of the Lord! [5] This is what the Sovereign Lord says: Look! I am going to put breath into you and make you live again! [6] I will put flesh and muscles on you and cover you with skin. I will put breath into you, and you will come to life. Then you will know that I am the Lord."'

[7] So I spoke this message, just as he told me. Suddenly as I spoke, there was a rattling noise all across the valley. The bones of each body came together and attached themselves as complete skeletons. [8] Then as I watched, muscles and flesh formed over the bones. Then skin formed to cover their bodies, but they still had no breath in them.

[9] Then he said to me, 'Speak a prophetic message to the winds, son of man. Speak a prophetic message and say, "This is what the Sovereign Lord says: Come, O breath, from the four winds! Breathe into these dead bodies so they may live again."'

[10] So I spoke the message as he commanded me, and breath came into their bodies. They all came to life and stood up on their feet – a great army.

[11] Then he said to me, 'Son of man, these bones represent the people of Israel. They are saying, "We have become old, dry bones – all hope is gone. Our nation is finished." [12] Therefore, prophesy to them and say, "This is what the Sovereign Lord says: O my people, I will open your graves of exile and cause you to rise again. Then I will bring you back to the land of Israel. [13] When this happens, O my people, you will know that I am the Lord. [14] I will put my Spirit in you, and you will live again and return home to your own land. Then you will know that I, the Lord, have spoken, and I have done what I said. Yes, the Lord has spoken!"'

## Where we end up

The Lord explains that this is what he will do for his people. He will bring them out of their graves and put his Spirit in them that they may live.

**Christ foreshadowed:** The Coming of the Holy Spirit – p. 257

# We Will Not Bow

## 36

### Main Theme
The Lord will stand with his servants to deliver them from the hands of the wicked.

### Setting
The Plain of Dura in Babylon (Israel in Exile)

### Characters
Shadrach, Meshach, Abednego, and Nebuchadnezzar

### Key Verse:
### Daniel 3:17–18
'If we are thrown into the blazing furnace, the God whom we serve is able to save us. He will rescue us from your power, Your Majesty. But even if he doesn't, we want to make it clear to you, Your Majesty, that we will never serve your gods or worship the gold statue you have set up.'

The three Hebrew boys are thrown into the fiery furnace.

## Key plot points

**v.1, 5** – Nebuchadnezzar sets up a golden statue and orders everyone in Babylon to fall down and worship it.

**v.12** – Three Hebrews, Shadrach, Meshach, and Abednego, refuse to worship the statue.

**v.13** – Nebuchadnezzar is enraged and brings them into question them.

## Read the story Daniel 3

¹ King Nebuchadnezzar made a golden statue thirty metres tall and three metres wide and set it up on the plain of Dura in the province of Babylon. ² Then he sent messages to the high officers, officials, governors, advisers, treasurers, judges, magistrates, and all the provincial officials to come to the dedication of the statue he had set up. ³ So all these officials came and stood before the statue King Nebuchadnezzar had set up.

⁴ Then a herald shouted out, 'People of all races and nations and languages, listen to the king's command! ⁵ When you hear the sound of the horn, flute, zither, lyre, harp, pipes, and other musical instruments, bow to the ground to worship King Nebuchadnezzar's gold statue. ⁶ Anyone who refuses to obey will immediately be thrown into a blazing furnace.'

⁷ So at the sound of the musical instruments, all the people, whatever their race or nation or language, bowed to the ground and worshipped the golden statue that King Nebuchadnezzar had set up.

⁸ But some of the astrologers went to the king and informed on the Jews. ⁹ They said to King Nebuchadnezzar, 'Long live the king! ¹⁰ You issued a decree requiring all the people to bow down and worship the golden statue when they hear the sound of the horn, flute, zither, lyre, harp, pipes, and other musical instruments. ¹¹ That decree also states that those who refuse to obey must be thrown into a blazing furnace. ¹² But there are some Jews – Shadrach, Meshach, and Abednego – whom you have put in charge of the province of Babylon. They pay no attention to you, Your Majesty. They refuse to serve your gods and do not worship the golden statue you have set up.'

¹³ Then Nebuchadnezzar flew into a rage and ordered that Shadrach, Meshach, and Abednego be brought before him. When they were brought in, ¹⁴ Nebuchadnezzar said to them, 'Is it true, Shadrach, Meshach, and Abednego, that you refuse to serve my gods or to worship the golden statue I have set up? ¹⁵ I will give you one more chance to bow down and worship the statue I have made when you hear the sound of the musical instruments. But if you refuse, you will be thrown immediately into the blazing furnace. And then what god will be able to rescue you from my power?'

<sup>16</sup> Shadrach, Meshach, and Abednego replied, 'O Nebuchadnezzar, we do not need to defend ourselves before you. <sup>17</sup> If we are thrown into the blazing furnace, the God whom we serve is able to save us. He will rescue us from your power, Your Majesty. <sup>18</sup> But even if he doesn't, we want to make it clear to you, Your Majesty, that we will never serve your gods or worship the golden statue you have set up.'

<sup>19</sup> Nebuchadnezzar was so furious with Shadrach, Meshach, and Abednego that his face became distorted with rage. He commanded that the furnace be heated seven times hotter than usual. <sup>20</sup> Then he ordered some of the strongest men of his army to bind Shadrach, Meshach, and Abednego and throw them into the blazing furnace. <sup>21</sup> So they tied them up and threw them into the furnace, fully dressed in their trousers, turbans, robes, and other garments. <sup>22</sup> And because the king, in his anger, had demanded such a hot fire in the furnace, the flames killed the soldiers as they threw the three men in. <sup>23</sup> So Shadrach, Meshach, and Abednego, securely tied, fell into the roaring flames.

<sup>24</sup> But suddenly, Nebuchadnezzar jumped up in amazement and exclaimed to his advisers, 'Didn't we tie up three men and throw them into the furnace?'

'Yes, Your Majesty, we certainly did,' they replied.

<sup>25</sup> 'Look!' Nebuchadnezzar shouted. 'I see four men, unbound, walking around in the fire unharmed! And the fourth looks like a god!'

<sup>26</sup> Then Nebuchadnezzar came as close as he could to the door of the flaming furnace and shouted: 'Shadrach, Meshach, and Abednego, servants of the Most High God, come out! Come here!'

So Shadrach, Meshach, and Abednego stepped out of the fire. <sup>27</sup> Then the high officers, officials, governors, and advisers crowded around them and saw that the fire had not touched them. Not a hair on their heads was singed, and their clothing was not scorched. They didn't even smell of smoke!

<sup>28</sup> Then Nebuchadnezzar said, 'Praise to the God of Shadrach, Meshach, and Abednego! He sent his angel to rescue his servants who trusted in him. They defied the king's command and were willing to die rather than serve or worship any god except their own God. <sup>29</sup> Therefore, I make this decree: If any people, whatever their race or nation or language, speak a word against the God of Shadrach, Meshach, and Abednego, they will be torn limb from limb, and their

**v.16–18** – Shadrach, Meshach, and Abednego refuse to bow down, choosing instead to be thrown into a fiery furnace.

**v.19** – Nebuchadnezzar turns the furnace up to seven times its normal heat and throws them in.

**v.25** – When he goes to look in, Nebuchadnezzar sees four men instead of three in the fire.

**v.26–27** – He calls Shadrach, Meshach, and Abednego out of the fire. When they come out they are not burned or hurt.

houses will be turned into heaps of rubble. There is no other god who can rescue like this!'

<sup>30</sup> Then the king promoted Shadrach, Meshach, and Abednego to even higher positions in the province of Babylon.

### Where we end up

Nebuchadnezzar forbids anyone in his kingdom from blaspheming against the Lord because of his great deliverance.

---

**My Reflections**

# Daniel

## 37

## Main Theme

The Lord will stand with his servants to deliver them from the hands of the wicked.

## Setting

The kingdom of the Medes and Persians (formerly Babylon)

## Characters

King Darius, Daniel, and government officials (satraps and high officials under Darius)

## Key Verse: Daniel 6:26–27

'I decree that everyone throughout my kingdom should tremble with fear before the God of Daniel. For he is the living God, and he will endure forever. His kingdom will never be destroyed, and his rule will never end. He rescues and saves his people; he performs miraculous signs and wonders in the heavens and on earth. He has rescued Daniel from the power of the lions.'

Daniel is thrown into the lions' den.

## Key plot points

**v.2–4** – Daniel excels as a government official and makes the other officials jealous.

**v.5–9** – In a plot against Daniel, some of the government officials convince Darius to make a decree that anyone who prays to someone other than the king should be thrown into the lions' den.

**v.10** – When Daniel hears of the decree, he continues to pray three times a day to the Lord.

## Read the story Daniel 6

[1] Darius the Mede decided to divide the kingdom into 120 provinces, and he appointed a high officer to rule over each province. [2] The king also chose Daniel and two others as administrators to supervise the high officers and protect the king's interests. [3] Daniel soon proved himself more capable than all the other administrators and high officers. Because of Daniel's great ability, the king made plans to place him over the entire empire.

[4] Then the other administrators and high officers began searching for some fault in the way Daniel was handling government affairs, but they couldn't find anything to criticise or condemn. He was faithful, always responsible, and completely trustworthy. [5] So they concluded, 'Our only chance of finding grounds for accusing Daniel will be in connection with the rules of his religion.'

[6] So the administrators and high officers went to the king and said, 'Long live King Darius! [7] We are all in agreement – we administrators, officials, high officers, advisers, and governors – that the king should make a law that will be strictly enforced. Give orders that for the next thirty days any person who prays to anyone, divine or human – except to you, Your Majesty – will be thrown into the den of lions. [8] And now, Your Majesty, issue and sign this law so it cannot be changed, an official law of the Medes and Persians that cannot be revoked.' [9] So King Darius signed the law.

[10] But when Daniel learned that the law had been signed, he went home and knelt down as usual in his upstairs room, with its windows open towards Jerusalem. He prayed three times a day, just as he had always done, giving thanks to his God. [11] Then the officials went together to Daniel's house and found him praying and asking for God's help. [12] So they went straight to the king and reminded him about his law. 'Did you not sign a law that for the next thirty days any person who prays to anyone, divine or human – except to you, Your Majesty – will be thrown into the den of lions?'

'Yes,' the king replied, 'that decision stands; it is an official law of the Medes and Persians that cannot be revoked.'

[13] Then they told the king, 'That man Daniel, one of the captives from Judah, is ignoring you and your law. He still prays to his God three times a day.'

¹⁴ Hearing this, the king was deeply troubled, and he tried to think of a way to save Daniel. He spent the rest of the day looking for a way to get Daniel out of this predicament.

¹⁵ In the evening the men went together to the king and said, 'Your Majesty, you know that according to the law of the Medes and the Persians, no law that the king signs can be changed.'

¹⁶ So at last the king gave orders for Daniel to be arrested and thrown into the den of lions. The king said to him, 'May your God, whom you serve so faithfully, rescue you.'

¹⁷ A stone was brought and placed over the mouth of the den. The king sealed the stone with his own royal seal and the seals of his nobles, so that no one could rescue Daniel. ¹⁸ Then the king returned to his palace and spent the night fasting. He refused his usual entertainment and couldn't sleep at all that night.

¹⁹ Very early the next morning, the king got up and hurried out to the lions' den. ²⁰ When he got there, he called out in anguish, 'Daniel, servant of the living God! Was your God, whom you serve so faithfully, able to rescue you from the lions?'

²¹ Daniel answered, 'Long live the king! ²² My God sent his angel to shut the lions' mouths so that they would not hurt me, for I have been found innocent in his sight. And I have not wronged you, Your Majesty.'

²³ The king was overjoyed and ordered that Daniel be lifted from the den. Not a scratch was found on him, for he had trusted in his God.

²⁴ Then the king gave orders to arrest the men who had maliciously accused Daniel. He had them thrown into the lions' den, along with their wives and children. The lions leaped on them and tore them apart before they even hit the floor of the den.

²⁵ Then King Darius sent this message to the people of every race and nation and language throughout the world: 'Peace and prosperity to you!

²⁶ 'I decree that everyone throughout my kingdom should tremble with fear before the God of Daniel.

For he is the living God,
and he will endure for ever.
His kingdom will never be destroyed,
and his rule will never end.

**v.14–16** — Although Darius is grieved, the officials hold him to his decree. He throws Daniel into the lions' den.

**v.19–22** — In the morning when Darius rushes to check on Daniel, he finds him alive and well. The Lord sent an angel to shut the mouths of the lions.

**v.23** — Darius removes Daniel from the lion's den

**v.24** — Darius throws the officials that had conspired against Daniel into the lions' den, and they are immediately torn apart by the lions.

**27** He rescues and saves his people;
> he performs miraculous signs and wonders
> in the heavens and on earth.
> He has rescued Daniel
> from the power of the lions.'

**28** So Daniel prospered during the reign of Darius and the reign of Cyrus the Persian.

## Where we end up

King Darius sends a message to all people, praising the Lord.

**Christ foreshadowed:** Paul, Ambassador in Chains – p. 264

## My Reflections

# Rebuilding the Temple

## 38

### Main Theme
The Lord will build a new Temple where his people will worship him in spirit and in truth.

### Setting
Jerusalem

### Characters
Jeshua (priest of the Lord), Zerubbabel (a leader of God's people), Haggai and Zechariah (prophets of the Lord), and King Darius

### Key Verse: Ezra 5:1–2
At that time the prophets Haggai and Zechariah son of Iddo prophesied to the Jews in Judah and Jerusalem. They prophesied in the name of the God of Israel who was over them. Zerubbabel son of Shealtiel and Jeshua son of Jehozadak responded by starting again to rebuild the Temple of God in Jerusalem. And the prophets of God were with them and helped them.

The Temple is rebuilt.

## Key plot points

**Introduction** – After Babylon falls to Persia, King Cyrus allows the Jewish people to return to Jerusalem.

**v.8** – Their first work is to rebuild the Temple.

## Read the story Ezra 3 – 6

**3** In early autumn, when the Israelites had settled in their towns, all the people assembled in Jerusalem with a unified purpose. ² Then Jeshua son of Jehozadak joined his fellow priests and Zerubbabel son of Shealtiel with his family in rebuilding the altar of the God of Israel. They wanted to sacrifice burnt offerings on it, as instructed in the Law of Moses, the man of God. ³ Even though the people were afraid of the local residents, they rebuilt the altar at its old site. Then they began to sacrifice burnt offerings on the altar to the LORD each morning and evening.

⁴ They celebrated the Festival of Shelters as prescribed in the Law, sacrificing the number of burnt offerings specified for each day of the festival. ⁵ They also offered the regular burnt offerings and the offerings required for the new moon celebrations and the annual festivals as prescribed by the LORD. The people also gave voluntary offerings to the LORD. ⁶ Fifteen days before the Festival of Shelters began, the priests had begun to sacrifice burnt offerings to the LORD. This was even before they had started to lay the foundation of the LORD's Temple.

⁷ Then the people hired masons and carpenters and bought cedar logs from the people of Tyre and Sidon, paying them with food, wine, and olive oil. The logs were brought down from the Lebanon mountains and floated along the coast of the Mediterranean Sea to Joppa, for King Cyrus had given permission for this.

⁸ The construction of the Temple of God began in mid-spring, during the second year after they arrived in Jerusalem. The workforce was made up of everyone who had returned from exile, including Zerubbabel son of Shealtiel, Jeshua son of Jehozadak and his fellow priests, and all the Levites. The Levites who were twenty years old or older were put in charge of rebuilding the LORD's Temple. ⁹ The workers at the Temple of God were supervised by Jeshua with his sons and relatives, and Kadmiel and his sons, all descendants of Hodaviah. They were helped in this task by the Levites of the family of Henadad.

¹⁰ When the builders completed the foundation of the LORD's Temple, the priests put on their robes and took their places to blow their trumpets. And the Levites, descendants of Asaph, clashed their cymbals to praise the LORD, just as King David had prescribed. ¹¹ With praise and thanks, they sang this song to the LORD:

'He is so good!
    His faithful love for Israel endures for ever!'

Then all the people gave a great shout, praising the LORD because the foundation of the LORD's Temple had been laid.

¹² But many of the older priests, Levites, and other leaders who had seen the first Temple wept aloud when they saw the new Temple's foundation. The others, however, were shouting for joy. ¹³ The joyful shouting and weeping mingled together in a loud noise that could be heard far in the distance.

**4** The enemies of Judah and Benjamin heard that the exiles were rebuilding a Temple to the LORD, the God of Israel. ² So they approached Zerubbabel and the other leaders and said, 'Let us build with you, for we worship your God just as you do. We have sacrificed to him ever since King Esarhaddon of Assyria brought us here.'

³ But Zerubbabel, Jeshua, and the other leaders of Israel replied, 'You may have no part in this work. We alone will build the Temple for the LORD, the God of Israel, just as King Cyrus of Persia commanded us.'

⁴ Then the local residents tried to discourage and frighten the people of Judah to keep them from their work. ⁵ They bribed agents to work against them and to frustrate their plans. This went on during the entire reign of King Cyrus of Persia and lasted until King Darius of Persia took the throne.

v.4 — They lay the foundation, but then they face opposition from neighbouring peoples.

. . .

**5** At that time the prophets Haggai and Zechariah son of Iddo prophesied to the Jews in Judah and Jerusalem. They prophesied in the name of the God of Israel who was over them. ² Zerubbabel son of Shealtiel and Jeshua son of Jehozadak responded by starting again to rebuild the Temple of God in Jerusalem. And the prophets of God were with them and helped them.

v.1 — The prophets Haggai and Zechariah urge the people on by prophesying in the name of the Lord.

v.2 — Zerubbabel and Jeshua lead the people to continue building in the face of the opposition.

³ But Tattenai, governor of the province west of the River Euphrates, and Shethar-bozenai and their colleagues soon arrived in Jerusalem and asked, 'Who gave you permission to rebuild this Temple and restore this structure?' ⁴ They also asked for the names of all the men working on the Temple. ⁵ But because their God was watching over them, the leaders of the Jews were not prevented from building until a report was sent to Darius and he returned his decision.

. . .

**6** So King Darius issued orders that a search be made in the Babylonian archives, which were stored in the treasury. **2** But it was at the fortress at Ecbatana in the province of Media that a scroll was found. This is what it said:

'Memorandum:
   **3** 'In the first year of King Cyrus's reign, a decree was sent out concerning the Temple of God at Jerusalem.
   'Let the Temple be rebuilt on the site where Jews used to offer their sacrifices, using the original foundations. Its height will be thirty metres, and its width will be thirty metres. **4** Every three layers of specially prepared stones will be topped by a layer of timber. All expenses will be paid by the royal treasury. **5** Furthermore, the gold and silver cups, which were taken to Babylon by Nebuchadnezzar from the Temple of God in Jerusalem, must be returned to Jerusalem and put back where they belong. Let them be taken back to the Temple of God.'

**6** So King Darius sent this message:

'Now therefore, Tattenai, governor of the province west of the River Euphrates, and Shethar-bozenai, and your colleagues and other officials west of the River Euphrates – stay away from there! **7** Do not disturb the construction of the Temple of God. Let it be rebuilt on its original site, and do not hinder the governor of Judah and the elders of the Jews in their work.
   **8** 'Moreover, I hereby decree that you are to help these elders of the Jews as they rebuild this Temple of God. You must pay the full construction costs, without delay, from my taxes collected in the province west of the River Euphrates so that the work will not be interrupted.
   **9** 'Give the priests in Jerusalem whatever is needed in the way of young bulls, rams, and male lambs for the burnt offerings presented to the God of heaven. And without fail, provide them with as much wheat, salt, wine, and olive oil as they need each day. **10** Then they will be able to offer acceptable sacrifices to the God of heaven and pray for the welfare of the king and his sons.

**v.7** – King Darius issues a decree that all the opposition to the Jews should cease, and that everything they need should be provided for them.

[11] 'Those who violate this decree in any way will have a beam pulled from their house. Then they will be lifted up and impaled on it, and their house will be reduced to a pile of rubble.

[12] May the God who has chosen the city of Jerusalem as the place to honour his name destroy any king or nation that violates this command and destroys this Temple.

'I, Darius, have issued this decree. Let it be obeyed with all diligence.'

[13] Tattenai, governor of the province west of the River Euphrates, and Shethar-bozenai and their colleagues complied at once with the command of King Darius. [14] So the Jewish elders continued their work, and they were greatly encouraged by the preaching of the prophets Haggai and Zechariah son of Iddo. The Temple was finally finished, as had been commanded by the God of Israel and decreed by Cyrus, Darius, and Artaxerxes, the kings of Persia. [15] The Temple was completed on 12 March, during the sixth year of King Darius's reign.

[16] The Temple of God was then dedicated with great joy by the people of Israel, the priests, the Levites, and the rest of the people who had returned from exile. [17] During the dedication ceremony for the Temple of God, 100 young bulls, 200 rams, and 400 male lambs were sacrificed. And 12 male goats were presented as a sin offering for the twelve tribes of Israel. [18] Then the priests and Levites were divided into their various divisions to serve at the Temple of God in Jerusalem, as prescribed in the Book of Moses.

[19] On 21 April the returned exiles celebrated Passover. [20] The priests and Levites had purified themselves and were ceremonially clean. So they slaughtered the Passover lamb for all the returned exiles, for their fellow priests, and for themselves. [21] The Passover meal was eaten by the people of Israel who had returned from exile and by the others in the land who had turned from their corrupt practices to worship the LORD, the God of Israel. [22] Then they celebrated the Festival of Unleavened Bread for seven days. There was great joy throughout the land because the LORD had caused the king of Assyria to be favourable to them, so that he helped them to rebuild the Temple of God, the God of Israel.

## Where we end up

They complete and dedicate the second Temple, and celebrate the Passover festival that year.

# 39 Rebuilding the Walls

## Main Theme
The Lord will build a new Jerusalem where his people will dwell in peace.

## Setting
Susa (capital of Persia) and Jerusalem

## Characters
King Artaxerxes of Persia, Nehemiah, Sanballat and Tobiah (enemies of the Jews), and Ezra

## Key Verse: Nehemiah 2:17
But now I said to them, 'You know very well what trouble we are in. Jerusalem lies in ruins, and its gates have been destroyed by fire. Let us rebuild the wall of Jerusalem and end this disgrace!'

The walls of Jerusalem are rebuilt.

# Read the story Nehemiah 2, 4, 6:15–19, 8

**2** Early the following spring, in the month of Nisan, during the twentieth year of King Artaxerxes' reign, I was serving the king his wine. I had never before appeared sad in his presence. **2** So the king asked me, 'Why are you looking so sad? You don't look sick to me. You must be deeply troubled.'

Then I was terrified, **3** but I replied, 'Long live the king! How can I not be sad? For the city where my ancestors are buried is in ruins, and the gates have been destroyed by fire.'

**4** The king asked, 'Well, how can I help you?'

With a prayer to the God of heaven, **5** I replied, 'If it please the king, and if you are pleased with me, your servant, send me to Judah to rebuild the city where my ancestors are buried.'

**6** The king, with the queen sitting beside him, asked, 'How long will you be gone? When will you return?' After I told him how long I would be gone, the king agreed to my request.

**7** I also said to the king, 'If it please the king, let me have letters addressed to the governors of the province west of the River Euphrates, instructing them to let me travel safely through their territories on my way to Judah. **8** And please give me a letter addressed to Asaph, the manager of the king's forest, instructing him to give me timber. I will need it to make beams for the gates of the Temple fortress, for the city walls, and for a house for myself.' And the king granted these requests, because the gracious hand of God was on me.

**9** When I came to the governors of the province west of the River Euphrates, I delivered the king's letters to them. The king, I should add, had sent along army officers and horsemen to protect me. **10** But when Sanballat the Horonite and Tobiah the Ammonite official heard of my arrival, they were very displeased that someone had come to help the people of Israel.

**11** So I arrived in Jerusalem. Three days later, **12** I slipped out during the night, taking only a few others with me. I had not told anyone about the plans God had put in my heart for Jerusalem. We took no pack animals with us except the donkey I was riding. **13** After dark I went out through the Valley Gate, past the Jackal's Well, and over to the Dung Gate to inspect the broken walls and burned gates. **14** Then I went to the Fountain Gate and to the King's Pool, but my donkey

# Key plot points

**Introduction** – Nehemiah is a cup-bearer for King Artaxerxes. When he hears of Jerusalem's poor condition he mourns, fasts, and prays.

**v.5** – Nehemiah asks the king for leave and assistance to go to repair the walls of Jerusalem.

**v.8** – The Lord gives Nehemiah favour with the king of Persia. Nehemiah returns and leads the people to rebuild the wall around Jerusalem.

couldn't get through the rubble. <sup>15</sup> So, though it was still dark, I went up the Kidron Valley instead, inspecting the wall before I turned back and entered again at the Valley Gate.

<sup>16</sup> The city officials did not know I had been out there or what I was doing, for I had not yet said anything to anyone about my plans. I had not yet spoken to the Jewish leaders – the priests, the nobles, the officials, or anyone else in the administration. <sup>17</sup> But now I said to them, 'You know very well what trouble we are in. Jerusalem lies in ruins, and its gates have been destroyed by fire. Let us rebuild the wall of Jerusalem and end this disgrace!' <sup>18</sup> Then I told them about how the gracious hand of God had been on me, and about my conversation with the king.

They replied at once, 'Yes, let's rebuild the wall!' So they began the good work.

<sup>19</sup> But when Sanballat, Tobiah, and Geshem the Arab heard of our plan, they scoffed contemptuously. 'What are you doing? Are you rebelling against the king?' they asked.

<sup>20</sup> I replied, 'The God of heaven will help us succeed. We, his servants, will start rebuilding this wall. But you have no share, legal right, or historic claim in Jerusalem.'

…

**4** Sanballat was very angry when he learned that we were rebuilding the wall. He flew into a rage and mocked the Jews, <sup>2</sup> saying in front of his friends and the Samarian army officers, 'What does this bunch of poor, feeble Jews think they're doing? Do they think they can build the wall in a single day by just offering a few sacrifices? Do they actually think they can make something of stones from a rubbish heap – and charred ones at that?'

<sup>3</sup> Tobiah the Ammonite, who was standing beside him, remarked, 'That stone wall would collapse if even a fox walked along the top of it!'

<sup>4</sup> Then I prayed, 'Hear us, our God, for we are being mocked. May their scoffing fall back on their own heads, and may they themselves become captives in a foreign land! <sup>5</sup> Do not ignore their guilt. Do not blot out their sins, for they have provoked you to anger here in front of the builders.'

<sup>6</sup> At last the wall was completed to half its height around the entire city, for the people had worked with enthusiasm.

<sup>7</sup> But when Sanballat and Tobiah and the Arabs, Ammonites, and Ashdodites heard that the work was going ahead and that the gaps in the wall of Jerusalem were being repaired, they were furious. <sup>8</sup> They

**v.7–8** – Sanballat and Tobiah are enemies of God's people who oppose the work on the walls. Their violent opposition slows but does not stop the building.

all made plans to come and fight against Jerusalem and throw us into confusion. ⁹ But we prayed to our God and guarded the city day and night to protect ourselves.

¹⁰ Then the people of Judah began to complain, 'The workers are getting tired, and there is so much rubble to be moved. We will never be able to build the wall by ourselves.'

¹¹ Meanwhile, our enemies were saying, 'Before they know what's happening, we will swoop down on them and kill them and end their work.'

¹² The Jews who lived near the enemy came and told us again and again, 'They will come from all directions and attack us!' ¹³ So I placed armed guards behind the lowest parts of the wall in the exposed areas. I stationed the people to stand guard by families, armed with swords, spears, and bows.

¹⁴ Then as I assessed the situation, I called together the nobles and the rest of the people and said to them, 'Don't be afraid of the enemy! Remember the LORD, who is great and glorious, and fight for your brothers, your sons, your daughters, your wives, and your homes!'

¹⁵ When our enemies heard that we knew of their plans and that God had frustrated them, we all returned to our work on the wall. ¹⁶ But from then on, only half my men worked while the other half stood guard with spears, shields, bows, and coats of mail. The leaders stationed themselves behind the people of Judah ¹⁷ who were building the wall. The labourers carried on their work with one hand supporting their load and one hand holding a weapon. ¹⁸ All the builders had a sword belted to their side. The trumpeter stayed with me to sound the alarm.

¹⁹ Then I explained to the nobles and officials and all the people, 'The work is very spread out, and we are widely separated from each other along the wall. ²⁰ When you hear the blast of the trumpet, rush to wherever it is sounding. Then our God will fight for us!'

²¹ We worked early and late, from sunrise to sunset. And half the men were always on guard. ²² I also told everyone living outside the walls to stay in Jerusalem. That way they and their servants could help with guard duty at night and work during the day. ²³ During this time, none of us – not I, nor my relatives, nor my servants, nor the guards who were with me – ever took off our clothes. We carried our weapons with us at all times, even when we went for water.

**v.15** – The wall is completed under Nehemiah's supervision.

**6** [15] So on 2 October the wall was finished – just fifty-two days after we had begun. [16] When our enemies and the surrounding nations heard about it, they were frightened and humiliated. They realized this work had been done with the help of our God.

[17] During those fifty-two days, many letters went back and forth between Tobiah and the nobles of Judah. [18] For many in Judah had sworn allegiance to him because his father-in-law was Shecaniah son of Arah, and his son Jehohanan was married to the daughter of Meshullam son of Berekiah. [19] They kept telling me about Tobiah's good deeds, and then they told him everything I said. And Tobiah kept sending threatening letters to intimidate me.

...

**v.1** – Ezra, a scribe, reads the Law for the people.

**8** In October, when the Israelites had settled in their towns, [1]all the people assembled with a unified purpose at the square just inside the Water Gate. They asked Ezra the scribe to bring out the Book of the Law of Moses, which the Lord had given for Israel to obey.

[2] So on 8 October Ezra the priest brought the Book of the Law before the assembly, which included the men and women and all the children old enough to understand. [3] He faced the square just inside the Water Gate from early morning until noon and read aloud to everyone who could understand. All the people listened closely to the Book of the Law.

[4] Ezra the scribe stood on a high wooden platform that had been made for the occasion. To his right stood Mattithiah, Shema, Anaiah, Uriah, Hilkiah, and Maaseiah. To his left stood Pedaiah, Mishael, Malkijah, Hashum, Hashbaddanah, Zechariah, and Meshullam. [5] Ezra stood on the platform in full view of all the people. When they saw him open the book, they all rose to their feet.

[6] Then Ezra praised the LORD, the great God, and all the people chanted, 'Amen! Amen!' As they lifted their hands. Then they bowed down and worshipped the LORD with their faces to the ground.

[7] The Levites – Jeshua, Bani, Sherebiah, Jamin, Akkub, Shabbethai, Hodiah, Maaseiah, Kelita, Azariah, Jozabad, Hanan, and Pelaiah – then instructed the people in the Law while everyone remained in their places. [8] They read from the Book of the Law of God and clearly explained the meaning of what was being read, helping the people understand each passage.

Ezra reads God's Law to the people.

⁹ Then Nehemiah the governor, Ezra the priest and scribe, and the Levites who were interpreting for the people said to them, 'Don't mourn or weep on such a day as this! For today is a sacred day before the LORD your God.' For the people had all been weeping as they listened to the words of the Law.

¹⁰ And Nehemiah continued, 'Go and celebrate with a feast of rich foods and sweet drinks, and share gifts of food with people who have nothing prepared. This is a sacred day before our LORD. Don't be dejected and sad, for the joy of the LORD is your strength!'

¹¹ And the Levites, too, quietened the people, telling them, 'Hush! Don't weep! For this is a sacred day.' ¹² So the people went away to eat and drink at a festive meal, to share gifts of food, and to celebrate with great joy because they had heard God's words and understood them.

¹³ On 9 October the family leaders of all the people, together with the priests and Levites, met with Ezra the scribe to go over the Law in greater detail. ¹⁴ As they studied the Law, they discovered that the LORD had commanded through Moses that the Israelites should live in shelters during the festival to be held that month. ¹⁵ He had said that a proclamation should be made throughout their towns and in Jerusalem, telling the people to go to the hills to get branches from olive, wild olive, myrtle, palm, and other leafy trees. They were to use these branches to make shelters in which they would live during the festival, as prescribed in the Law.

¹⁶ So the people went out and cut branches and used them to build shelters on the roofs of their houses, in their courtyards, in the courtyards of God's Temple, or in the squares just inside the Water Gate and the Ephraim Gate. ¹⁷ So everyone who had returned from captivity lived in these shelters during the festival, and they were all filled with great joy! The Israelites had not celebrated like this since the days of Joshuam son of Nun.

¹⁸ Ezra read from the Book of the Law of God on each of the seven days of the festival. Then on the eighth day they held a solemn assembly, as was required by law.

### Where we end up

When the people are grieved by hearing the Law, Nehemiah tells them that the joy of the Lord is their strength and calls for celebration.

# 40 Queen Esther

**Main Theme**

The Lord's deliverer will save God's people through self-sacrifice.

**Setting**

The citadel of Susa

**Characters**

King Ahasuerus (Xerxes), Esther, Mordecai, and Haman

**Key Verse: Esther 4.14**

'If you keep quiet at a time like this, deliverance and relief for the Jews will arise from some other place, but you and your relatives will die. Who knows if perhaps you were made queen for just such a time as this?'

Esther approaches the king of Persia.

# Read the story Esther 3 – 5:7, 7 – 8

**3** Some time later King Xerxes promoted Haman son of Hammedatha the Agagite over all the other nobles, making him the most powerful official in the empire. ² All the king's officials would bow down before Haman to show him respect whenever he passed by, for so the king had commanded. But Mordecai refused to bow down or show him respect.

³ Then the palace officials at the king's gate asked Mordecai, 'Why are you disobeying the king's command?' ⁴ They spoke to him day after day, but still he refused to comply with the order. So they spoke to Haman about this to see if he would tolerate Mordecai's conduct, since Mordecai had told them he was a Jew.

⁵ When Haman saw that Mordecai would not bow down or show him respect, he was filled with rage. ⁶ He had learned of Mordecai's nationality, so he decided it was not enough to lay hands on Mordecai alone. Instead, he looked for a way to destroy all the Jews throughout the entire empire of Xerxes.

⁷ So in the month of April, during the twelfth year of King Xerxes' reign, lots were cast in Haman's presence (the lots were called purim) to determine the best day and month to take action. And the day selected was 7 March, nearly a year later.

⁸ Then Haman approached King Xerxes and said, 'There is a certain race of people scattered through all the provinces of your empire who keep themselves separate from everyone else. Their laws are different from those of any other people, and they refuse to obey the laws of the king. So it is not in the king's interest to let them live. ⁹ If it please the king, issue a decree that they be destroyed, and I will give 10,000 large sacks of silver to the government administrators to be deposited in the royal treasury.'

¹⁰ The king agreed, confirming his decision by removing his signet ring from his finger and giving it to Haman son of Hammedatha the Agagite, the enemy of the Jews. ¹¹ The king said, 'The money and the people are both yours to do with as you see fit.'

¹² So on 17 April the king's secretaries were summoned, and a decree was written exactly as Haman dictated. It was sent to the king's highest officers, the governors of the respective provinces, and the nobles of each province in their own scripts and languages. The

## Key plot points

**Introduction** – Esther becomes queen of Persia when the former queen is deposed.

**v.1–2** – Haman is an exalted servant of the king. Mordecai, Esther's cousin, refuses to bow down before Haman.

**v.8–9** – Haman, out of hatred for Mordecai, persuades the king to order the annihilation of the Jews.

decree was written in the name of King Xerxes and sealed with the king's signet ring. [13] Dispatches were sent by swift messengers into all the provinces of the empire, giving the order that all Jews – young and old, including women and children – must be killed, slaughtered, and annihilated on a single day. This was scheduled to happen on 7 March of the next year. The property of the Jews would be given to those who killed them.

[14] A copy of this decree was to be issued as law in every province and proclaimed to all peoples, so that they would be ready to do their duty on the appointed day. [15] At the king's command, the decree went out by swift messengers, and it was also proclaimed in the fortress of Susa. Then the king and Haman sat down to drink, but the city of Susa fell into confusion.

**4** When Mordecai learned about all that had been done, he tore his clothes, put on sackcloth and ashes, and went out into the city, crying with a loud and bitter wail. [2] He went as far as the gate of the palace, for no one was allowed to enter the palace gate while wearing clothes of mourning. [3] And as news of the king's decree reached all the provinces, there was great mourning among the Jews. They fasted, wept, and wailed, and many people lay in sackcloth and ashes.

[4] When Queen Esther's maids and eunuchs came and told her about Mordecai, she was deeply distressed. She sent clothing to him to replace the sackcloth, but he refused it. [5] Then Esther sent for Hathach, one of the king's eunuchs who had been appointed as her attendant. She ordered him to go to Mordecai and find out what was troubling him and why he was in mourning. [6] So Hathach went out to Mordecai in the square in front of the palace gate.

[7] Mordecai told him the whole story, including the exact amount of money Haman had promised to pay into the royal treasury for the destruction of the Jews. [8] Mordecai gave Hathach a copy of the decree issued in Susa that called for the death of all Jews. He asked Hathach to show it to Esther and explain the situation to her. He also asked Hathach to direct her to go to the king to beg for mercy and plead for her people. [9] So Hathach returned to Esther with Mordecai's message.

[10] Then Esther told Hathach to go back and relay this message to Mordecai: [11] 'All the king's officials and even the people in the provinces know that anyone who appears before the king in his inner court without being invited is doomed to die unless the king holds out

**v.8** – Mordecai asks Esther to talk to the king about saving the Jews.

his golden sceptre. And the king has not called for me to come to him for thirty days.' ¹² So Hathach gave Esther's message to Mordecai.

¹³ Mordecai sent this reply to Esther: 'Don't think for a moment that because you're in the palace you will escape when all other Jews are killed. ¹⁴ If you keep quiet at a time like this, deliverance and relief for the Jews will arise from some other place, but you and your relatives will die. Who knows if perhaps you were made queen for just such a time as this?'

¹⁵ Then Esther sent this reply to Mordecai: ¹⁶ 'Go and gather together all the Jews of Susa and fast for me. Do not eat or drink for three days, night or day. My maids and I will do the same. And then, though it is against the law, I will go in to see the king. If I must die, I must die.' ¹⁷ So Mordecai went away and did everything as Esther had ordered him.

5 On the third day of the fast, Esther put on her royal robes and entered the inner court of the palace, just across from the king's hall. The king was sitting on his royal throne, facing the entrance. ² When he saw Queen Esther standing there in the inner court, he welcomed her and held out the golden sceptre to her. So Esther approached and touched the end of the sceptre.

³ Then the king asked her, 'What do you want, Queen Esther? What is your request? I will give it to you, even if it is half the kingdom!'

⁴ And Esther replied, 'If it please the king, let the king and Haman come today to a banquet I have prepared for the king.'

⁵ The king turned to his attendants and said, 'Tell Haman to come quickly to a banquet, as Esther has requested.' So the king and Haman went to Esther's banquet.

⁶ And while they were drinking wine, the king said to Esther, 'Now tell me what you really want. What is your request? I will give it to you, even if it is half the kingdom!'

⁷ Esther replied, 'This is my request and deepest wish. ⁸ If I have found favour with the king, and if it pleases the king to grant my request and do what I ask, please come with Haman tomorrow to the banquet I will prepare for you. Then I will explain what this is all about.'

···

7 So the king and Haman went to Queen Esther's banquet. ² On this second occasion, while they were drinking wine, the king again

**v.10–14** – Esther is afraid to go in before the king uninvited, but Mordecai tells her that it may be for this very time that she has been put in her position as queen.

**v.1–2** – Esther risks her own life and approaches the king.

said to Esther, 'Tell me what you want, Queen Esther. What is your request? I will give it to you, even if it is half the kingdom!'

³ Queen Esther replied, 'If I have found favour with the king, and if it pleases the king to grant my request, I ask that my life and the lives of my people will be spared. ⁴ For my people and I have been sold to those who would kill, slaughter, and annihilate us. If we had merely been sold as slaves, I could remain quiet, for that would be too trivial a matter to warrant disturbing the king.'

⁵ 'Who would do such a thing?' King Xerxes demanded. 'Who would be so presumptuous as to touch you?'

⁶ Esther replied, 'This wicked Haman is our adversary and our enemy.' Haman grew pale with fright before the king and queen. ⁷ Then the king jumped to his feet in a rage and went out into the palace garden.

Haman, however, stayed behind to plead for his life with Queen Esther, for he knew that the king intended to kill him. ⁸ In despair he fell on the couch where Queen Esther was reclining, just as the king was returning from the palace garden.

The king exclaimed, 'Will he even assault the queen right here in the palace, before my very eyes?' And as soon as the king spoke, his attendants covered Haman's face, signalling his doom.

⁹ Then Harbona, one of the king's eunuchs, said, 'Haman has set up a sharpened pole that stands twenty-five metres tall in his own courtyard. He intended to use it to impale Mordecai, the man who saved the king from assassination.'

'Then impale Haman on it!' the king ordered. ¹⁰ So they impaled Haman on the pole he had set up for Mordecai, and the king's anger subsided.

**8** On that same day King Xerxes gave the property of Haman, the enemy of the Jews, to Queen Esther. Then Mordecai was brought before the king, for Esther had told the king how they were related. ² The king took off his signet ring – which he had taken back from Haman – and gave it to Mordecai. And Esther appointed Mordecai to be in charge of Haman's property.

³ Then Esther went again before the king, falling down at his feet and begging him with tears to stop the evil plot devised by Haman the Agagite against the Jews. ⁴ Again the king held out the golden sceptre to Esther. So she rose and stood before him.

⁵ Esther said, 'If it please the king, and if I have found favour with him, and if he thinks it is right, and if I am pleasing to him, let there be a decree that reverses the orders of Haman son of Hammedatha the Agagite, who ordered that Jews throughout all the king's provinces should be destroyed. ⁶ For how can I endure to see my people and my family slaughtered and destroyed?'

⁷ Then King Xerxes said to Queen Esther and Mordecai the Jew, 'I have given Esther the property of Haman, and he has been impaled on a pole because he tried to destroy the Jews. ⁸ Now go ahead and send a message to the Jews in the king's name, telling them whatever you want, and seal it with the king's signet ring. But remember that whatever has already been written in the king's name and sealed with his signet ring can never be revoked.'

⁹ So on 25 June the king's secretaries were summoned, and a decree was written exactly as Mordecai dictated. It was sent to the Jews and to the highest officers, the governors, and the nobles of all the 127 provinces stretching from India to Ethiopia. The decree was written in the scripts and languages of all the peoples of the empire, including that of the Jews. ¹⁰ The decree was written in the name of King Xerxes and sealed with the king's signet ring. Mordecai sent the dispatches by swift messengers, who rode fast horses especially bred for the king's service.

¹¹ The king's decree gave the Jews in every city authority to unite to defend their lives. They were allowed to kill, slaughter, and annihilate anyone of any nationality or province who might attack them or their children and wives, and to take the property of their enemies. ¹² The day chosen for this event throughout all the provinces of King Xerxes was 7 March of the next year.

¹³ A copy of this decree was to be issued as law in every province and proclaimed to all people, so that the Jews would be ready to take revenge on their enemies on the appointed day. ¹⁴ So urged on by the king's command, the messengers rode out swiftly on fast horses bred for the king's service. The same decree was also proclaimed in the fortress of Susa.

¹⁵ Then Mordecai left the king's presence, wearing the royal robe of blue and white, the great crown of gold, and an outer cloak of fine linen and purple. And the people of Susa celebrated the new decree. ¹⁶ The Jews were filled with joy and gladness and were honoured

everywhere. [17] In every province and city, wherever the king's decree arrived, the Jews rejoiced and had a great celebration and declared a public festival and holiday. And many of the people of the land became Jews themselves, for they feared what the Jews might do to them.

## Where we end up

The Jews are delivered by a second kingly decree, warning them of the plot and urging them to defend themselves.

**My Reflections**

# The Prophetic Promise

**Main Theme**

The Lord will send the Messiah, a new king full of the Holy Spirit who will bring the blessing of God's Kingdom to all creation.

**Setting**

A prophetic word

**Characters**

Isaiah the Prophet, the Messiah (the coming King) and the Spirit of the Lord

**Key Verse: Isaiah 11:2**

And the Spirit of the LORD will rest on him – the Spirit of wisdom and understanding, the Spirit of counsel and might, the Spirit of knowledge and the fear of the LORD.

'Thus says the Lord . . .'

## Key plot points

**Introduction** – Isaiah, along with all the Law and the Prophets, predicts the coming of Messiah, the King of God's Kingdom.

**v.1** – He says a shoot will come from the stump of Jesse. The coming King will be born in the line of David.

**v.2** – The Spirit of God will rest on the King.

**v.3–4** – The King will fear the Lord, ruling with justice and righteousness.

**v.6** – He will usher in the age of God's Kingdom where violence and death are no more.

**v.9** – He will bring the knowledge of the Lord across the whole earth.

## Read the story Isaiah 11:1–9

¹ Out of the stump of David's family will grow a shoot –
yes, a new Branch bearing fruit from the old root.
² And the Spirit of the LORD will rest on him –
the Spirit of wisdom and understanding,
the Spirit of counsel and might,
the Spirit of knowledge and the fear of the LORD.
³ He will delight in obeying the LORD.
He will not judge by appearance
nor make a decision based on hearsay.
⁴ He will give justice to the poor
and make fair decisions for the exploited.
The earth will shake at the force of his word,
and one breath from his mouth will destroy the wicked.
⁵ He will wear righteousness like a belt
and truth like an undergarment.
⁶ In that day the wolf and the lamb will live together;
the leopard will lie down with the baby goat.
The calf and the yearling will be safe with the lion,
and a little child will lead them all.
⁷ The cow will graze near the bear.
The cub and the calf will lie down together.
The lion will eat hay like a cow.
⁸ The baby will play safely near the hole of a cobra.
Yes, a little child will put its hand in a nest of deadly
snakes without harm.
⁹ Nothing will hurt or destroy in all my holy mountain,
for as the waters fill the sea,
so the earth will be filled with people who know the LORD.

## Where we end up

The whole Old Testament builds anticipation for this one who would come and reign forever . . .

**Christ foreshadowed:**
Journey to Bethlehem – p. 171
The Triumphal Entry – p. 221
The Coming of the Holy Spirit – p. 257

# The Story of God in Christ:
# The Fullness of Time

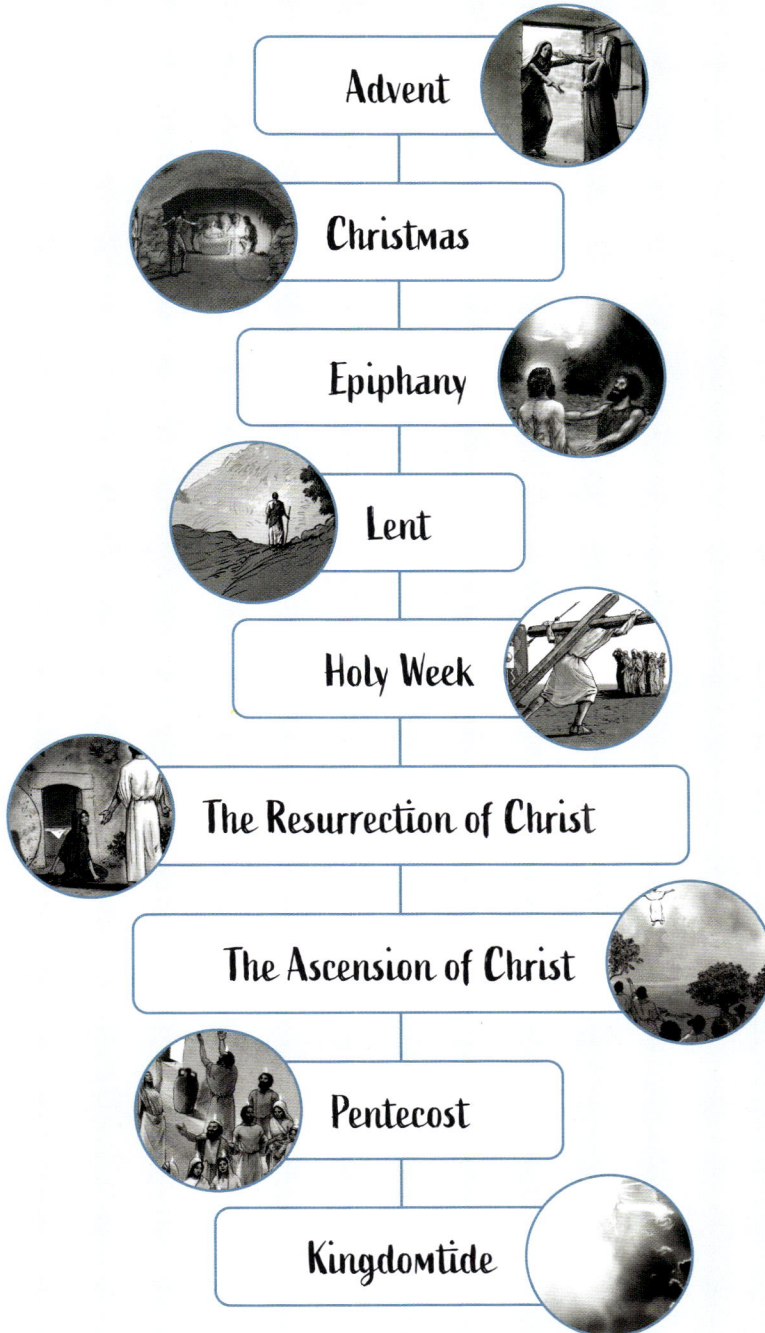

Advent

Christmas

Epiphany

Lent

Holy Week

The Resurrection of Christ

The Ascension of Christ

Pentecost

Kingdomtide

# 42  The Annunciation

**Main Theme**

The Lord announces the arrival of his Messiah, a son of David, to establish his Kingdom.

**Setting**

Nazareth (a small town in northern Israel)

**Key Verse: Luke 1:31**

'You will conceive and give birth to a son, and you will name him Jesus.'

**Characters**

Mary (a young woman of Nazareth) and Gabriel (the angel)

The angel Gabriel visits the Virgin Mary to announce the arrival of the Messiah.

# Read the story Luke 1:26–38

[26] In the sixth month of Elizabeth's pregnancy, God sent the angel Gabriel to Nazareth, a village in Galilee, [27] to a virgin named Mary. She was engaged to be married to a man named Joseph, a descendant of King David. [28] Gabriel appeared to her and said, 'Greetings, favoured woman! The Lord is with you!'

[29] Confused and disturbed, Mary tried to think what the angel could mean. [30] 'Don't be afraid, Mary,' the angel told her, 'for you have found favour with God! [31] You will conceive and give birth to a son, and you will name him Jesus. [32] He will be very great and will be called the Son of the Most High. The Lord God will give him the throne of his ancestor David. [33] And he will reign over Israel for ever; his Kingdom will never end!'

[34] Mary asked the angel, 'But how can this happen? I am a virgin.'

[35] The angel replied, 'The Holy Spirit will come upon you, and the power of the Most High will overshadow you. So the baby to be born will be holy, and he will be called the Son of God. [36] What's more, your relative Elizabeth has become pregnant in her old age! People used to say she was barren, but she has conceived a son and is now in her sixth month. [37] For the word of God will never fail.'

[38] Mary responded, 'I am the Lord's servant. May everything you have said about me come true.' And then the angel left her.

**v.26–27** – Mary is a young woman living in Nazareth. She is an unmarried virgin.

**v.28** – The Lord sends the angel Gabriel to announce to Mary that, though she is a virgin, she will conceive a child and name him Jesus.

**v.32** – This child will be the Son of God and the Lord will give him the throne of David and Kingdom that will never end.

**v.34** – Mary asks how this is possible since she is a virgin.

**v.35** – The angel explains that the child will be conceived by the Holy Spirit.

**v.36** – He also tells Mary that her relative, Elizabeth has also conceived a child in her olc age.

## Where we end up

Mary says she is the servant of the Lord and accepts the word of the angel, and the angel departs.

## Old Testament Foundation: The Promise of a Saviour

**The Promise to Adam and Eve** (Genesis 3:15) – p. 21. The Messiah is born of a woman.

**The Promise to Abram** (Genesis 12:1–3, 15:5) – p. 32. The Messiah is a descendant of Abraham, Isaac, and Jacob, an heir of God's promise and blessing.

**The Covenant with David**: 'Your house and your kingdom will continue before me for all time, and your throne will be secure forever' (2 Samuel 7:16). The Messiah is born in the family of David, the line of God's covenant king.

# 43  The Visitation

**Main Theme**

The Lord gives his servants joy by confirming the arrival of the Messiah.

**Setting**

The house of Zechariah and Elizabeth in a Judean town in the hill country

**Characters**

Mary, Elizabeth, and the unborn babies of Mary and Elizabeth

**Key Verse: Luke 1:46–47**

Mary responded, 'Oh, how my soul praises the Lord. How my spirit rejoices in God my Saviour!'

Elizabeth receives Mary, the mother of the Messiah.

# Read the story Luke 1:39–56

[39] A few days later Mary hurried to the hill country of Judea, to the town [40] where Zechariah lived. She entered the house and greeted Elizabeth. [41] At the sound of Mary's greeting, Elizabeth's child leaped within her, and Elizabeth was filled with the Holy Spirit.

[42] Elizabeth gave a glad cry and exclaimed to Mary, 'God has blessed you above all women, and your child is blessed. [43] Why am I so honoured, that the mother of my Lord should visit me? [44] When I heard your greeting, the baby in my womb jumped for joy. [45] You are blessed because you believed that the Lord would do what he said.'

[46] Mary responded,

'Oh, how my soul praises the Lord.
[47]     How my spirit rejoices in God my Saviour!
[48] For he took notice of his lowly servant girl,
          and from now on all generations will call me blessed.
[49] For the Mighty One is holy,
          and he has done great things for me.
[50] He shows mercy from generation to generation
          to all who fear him.
[51] His mighty arm has done tremendous things!
          He has scattered the proud and haughty ones.
[52] He has brought down princes from their thrones
          and exalted the humble.
[53] He has filled the hungry with good things
          and sent the rich away with empty hands.
[54] He has helped his servant Israel
          and remembered to be merciful.
[55] For he made this promise to our ancestors,
          to Abraham and his children for ever.'

[56] Mary stayed with Elizabeth about three months and then went back to her own home.

## Key plot points

**v.40** – After the visitation of Gabriel, Mary goes to visit her relative Elizabeth.

**v.41** – When Mary arrives, the baby in Elizabeth's womb leaps for joy.

**v.42** – Elizabeth greets Mary with a blessing.

**v.45** – Elizabeth tells Mary of her baby leaping in her womb and blesses her for believing the Lord.

**v.46–55** – Mary responds with a beautiful hymn of praise (often called The Magnificat).

## Where we end up

Mary remains with Elizabeth for three months.

# 44  The Ministry of John the Baptist

**Main Theme**

The Lord prepares the way for the Messiah, the true seed of Abraham, to establish his Kingdom.

**Setting**

The Wilderness of Judea near the River Jordan

**Characters**

John the Baptist, Jewish people, and Pharisees and Sadducees (Jewish religious leaders)

**Key Verse: Matthew 3:11**

'I baptize with water those who repent of their sins and turn to God. But someone is coming soon who is greater than I am — so much greater that I'm not worthy even to be his slave and carry his sandals. He will baptize you with the Holy Spirit and with fire.'

John the Baptist prepares the way for the Messiah.

# Read the story Matthew 3:1–12

[1] In those days John the Baptist came to the Judean wilderness and began preaching. His message was, [2] 'Repent of your sins and turn to God, for the Kingdom of Heaven is near.' [3] The prophet Isaiah was speaking about John when he said,

'He is a voice shouting in the wilderness,
"Prepare the way for the LORD's coming!
    Clear the road for him!"'

[4] John's clothes were woven from coarse camel hair, and he wore a leather belt around his waist. For food he ate locusts and wild honey. [5] People from Jerusalem and from all of Judea and all over the Jordan Valley went out to see and hear John. [6] And when they confessed their sins, he baptized them in the River Jordan.

[7] But when he saw many Pharisees and Sadducees coming to watch him baptize, he denounced them. 'You brood of snakes!' he exclaimed. 'Who warned you to flee the coming wrath? [8] Prove by the way you live that you have repented of your sins and turned to God. [9] Don't just say to each other, "We're safe, for we are descendants of Abraham." That means nothing, for I tell you, God can create children of Abraham from these very stones. [10] Even now the axe of God's judgement is poised, ready to sever the roots of the trees. Yes, every tree that does not produce good fruit will be chopped down and thrown into the fire.

[11] 'I baptize with water those who repent of their sins and turn to God. But someone is coming soon who is greater than I am – so much greater that I'm not worthy even to be his slave and carry his sandals. He will baptize you with the Holy Spirit and with fire. [12] He is ready to separate the chaff from the wheat with his winnowing fork. Then he will clean up the threshing area, gathering the wheat into his barn but burning the chaff with never-ending fire.'

## Key plot points

**v.1, 4** – John is a wild man who wears rough clothing and eats wild locusts and honey.

**v.2** – He preaches in the wilderness that the Kingdom of God is at hand.

**v.6** – He calls for repentance ahead of the arrival of the Messiah and baptizes many Jewish people in the River Jordan.

**v.7** – The Pharisees and Sadducees are Jewish religious leaders who come to see what John is doing. When he sees them, John calls them a brood of vipers.

**v.8–9** – John tells them that they must repent instead of relying on their ancestry for God's favour.

## Where we end up

John says that while he baptizes in water for repentance, the Messiah will come and baptize with the Holy Spirit and with fire. He warns the religious leaders that the Messiah will bring the wrath of God against them if they do not repent.

**Sodom and Gomorrah** (Genesis 19) – p. 38. The messenger is sent ahead to warn the people to flee the wrath to come. God's rescue of Lot foreshadows God's rescue of humanity by grace from the coming judgement.

## My Reflections

# Journey to Bethlehem

## 45

**Main Theme**

Jesus is the promised Messiah, the son of David, the new king of God's Kingdom.

**Setting**

The road from Nazareth to Bethlehem

**Characters**

Joseph and Mary

**Key Verse: Luke 2:4**

And because Joseph was a descendant of King David, he had to go to Bethlehem in Judea, David's ancient home. He travelled there from the village of Nazareth in Galilee.

Mary and Joseph journey to Bethlehem.

## Key plot points

**v.1** – The Roman Emperor Augustus calls for a census.

**v.3** – Everyone has to return to their hometown to be registered.

**v.4** – Joseph must return to Bethlehem, his hometown, because he is of the house and family of David.

**v.5** – Mary, his betrothed, is pregnant with Jesus. They make the journey together, and it is likely that they travelled by donkey.

## Read the story Luke 2:1–5

[1] At that time the Roman emperor, Augustus, decreed that a census should be taken throughout the Roman Empire. [2] (This was the first census taken when Quirinius was governor of Syria.) [3] All returned to their own ancestral towns to register for this census. [4] And because Joseph was a descendant of King David, he had to go to Bethlehem in Judea, David's ancient home. He travelled there from the village of Nazareth in Galilee. [5] He took with him Mary, to whom he was engaged, who was now expecting a child.

### Where we end up

The stage for the arrival of the Lord's Messiah is set. Mary and Joseph are making the final leg of the journey of hope and anticipation that began all the way back in the Garden of Eden.

### Old Testament Foundation: The Deliverer Is Born

**The Prophetic Promise:** 'But you, O Bethlehem Ephrathah, are only a small village among all the people of Judah. Yet a ruler of Israel, whose origins are in the distant past, will come from you on my behalf' (Micah 5:2). All of the prophets anticipate the arrival of the Lord's Messiah. Micah foretold that the Messiah would be born in Bethlehem.

# The Birth of Jesus

## 46

## Main Theme

Jesus is the Christ, the Son of God, born of a virgin.

## Setting

Nazareth (the town where Joseph and Mary live) and Bethlehem (where Jesus is born)

## Key Verse: Luke 2:7

She gave birth to her first-born son. She wrapped him snugly in strips of cloth and laid him in a manger, because there was no lodging available for them.

## Characters

Joseph, Mary, the angel of the Lord, and Jesus

Christ is born in Bethlehem.

## Key plot points

**v.18** – Mary is pregnant, and Joseph knows that he is not the father.

**v.19** – Joseph plans to call off their engagement quietly.

**v.20** – The angel of the Lord appears to Joseph in a dream and tells him to take Mary as his wife. The angel confirms that the child in Mary's womb was conceived by the Holy Spirit.

**v.24** – Joseph takes Mary as his wife.

## Read the story Matthew 1:18–25 and Luke 2:6–7

**1** [18] This is how Jesus the Messiah was born. His mother, Mary, was engaged to be married to Joseph. But before the marriage took place, while she was still a virgin, she became pregnant through the power of the Holy Spirit. [19] Joseph, to whom she was engaged, was a righteous man and did not want to disgrace her publicly, so he decided to break the engagement quietly.

[20] As he considered this, an angel of the Lord appeared to him in a dream. 'Joseph, son of David,' the angel said, 'do not be afraid to take Mary as your wife. For the child within her was conceived by the Holy Spirit. [21] And she will have a son, and you are to name him Jesus, for he will save his people from their sins.'

[22] All of this occurred to fulfil the Lord's message through his prophet:

[23] 'Look! The virgin will conceive a child!
　　She will give birth to a son,
and they will call him Immanuel,
　　which means "God is with us".'

[24] When Joseph woke up, he did as the angel of the Lord commanded and took Mary as his wife. [25] But he did not have sexual relations with her until her son was born. And Joseph named him Jesus.

…

**2** [6] And while they were there, the time came for her baby to be born. [7] She gave birth to her first-born son. She wrapped him snugly in strips of cloth and laid him in a manger, because there was no lodging available for them.

## Where we end up

Mary gives birth to Jesus in a stable in Bethlehem and lays him in a manger because there is no room for them in the inn.

# The Announcement of Christ's Birth to the Shepherds

## 47

**Main Theme**

The arrival of Christ the Lord is good news of great joy for all people!

**Characters**

Shepherds, the angel of the Lord, Mary and Joseph, and Jesus

**Key Verse: Luke 2:14**

'Glory to God in highest heaven, and peace on earth to those with whom God is pleased.'

**Setting**

The fields around Bethlehem

The angels announce the birth of Jesus to the shepherds.

## Key plot points

**v.8** – Around Bethlehem many shepherds are keeping watch over their flocks by night.

**v.9, 13** – Suddenly, the angel of the Lord appears to them with a great multitude of other angels.

**v.11–12** – He tells them to go and find the Messiah (or Christ), who has been born this very night in Bethlehem.

**v.16** – The shepherds hurry to Bethlehem. They find Mary and Joseph, and Jesus, the newborn Lord, wrapped in swaddling clothes, and lying in a manger.

**v.17** – The shepherds tell Mary and Joseph about the announcement of the angels.

**v.18** – Everyone is amazed by what the shepherds say.

## Read the story Luke 2:8–20

[8] That night there were shepherds staying in the fields nearby, guarding their flocks of sheep. [9] Suddenly, an angel of the Lord appeared among them, and the radiance of the Lord's glory surrounded them. They were terrified, [10] but the angel reassured them. 'Don't be afraid!' he said. 'I bring you good news that will bring great joy to all people. [11] The Saviour – yes, the Messiah, the Lord – has been born today in Bethlehem, the city of David! [12] And you will recognize him by this sign: You will find a baby wrapped snugly in strips of cloth, lying in a manger.'

[13] Suddenly, the angel was joined by a vast host of others – the armies of heaven – praising God and saying,

[14] 'Glory to God in highest heaven,
and peace on earth to those with whom God is pleased.'

[15] When the angels had returned to heaven, the shepherds said to each other, 'Let's go to Bethlehem! Let's see this thing that has happened, which the Lord has told us about'.

[16] They hurried to the village and found Mary and Joseph. And there was the baby, lying in the manger. [17] After seeing him, the shepherds told everyone what had happened and what the angel had said to them about this child. [18] All who heard the shepherds' story were astonished, [19] but Mary kept all these things in her heart and thought about them often. [20] The shepherds went back to their flocks, glorifying and praising God for all they had heard and seen. It was just as the angel had told them.

### Where we end up

Mary treasures the shepherds' words in her heart, and the shepherds return to their flocks praising the Lord.

## 48

# The Presentation of the Lord in the Temple

### Main Theme

Christ is the fulfilment of the Lord's promise of salvation for the world.

### Setting

The Temple in Jerusalem

### Characters

Simeon, Anna, Mary, Joseph, and Jesus

### Key Verse: Luke 2:29–32

'Sovereign Lord, now let your servant die in peace, as you have promised. I have seen your salvation, which you have prepared for all people. He is a light to reveal God to the nations, and he is the glory of your people Israel!'

### Key Verse: Luke 2:38

She came along just as Simeon was talking with Mary and Joseph, and she began praising God. She talked about the child to everyone who had been waiting expectantly for God to rescue Jerusalem.

Simeon takes Jesus in his arms and praises God.

## Key plot points

**v.21–24** – Eight days after his birth, Mary and Joseph bring Jesus to the Temple according to the requirements of Old Testament Law.

## Read the story Luke 2:21–39

[21] Eight days later, when the baby was circumcised, he was named Jesus, the name given him by the angel even before he was conceived.

[22] Then it was time for their purification offering, as required by the law of Moses after the birth of a child; so his parents took him to Jerusalem to present him to the Lord. [23] The law of the Lord says, 'If a woman's first child is a boy, he must be dedicated to the LORD.' [24] So they offered the sacrifice required in the law of the Lord – 'either a pair of turtledoves or two young pigeons'.

[25] At that time there was a man in Jerusalem named Simeon. He was righteous and devout and was eagerly waiting for the Messiah to come and rescue Israel. The Holy Spirit was upon him [26] and had revealed to him that he would not die until he had seen the Lord's Messiah.

The prophetess Anna praises God and tells others about Jesus.

<sup>27</sup> That day the Spirit led him to the Temple. So when Mary and Joseph came to present the baby Jesus to the Lord as the law required, <sup>28</sup> Simeon was there. He took the child in his arms and praised God, saying,

<sup>29</sup> 'Sovereign Lord, now let your servant die in peace,
    as you have promised.
<sup>30</sup> I have seen your salvation,
<sup>31</sup>    which you have prepared for all people.
<sup>32</sup> He is a light to reveal God to the nations,
    and he is the glory of your people Israel!'

<sup>33</sup> Jesus' parents were amazed at what was being said about him. <sup>34</sup> Then Simeon blessed them, and he said to Mary, the baby's mother, 'This child is destined to cause many in Israel to fall, and many others to rise. He has been sent as a sign from God, but many will oppose him. <sup>35</sup> As a result, the deepest thoughts of many hearts will be revealed. And a sword will pierce your very soul.'

<sup>36</sup> Anna, a prophet, was also there in the Temple. She was the daughter of Phanuel from the tribe of Asher, and she was very old. Her husband died when they had been married only seven years. <sup>37</sup> Then she lived as a widow to the age of eighty-four. She never left the Temple but stayed there day and night, worshipping God with fasting and prayer. <sup>38</sup> She came along just as Simeon was talking with Mary and Joseph, and she began praising God. She talked about the child to everyone who had been waiting expectantly for God to rescue Jerusalem.

<sup>39</sup> When Jesus' parents had fulfilled all the requirements of the law of the Lord, they returned home to Nazareth in Galilee.

**v.27** – The Holy Spirit leads Simeon, a righteous and holy man, into the Temple at this same time.

**v.28–32** – He takes Jesus in his arms and praises God for allowing him to see the Messiah.

**v.34–35** – He then speaks a prophecy to Mary that Jesus, as the Messiah, is destined for opposition and that her own soul would be pierced.

**v.36,38** – Anna, a prophet of the Lord, is also there and she begins to tell everyone around about Jesus.

## Where we end up

Mary and Joseph return home where Jesus grows strong and wise with the favour of God upon him.

## Old Testament Foundation: The Deliverer Is Recognized

**The Lord Gives the Law:** When Moses came down Mount Sinai carrying the two stone tablets inscribed with the terms of the covenant, he wasn't aware that his face had become radiant because he had spoken to the Lord (Exodus 34:29). In his arrival, the Messiah comes not to abolish the Law, but to fulfil it.

# 49 The Adoration of the Magi

### Main Theme

All nations will come to the light of Christ, the king of the Jews.

### Setting

Jerusalem and Bethlehem

### Characters

The Magi from the East, King Herod, Jesus, and Mary

### Key Verse: Matthew 2:11

They entered the house and saw the child with his mother, Mary, and they bowed down and worshipped him. Then they opened their treasure chests and gave him gifts of gold, frankincense, and myrrh.

The Magi give gifts to Jesus.

# Read the story Matthew 2:1–12

[1] Jesus was born in Bethlehem in Judea, during the reign of King Herod. About that time some wise men from eastern lands arrived in Jerusalem, asking, [2] 'Where is the newborn king of the Jews? We saw his star as it rose, and we have come to worship him.'

[3] King Herod was deeply disturbed when he heard this, as was everyone in Jerusalem. [4] He called a meeting of the leading priests and teachers of religious law and asked, 'Where is the Messiah supposed to be born?'

[5] 'In Bethlehem in Judea,' they said, 'for this is what the prophet wrote:

[6] "And you, O Bethlehem in the land of Judah,
    are not least among the ruling cities of Judah,
for a ruler will come from you
    who will be the shepherd for my people Israel."'

[7] Then Herod called for a private meeting with the wise men, and he learned from them the time when the star first appeared. [8] Then he told them, 'Go to Bethlehem and search carefully for the child. And when you find him, come back and tell me so that I can go and worship him, too!'

[9] After this interview the wise men went their way. And the star they had seen in the east guided them to Bethlehem. It went ahead of them and stopped over the place where the child was. [10] When they saw the star, they were filled with joy! [11] They entered the house and saw the child with his mother, Mary, and they bowed down and worshipped him. Then they opened their treasure chests and gave him gifts of gold, frankincense, and myrrh.

[12] When it was time to leave, they returned to their own country by another route, for God had warned them in a dream not to return to Herod.

**v.1–2** – Magi (wise men) from the East arrive in Jerusalem seeking the newborn king of the Jews. They observed his star rising and have come to worship him.

**v.3, 7** – King Herod is greatly troubled by the news and calls a secret meeting with the Magi.

**v.8** – Herod sends them on to Bethlehem but asks them to report back to him on where they find the child.

**v.9** – The Magi go to Bethlehem and the star they are following leads them directly to the house where Mary and Jesus are.

**v.11** – They kneel before Jesus and give him gifts of gold, frankincense, and myrrh.

## Where we end up

The Magi are warned in a dream not to return to Herod for he intends to harm Jesus, so they leave Bethlehem and return to their homeland without going back through Jerusalem.

# 50 The Baptism of the Lord

**Main Theme**

Christ is the beloved Son of God the Father

**Setting**

The River Jordan

**Characters**

John the Baptist, Jesus, and God the Father

**Key Verse: Matthew 3:16–17**

After his baptism, as Jesus came up out of the water, the heavens were opened and he saw the Spirit of God descending like a dove and settling on him. And a voice from heaven said, 'This is my dearly loved Son, who brings me great joy.'

John baptizes Jesus in the River Jordan.

# Read the story Matthew 3:13–17

13 Then Jesus went from Galilee to the River Jordan to be baptized by John. 14 But John tried to talk him out of it. 'I am the one who needs to be baptized by you', he said, 'so why are you coming to me?'

15 But Jesus said, 'It should be done, for we must carry out all that God requires.' So John agreed to baptize him.

16 After his baptism, as Jesus came up out of the water, the heavens were opened and he saw the Spirit of God descending like a dove and settling on him. 17 And a voice from heaven said, 'This is my dearly loved Son, who brings me great joy.'

# Key plot points

**v.13** – Jesus comes down to the River Jordan to be baptized by John.

**v.14** – John objects saying that he needs to be baptized by Jesus.

**v.15** – Jesus convinces John to baptize him by saying that it is necessary to fulfill all righteousness.

**v.16** – As Jesus comes up from the water, the Spirit of God descends like a dove and rests on him.

## Where we end up

The voice of the Father comes from heaven and declares Jesus as his Son and beloved.

## Old Testament Foundation: Fully Human and Fully Divine

**Noah's Ark** (Genesis 6 – 9) – p. 26. As the Lord rescued Noah and his family through the waters, so too Christ enters the waters in order to fulfil all righteousness and bring about a great rescue from the coming destruction.

**The Red Sea** (Exodus 14 – 15) – p. 61. As Moses and the people passed through the Red Sea and then were led up into the wilderness to be tested, so too Christ passes through the waters and is led into the wilderness.

**David is Anointed** (1 Samuel 16:1–13) – p. 103. As Samuel anointed David to be king over Israel, so the Spirit of God anointed Jesus to be King of the universe.

## My Reflections

# 51 The Temptation of Our Lord

**Main Theme**

Christ came to destroy the works of the devil and deliver humanity from his power.

**Characters**

The Holy Spirit, Jesus, and Satan (the tempter)

**Key Verse: Matthew 4:4**

But Jesus told him, 'No! The Scriptures say, "People do not live by bread alone, but by every word that comes from the mouth of God."'

**Setting**

The wilderness

Jesus spends forty days and nights in the wilderness.

# Read the story Matthew 4:1–11

[1] Then Jesus was led by the Spirit into the wilderness to be tempted there by the devil. [2] For forty days and forty nights he fasted and became very hungry.

[3] During that time the devil came and said to him, 'If you are the Son of God, tell these stones to become loaves of bread.'

[4] But Jesus told him, 'No! The Scriptures say,

"People do not live by bread alone,
   but by every word that comes from the mouth of God."'

[5] Then the devil took him to the holy city, Jerusalem, to the highest point of the Temple, [6] and said, 'If you are the Son of God, jump off! For the Scriptures say,

"He will order his angels to protect you.
 And they will hold you up with their hands
   so you won't even hurt your foot on a stone."'

# Key plot points

**v.1** – The Holy Spirit leads Jesus into the wilderness to be tempted by the devil.

**v.2** – Jesus fasts for forty days and nights.

The tempter comes to Jesus and gives him three temptations. Each time Jesus responds with Scripture.

**v.3–4** – He tempts Jesus to turn stones into bread. Jesus responds that he lives not by bread alone, but by the Word of God.

**v.5–7** – Satan tempts Jesus to throw himself off the pinnacle of the Temple to see if the angels will catch him. Jesus refuses to put God to the test.

Jesus being tempted by the devil in the wilderness.

**v.8–10** – Satan then takes Jesus to a high mountain and tempts him with authority over all the nations of the world, if only Jesus will worship him. Jesus responds that he will worship and serve only the Lord.

7 Jesus responded, 'The Scriptures also say, "You must not test the Lord your God."'

8 Next the devil took him to the peak of a very high mountain and showed him all the kingdoms of the world and their glory. 9 'I will give it all to you', he said, 'if you will kneel down and worship me.'

10 'Get out of here, Satan,' Jesus told him. 'For the Scriptures say,

"You must worship the Lord your God
and serve only him."'

11 Then the devil went away, and angels came and took care of Jesus.

## Where we end up

The devil leaves Jesus and the angels attend to him.

## Old Testament Foundation: Overcoming Temptation

**The Serpent in the Garden** (Genesis 3:1–7) – p. 18. Where Adam and Eve fell to the temptation of Satan, Christ resists and overcomes temptation.

**Wilderness Wanderings** (Numbers 14:11–45) – p. 72. As Israel faced temptations in the wilderness, so Christ is led into the wilderness to be tempted.

## My Reflections

# The Calling of the Disciples

## 52

## Main Theme

Christ calls disciples who will gather his people into his Kingdom.

## Setting

The Sea of Galilee

## Characters

Jesus, Simon (also known as Peter) and Andrew (brothers, fishermen), James and John (brothers, fishermen), and Zebedee (father of James and John)

## Key Verse: Matthew 4:19

Jesus called out to them, 'Come, follow me, and I will show you how to fish for people!'

Jesus calls his first disciples.

## Key plot points

**v.18** – Simon and Andrew are fishing on the Sea of Galilee.

**v.19** – Jesus is walking and calls the brothers to follow him as his disciples. He promises that from now on, they will fish for people.

**v.20** – Immediately, they leave their work and follow Jesus.

**v.21** – The scene is repeated with brothers James and John. They are mending nets with their father Zebedee when Jesus calls them.

**v.22** – Immediately, they leave their father and their work to follow Jesus.

## Read the story Matthew 4:18–22

18 One day as Jesus was walking along the shore of the Sea of Galilee, he saw two brothers – Simon, also called Peter, and Andrew – throwing a net into the water, for they fished for a living. 19 Jesus called out to them, 'Come, follow me, and I will show you how to fish for people!' 20 And they left their nets at once and followed him.

21 A little farther up the shore he saw two other brothers, James and John, sitting in a boat with their father, Zebedee, repairing their nets. And he called them to come, too. 22 They immediately followed him, leaving the boat and their father behind.

### Where we end up

Jesus calls his first disciples to follow him and help him with his work to share the good news that the Kingdom of Heaven is near.

### Old Testament Foundation: God's Reign and the End of the Curse

**The Promise to Abraham** (Genesis 12:15) – p. 32. The promise that God made to Abraham to make his descendants as numerous as the stars is being fulfilled in Christ, who calls all people to become children of Abraham by faith.

### My Reflections

........................................................

........................................................

........................................................

........................................................

# The Feeding of the Five Thousand

53

### Main Theme
Christ is the true bread of heaven.

### Setting
The eastern side of the Sea of Galilee

### Characters
Jesus, Jesus' disciples, and a large crowd of about 5,000

### Key Verse: John 6:11
Then Jesus took the loaves, gave thanks to God, and distributed them to the people. Afterwards he did the same with the fish. And they all ate as much as they wanted.

Jesus feeds 5,000 with a young boy's lunch.

## Read the story John 6:1–15

[1] After this, Jesus crossed over to the far side of the Sea of Galilee, also known as the Sea of Tiberias. [2] A huge crowd kept following him wherever he went, because they saw his miraculous signs as he healed the sick. [3] Then Jesus climbed a hill and sat down with his disciples around him. [4] (It was nearly time for the Jewish Passover celebration.)

## Key plot points

**v.1** – Because of the miracles he is performing, a large crowd of about 5,000 people follow Jesus to the east of the Sea of Galilee.

**v.5** – Jesus asks his disciple Philip how they are going to get food for the crowd.

**v.7** – Philip replies that several months' wages would not buy enough food for them.

**v.8–9** – Andrew finds a young boy who has five loaves of bread and two fish.

**v.11** – Jesus takes the small meal, gives thanks to God, and begins to distribute the bread and fish to all those around. Everyone is able to eat as much as they want.

**v.13** – When everyone is full, the disciples pick up twelve baskets full of leftover fragments.

⁵ Jesus soon saw a huge crowd of people coming to look for him. Turning to Philip, he asked, 'Where can we buy bread to feed all these people?' ⁶ He was testing Philip, for he already knew what he was going to do.

⁷ Philip replied, 'Even if we worked for months, we wouldn't have enough money to feed them!'

⁸ Then Andrew, Simon Peter's brother, spoke up. ⁹ 'There's a young boy here with five barley loaves and two fish. But what good is that with this huge crowd?'

¹⁰ 'Tell everyone to sit down,' Jesus said. So they all sat down on the grassy slopes. (The men alone numbered about 5,000.) ¹¹ Then Jesus took the loaves, gave thanks to God, and distributed them to the people. Afterwards he did the same with the fish. And they all ate as much as they wanted. ¹² After everyone was full, Jesus told his disciples, 'Now gather the leftovers, so that nothing is wasted.' ¹³ So they picked up the pieces and filled twelve baskets with scraps left by the people who had eaten from the five barley loaves.

¹⁴ When the people saw him do this miraculous sign, they exclaimed, 'Surely, he is the Prophet we have been expecting!' ¹⁵ When Jesus saw that they were ready to force him to be their king, he slipped away into the hills by himself.

## Where we end up

The people proclaim that Jesus is the Lord's prophet.

## My Reflections

# The Gerasene Demoniac

## 54

**Main Theme**

Christ came to destroy the works of the devil and deliver humanity from his power.

**Setting**

The country of the Gerasenes (east side of the Sea of Galilee)

**Key Verse: Mark 5:19**

But Jesus said, 'No, go home to your family, and tell them everything the Lord has done for you and how merciful he has been.'

**Characters**

Jesus, the disciples, unnamed demoniac, a legion of demons, and the townspeople

A Gerasene man is possessed by evil spirits.

## Key plot points

**v.1** – Jesus crosses the Sea of Galilee by boat.

**v.2** – As soon as Jesus steps ashore, a demoniac who lives in the tombs begins to run toward him and shout at him.

**v.3–5** – The demoniac lives among the tombs, howling and hurting himself, and no one can control him.

**v.7** – The demoniac asks Jesus not to torment him.

## Read the story Mark 5:1–20

[1] So they arrived at the other side of the lake, in the region of the Gerasenes. [2] When Jesus climbed out of the boat, a man possessed by an evil spirit came out from the tombs to meet him. [3] This man lived in the burial caves and could no longer be restrained, even with a chain. [4] Whenever he was put into chains and shackles – as he often was – he snapped the chains from his wrists and smashed the shackles. No one was strong enough to subdue him. [5] Day and night he wandered among the burial caves and in the hills, howling and cutting himself with sharp stones.

[6] When Jesus was still some distance away, the man saw him, ran to meet him, and bowed low before him. [7] With a shriek, he screamed, 'Why are you interfering with me, Jesus, Son of the Most High God?

Jesus heals the Gerasene man.

In the name of God, I beg you, don't torture me!' [8] For Jesus had already said to the spirit, 'Come out of the man, you evil spirit.'

[9] Then Jesus demanded, 'What is your name?'

And he replied, 'My name is Legion, because there are many of us inside this man.' [10] Then the evil spirits begged him again and again not to send them to some distant place.

[11] There happened to be a large herd of pigs feeding on the hillside nearby. [12] 'Send us into those pigs,' the spirits begged. 'Let us enter them.'

[13] So Jesus gave them permission. The evil spirits came out of the man and entered the pigs, and the entire herd of about 2,000 pigs plunged down the steep hillside into the lake and drowned in the water.

[14] The herdsmen fled to the nearby town and the surrounding countryside, spreading the news as they ran. People rushed out to see what had happened. [15] A crowd soon gathered around Jesus, and they saw the man who had been possessed by the legion of demons. He was sitting there fully clothed and perfectly sane, and they were all afraid. [16] Then those who had seen what happened told the others about the demon-possessed man and the pigs. [17] And the crowd began pleading with Jesus to go away and leave them alone.

[18] As Jesus was getting into the boat, the man who had been demon possessed begged to go with him. [19] But Jesus said, 'No, go home to your family, and tell them everything the Lord has done for you and how merciful he has been.' [20] So the man started off to visit the Ten Towns of that region and began to proclaim the great things Jesus had done for him; and everyone was amazed at what he told them.

**v.9** – When Jesus asks his name, he responds that there is a legion of evil spirits in him.

**v.12–13** – The evil spirits ask to be sent into a herd of pigs on the hillside. Jesus grants this request, and the pigs rush off the hill and drown themselves in the sea.

**v.14** – The pig herders run off to get the townspeople.

**v.17** – When the townspeople arrive, they ask Jesus to leave their region.

**v.18–19** – The man who had the legion of evil spirits begs to follow Jesus. Jesus tells him to go tell everyone what the Lord has done for him.

## Where we end up
The man amazes everyone with his story.

## Old Testament Foundation: Battles Won

**Winning Canaan** (Joshua 5:13 – 6:27) – p. 79. As an angel appeared to lead Joshua and his people to victory, so Christ appeared to defeat the power of the devil (1 John 3:8).

# 55 Jairus' Daughter

**Main Theme**

Christ overcomes the curse and conquers death itself.

**Setting**

A town on the Sea of Galilee

**Characters**

Jesus, Jairus (a synagogue leader), Jairus' daughter, and a crowd of mourners

**Key Verse: Mark 5:36**

But Jesus overheard them and said to Jairus, 'Don't be afraid. Just have faith.'

Jesus heals Jairus' daughter.

# Read the story Mark 5:21–24, 35–43

²¹ Jesus got into the boat again and went back to the other side of the lake, where a large crowd gathered around him on the shore. ²² Then a leader of the local synagogue, whose name was Jairus, arrived. When he saw Jesus, he fell at his feet, ²³ pleading fervently with him. 'My little daughter is dying,' he said. 'Please come and lay your hands on her; heal her so she can live.'

²⁴ Jesus went with him, and all the people followed, crowding around him.

…

³⁵ While he was still speaking to her, messengers arrived from the home of Jairus, the leader of the synagogue. They told him, 'Your daughter is dead. There's no use troubling the Teacher now.'

³⁶ But Jesus overheard them and said to Jairus, 'Don't be afraid. Just have faith.'

³⁷ Then Jesus stopped the crowd and wouldn't let anyone go with him except Peter, James, and John (the brother of James). ³⁸ When they came to the home of the synagogue leader, Jesus saw much commotion and weeping and wailing. ³⁹ He went inside and asked, 'Why all this commotion and weeping? The child isn't dead; she's only asleep.'

⁴⁰ The crowd laughed at him. But he made them all leave, and he took the girl's father and mother and his three disciples into the room where the girl was lying. ⁴¹ Holding her hand, he said to her, 'Talitha koum,' which means 'Little girl, get up!' ⁴² And the girl, who was twelve years old, immediately stood up and walked around! They were overwhelmed and totally amazed. ⁴³ Jesus gave them strict orders not to tell anyone what had happened, and then he told them to give her something to eat.

### Where we end up

Everyone is amazed at Jesus, but he orders them to tell no one about this.

# Key plot points

**v.22** – Jairus, a synagogue leader, approaches Jesus because his daughter is on the verge of death.

**v.24, 35** – Jesus goes with Jairus to the girl, but he gets delayed. Before Jesus arrives, someone comes from Jairus' house and announces that the girl has died.

**v.38** – They arrive at Jairus' house to find a large crowd of mourners weeping and wailing.

**v.39–40** – The crowd laughs at Jesus when he says the girl is merely asleep.

**v.41** – Jesus takes only a few people into the room. He tells the little girl to get up.

**v.42** – Immediately, the girl gets up and walks around the house.

# 56 The Bleeding Woman

**Main Theme**

Christ brings the healing and wholeness of God's Kingdom.

**Setting**

On the road to Jairus' house

**Characters**

Jesus, an unnamed woman who has been constantly bleeding for 12 years, a large crowd, and the disciples

**Key Verse: Mark 5:34**

And he said to her, 'Daughter, your faith has made you well. Go in peace. Your suffering is over.'

A woman is healed after 12 years of constant bleeding.

# Read the story Mark 5:25–34

²⁵ A woman in the crowd had suffered for twelve years with constant bleeding. ²⁶ She had suffered a great deal from many doctors, and over the years she had spent everything she had to pay them, but she got no better. In fact, she was worse. ²⁷ She had heard about Jesus, so she came up behind him through the crowd and touched his robe. ²⁸ For she thought to herself, 'If I can just touch his robe, I will be healed.' ²⁹ Immediately the bleeding stopped, and she could feel in her body that she had been healed of her terrible condition.

³⁰ Jesus realized at once that healing power had gone out from him, so he turned around in the crowd and asked, 'Who touched my robe?'

³¹ His disciples said to him, 'Look at this crowd pressing around you. How can you ask, "Who touched me?"'

³² But he kept on looking around to see who had done it. ³³ Then the frightened woman, trembling at the realization of what had happened to her, came and fell to her knees in front of him and told him what she had done. ³⁴ And he said to her, 'Daughter, your faith has made you well. Go in peace. Your suffering is over.'

# Key plot points

**v.25** – A woman who has suffered with constant bleeding for twelve years seeks out Jesus.

**v.26** – She has spent everything on doctors but has not got any better.

**v.27–28** – She believes that if she can touch Jesus' cloak she will be healed, so she makes her way through the crowd.

**v.29** – As soon as she touches Jesus' cloak, she stops bleeding.

**v.30** – As Jesus is journeying to heal Jairus' daughter, he stops and looks around. He asks who touched him. Jesus feels that power has gone out from him.

**v.31** – The disciples are shocked that Jesus asks this in a large crowd.

**v.32** – The woman comes before Jesus and tells him the truth.

## Where we end up
Jesus tells her that she can go in peace, and that her faith has healed her.

## My Reflections

# 57 The Parable of the Sower and the Soils

## Main Theme
The good news of Christ and his Kingdom is only fruitful in some who hear it.

## Setting
Beside the Sea of Galilee (a large lake)

## Characters
Jesus (the storyteller), a crowd of people, the disciples, the sower, and the evil one

## Key Verse: Matthew 13:23
'The seed that fell on good soil represents those who truly hear and understand God's word and produce a harvest of thirty, sixty, or even a hundred times as much as had been planted!'

Jesus tells a parable about the sower and the soils.

# Read the story Matthew 13:1–10, 18–23

[1] Later that same day Jesus left the house and sat beside the lake. [2] A large crowd soon gathered around him, so he got into a boat. Then he sat there and taught as the people stood on the shore. [3] He told many stories in the form of parables, such as this one:

'Listen! A farmer went out to plant some seeds. [4] As he scattered them across his field, some seeds fell on a footpath, and the birds came and ate them.

[5] Other seeds fell on shallow soil with underlying rock. The seeds sprouted quickly because the soil was shallow. [6] But the plants soon wilted under the hot sun, and since they didn't have deep roots, they died. [7] Other seeds fell among thorns that grew up and choked out the tender plants.

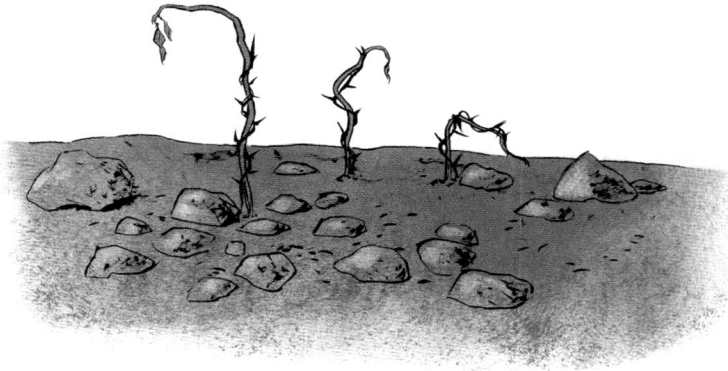

[8] Still other seeds fell on fertile soil, and they produced a crop that was thirty, sixty, and even a hundred times as much as had been planted! [9] Anyone with ears to hear should listen and understand.'

[10] His disciples came and asked him, 'Why do you use parables when you talk to the people?'

…

# Key plot points

**v.1–8** – Jesus tells a story to a crowd of people while he sits by the lake.

**v.10** – Later, when they are alone, the disciples ask him to explain the parable.

**v.19** — A sower goes to sow some seed. This seed is the word of the Kingdom. Some seed falls by the path and is eaten by the birds. This represents one who hears the word, but the evil one comes and snatches it away.

**v.20–21** — Some seed falls into rocky soil where it sprouts quickly but dies. This represents one who hears and receives the word, but who quickly falls away because of difficulties.

**v.22** — Some seed falls among thorns and is choked. This represents those who hear the word and receive it, but the world chokes out any fruitfulness.

18 'Now listen to the explanation of the parable about the farmer planting seeds: 19 The seed that fell on the footpath represents those who hear the message about the Kingdom and don't understand it. Then the evil one comes and snatches away the seed that was planted in their hearts. 20 The seed on the rocky soil represents those who hear the message and immediately receive it with joy. 21 But since they don't have deep roots, they don't last long. They fall away as soon as they have problems or are persecuted for believing God's word. 22 The seed that fell among the thorns represents those who hear God's word, but all too quickly the message is crowded out by the worries of this life and the lure of wealth, so no fruit is produced.

**v.23** — Some seed falls on fertile soil and yields a crop of thirty, sixty or a hundredfold. This represents those who hear the word and receive it, and who bear the fruit of the Kingdom.

23 The seed that fell on good soil represents those who truly hear and understand God's word and produce a harvest of thirty, sixty, or even a hundred times as much as had been planted!'

### Where we end up

Jesus concludes his parable, saying, 'He who has ears, let him hear.'

# The Mustard Seed

## 58

## Main Theme

Starting with a few disciples, Christ's Kingdom will grow to encompass all nations and all creation.

## Setting

Beside the Sea of Galilee

## Characters

Jesus (the storyteller) and a sower

## Key Verse: Matthew 13:31

Here is another illustration Jesus used: 'The Kingdom of Heaven is like a mustard seed planted in a field.'

Birds make nests in the branches of the mustard bush.

## Key plot points

**v.31** – Jesus is using parables and images to describe God's Kingdom. He says the Kingdom of Heaven is like a mustard seed that a sower sows in his field.

**v.32** – It begins as the tiniest of seeds. However, when it is fully grown it is the largest of shrubs and becomes a tree. All the birds of the air can come and make their nests in the branches of this great tree.

## Read the story Matthew 13:31–32

[31] Here is another illustration Jesus used: 'The Kingdom of Heaven is like a mustard seed planted in a field. [32] It is the smallest of all seeds, but it becomes the largest of garden plants; it grows into a tree, and birds come and make nests in its branches.'

Jesus compares the Kingdom of God to a mustard bush.

## Where we end up
Jesus continues to use stories and illustrations to explain God's Kingdom and his work.

# Jesus Walks on the Water

## 59

**Main Theme**

Christ is the Son of God, the Lord of all creation.

**Setting**

A lonely mountain and the Sea of Galilee

**Key Verse: Matthew 14:33**

Then the disciples worshipped him. 'You really are the Son of God!' they exclaimed.

**Characters**

Jesus, Peter, and the other disciples

Jesus walks on the water.

## Key plot points

**v.22–23** – After dismissing the crowds and sending his disciples ahead in a boat, Jesus goes up on a mountain by himself to pray.

**v.24** – The boat is battered by winds and waves, and drifts far away from the shore.

**v.25** – Jesus comes to them, walking on the water.

**v.26–27** – The disciples are terrified that it is a ghost until Jesus calls out to them and calms them.

**v.28–30** – Peter gets out of the boat and begins to walk toward Jesus on the water. He begins to sink when he looks around and sees the wind whipping up.

**v.31** – Jesus catches him by the arm and saves him from sinking, but asks Peter why he doubted.

## Read the story Matthew 14:22–33

22 Immediately after this, Jesus insisted that his disciples get back into the boat and cross to the other side of the lake, while he sent the people home. 23 After sending them home, he went up into the hills by himself to pray. Night fell while he was there alone.

24 Meanwhile, the disciples were in trouble far away from land, for a strong wind had risen, and they were fighting heavy waves. 25 About three o'clock in the morning Jesus came towards them, walking on the water. 26 When the disciples saw him walking on the water, they were terrified. In their fear, they cried out, 'It's a ghost!'

27 But Jesus spoke to them at once. 'Don't be afraid,' he said. 'Take courage. I am here!'

28 Then Peter called to him, 'Lord, if it's really you, tell me to come to you, walking on the water.'

29 'Yes, come,' Jesus said.

So Peter went over the side of the boat and walked on the water towards Jesus. 30 But when he saw the strong wind and the waves, he was terrified and began to sink. 'Save me, Lord!' he shouted.

31 Jesus immediately reached out and grabbed him. 'You have so little faith,' Jesus said. 'Why did you doubt me?'

32 When they climbed back into the boat, the wind stopped. 33 Then the disciples worshipped him. 'You really are the Son of God!' they exclaimed.

## Where we end up

When they get back in the boat, the disciples worship him, saying that he truly is the Son of God.

## My Reflections

..............................................................................................................

..............................................................................................................

..............................................................................................................

..............................................................................................................

# The Transfiguration

## 60

## Main Theme

Christ is the Son who shines the Father's glory and truth into the world.

## Setting

A high mountain

## Characters

Jesus, Peter, James, and John (Jesus' inner circle of disciples), Moses, Elijah, and God the Father

## Key Verse: Matthew 17:5

But even as he spoke, a bright cloud overshadowed them, and a voice from the cloud said, 'This is my dearly loved Son, who brings me great joy. Listen to him.'

Peter, James, and John see the transfiguration of Christ.

## Key plot points

**v.1** – Jesus takes Peter, James, and John up a high mountain to be alone.

**v.2** – When they get up there, Jesus' face and clothes are transfigured and begin to shine brightly.

**v.3** – Moses and Elijah appear with Jesus, speaking with him.

**v.4** – Peter suggests that they build three tents on the mountain.

**v.5** – As he is saying this, a bright cloud envelops them and the voice of the Father tells them to listen to Jesus, his beloved Son.

**v.6** – The disciples fall on their faces terrified.

**v.8** – When they look up again, they see only Jesus standing there.

## Read the story Matthew 17:1–9

¹ Six days later Jesus took Peter and the two brothers, James and John, and led them up a high mountain to be alone. ² As the men watched, Jesus' appearance was transformed so that his face shone like the sun, and his clothes became as white as light. ³ Suddenly, Moses and Elijah appeared and began talking with Jesus.

⁴ Peter exclaimed, 'Lord, it's wonderful for us to be here! If you want, I'll make three shelters as memorials – one for you, one for Moses, and one for Elijah.'

⁵ But even as he spoke, a bright cloud overshadowed them, and a voice from the cloud said, 'This is my dearly loved Son, who brings me great joy. Listen to him.' ⁶ The disciples were terrified and fell face down on the ground.

⁷ Then Jesus came over and touched them. 'Get up,' he said. 'Don't be afraid.' ⁸ And when they looked up, Moses and Elijah were gone, and they saw only Jesus.

⁹ As they went back down the mountain, Jesus commanded them, 'Don't tell anyone what you have seen until the Son of Man has been raised from the dead.'

### Where we end up

Jesus asks the three disciples not to tell anyone about what they have seen until after he has been raised from the dead.

### Old Testament Foundation: The Messiah as Prophet and Law Giver

**Moses' Shining Face:** 'When Moses came down Mount Sinai carrying the two stone tablets inscribed with the terms of the covenant, he wasn't aware that his face had become radiant because he had spoken to the LORD' (Exodus 34:29). As Moses' face shone when he had been on the mountain with the Lord, so Jesus' face shines on the mountain of transfiguration.

# The Great Confession

## 61

**Main Theme**

Jesus, the Messiah, will establish his Kingdom by suffering, dying, and rising again.

**Setting**

The villages around Caesarea Philippi

**Key Verse: Mark 8:34**

Then, calling the crowd to join his disciples, he said, 'If any of you wants to be my follower, you must give up your own way, take up your cross, and follow me.'

**Characters**

Jesus, Peter, and the other disciples

'Get away from me, Satan!'

## Key plot points

**v.27** – Jesus asks his disciples who people are saying that he is.

**v.28** – They say that the crowds think he is either John the Baptist or Elijah.

**v.29** – Jesus then asks who they (his disciples) say he is, and Peter speaks for the group and declares, "You are the Christ."

**v.31** – Jesus begins to teach them that the Christ came to suffer, to die, and to rise again.

**v.32** – Peter rebukes Jesus for saying this.

**v.33** – Jesus in turn rebukes Peter, saying, 'Get away from me, Satan.'

**v.34** – Jesus explains that his followers must deny themselves, take up their cross, and follow him.

## Read the story Mark 8:27 – 9:1

**8** [27] Jesus and his disciples left Galilee and went up to the villages near Caesarea Philippi. As they were walking along, he asked them, 'Who do people say I am?'

[28] 'Well,' they replied, 'some say John the Baptist, some say Elijah, and others say you are one of the other prophets.'

[29] Then he asked them, 'But who do you say I am?'

Peter replied, 'You are the Messiah.'

[30] But Jesus warned them not to tell anyone about him.

[31] Then Jesus began to tell them that the Son of Man must suffer many terrible things and be rejected by the elders, the leading priests, and the teachers of religious law. He would be killed, but three days later he would rise from the dead. [32] As he talked about this openly with his disciples, Peter took him aside and began to reprimand him for saying such things.

[33] Jesus turned around and looked at his disciples, then reprimanded Peter. 'Get away from me, Satan!' he said. 'You are seeing things merely from a human point of view, not from God's.'

[34] Then, calling the crowd to join his disciples, he said, 'If any of you wants to be my follower, you must give up your own way, take up your cross, and follow me. [35] If you try to hang on to your life, you will lose it. But if you give up your life for my sake and for the sake of the Good News, you will save it. [36] And what do you benefit if you gain the whole world but lose your own soul? [37] Is anything worth more than your soul? [38] If anyone is ashamed of me and my message in these adulterous and sinful days, the Son of Man will be ashamed of that person when he returns in the glory of his Father with the holy angels.'

**9** Jesus went on to say, 'I tell you the truth, some standing here right now will not die before they see the Kingdom of God arrive in great power!'

## Where we end up

Jesus declares that his followers must be willing to lose their lives for his sake.

# The Good Samaritan

## 62

**Main Theme**

Christ's Kingdom demands that we love others as ourselves.

**Setting**

Jesus is telling a parable to a self-righteous lawyer

**Characters**

Jesus, a lawyer (an expert in the Law of Moses), a man beaten and left for dead, a priest, a Levite and a Samaritan

**Key Verse: Luke 10:29**

The man wanted to justify his actions, so he asked Jesus, 'And who is my neighbour?'

**Key Verse: Luke 10:36–37**

'Now which of these three would you say was a neighbour to the man who was attacked by bandits?' Jesus asked. The man replied, 'The one who showed him mercy.' Then Jesus said, 'Yes, now go and do the same.'

Jesus tells a parable of a man who is beaten and left for dead.

## Key plot points

**v.25** – A lawyer, who wants to justify himself, asks Jesus what he must do to fulfil the command to love his neighbour and inherit eternal life.

**v.30** – In response, Jesus tells him a parable about a man who is travelling from Jerusalem to Jericho when he is robbed, beaten, and left for dead.

**v.31–32** – Both a priest and Levite pass by and do not help the man.

## Read the story Luke 10:25–37

²⁵ One day an expert in religious law stood up to test Jesus by asking him this question: 'Teacher, what should I do to inherit eternal life?'

²⁶ Jesus replied, 'What does the law of Moses say? How do you read it?'

²⁷ The man answered, '"You must love the LORD your God with all your heart, all your soul, all your strength, and all your mind." And, "Love your neighbour as yourself."'

²⁸ 'Right!' Jesus told him. 'Do this and you will live!'

²⁹ The man wanted to justify his actions, so he asked Jesus, 'And who is my neighbour?'

³⁰ Jesus replied with a story: 'A Jewish man was travelling from Jerusalem down to Jericho, and he was attacked by bandits. They stripped him of his clothes, beat him up, and left him half dead beside the road.

A Levite avoids the man.

³¹ 'By chance a priest came along. But when he saw the man lying there, he crossed to the other side of the road and passed him by. ³² A Temple assistant walked over and looked at him lying there, but he also passed by on the other side.

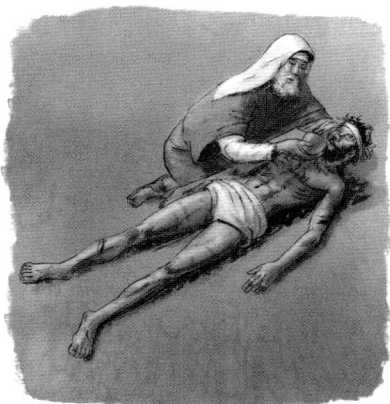

The Samaritan helps the man.

<sup>33</sup> 'Then a despised Samaritan came along, and when he saw the man, he felt compassion for him. <sup>34</sup> Going over to him, the Samaritan soothed his wounds with olive oil and wine and bandaged them. Then he put the man on his own donkey and took him to an inn, where he took care of him. <sup>35</sup> The next day he handed the innkeeper two silver coins, telling him, "Look after this man. If his bill runs higher than this, I'll pay you the next time I'm here."

<sup>36</sup> 'Now which of these three would you say was a neighbour to the man who was attacked by bandits?' Jesus asked.

<sup>37</sup> The man replied, 'The one who showed him mercy.'

Then Jesus said, 'Yes, now go and do the same.'

**v.33–34** — A despised Samaritan passes by and helps the man. He bandages his wounds, brings him to an inn, and pays for the man to stay while he heals.

## Where we end up

Jesus asks the lawyer who fulfilled the commandment to love one's neighbour. When the lawyer indicates that it is the Samaritan, Jesus commands him to go and do likewise.

## My Reflections

.................................................................................................

.................................................................................................

.................................................................................................

.................................................................................................

# 63  The Lost Sheep

**Main Theme**

Christ came to seek and save what was lost.

**Setting**

The Pharisees are upset that Jesus welcomes tax collectors and sinners

**Characters**

Jesus (the storyteller), a shepherd, and the sheep

**Key Verse: Luke 15:7**

In the same way, there is more joy in heaven over one lost sinner who repents and returns to God than over ninety-nine others who are righteous and haven't strayed away!

The shepherd leaves the ninety-nine to find the one lost sheep.

# Read the story Luke 15:1–7

[1] Tax collectors and other notorious sinners often came to listen to Jesus teach. [2] This made the Pharisees and teachers of religious law complain that he was associating with such sinful people – even eating with them!

The shepherd saves the one lost sheep.

[3] So Jesus told them this story: [4] 'If a man has a hundred sheep and one of them gets lost, what will he do? Won't he leave the ninety-nine others in the wilderness and go to search for the one that is lost until he finds it? [5] And when he has found it, he will joyfully carry it home on his shoulders. [6] When he arrives, he will call together his friends and neighbours, saying, "Rejoice with me because I have found my lost sheep." [7] In the same way, there is more joy in heaven over one lost sinner who repents and returns to God than over ninety-nine others who are righteous and haven't strayed away!'

## Where we end up

Jesus explains that all heaven rejoices greatly over one sinner who repents.

## Key plot points

**v.1–2** – Jesus tells a parable to a group of Pharisees who are grumbling that he welcomes tax collectors and sinners.

**v.4** – A shepherd has a flock of one hundred sheep. One sheep wanders away into the wilderness, but ninety-nine stay together. The shepherd leaves the ninety-nine to seek and save the one lost sheep.

**v.5–6** – When he finds the sheep, he calls together his friends and neighbours to celebrate that he has found his lost sheep.

# 64  The Prodigal Son

### Main Theme
The Lord and his Kingdom celebrate when the lost come home to him.

### Setting
The Pharisees are upset that Jesus welcomes tax collectors and sinners

### Characters
Jesus (the storyteller), the father, the younger son, and the older brother

### Key Verse: Luke 15:13
A few days later this younger son packed all his belongings and moved to a distant land, and there he wasted all his money in wild living.

### Key Verse: Luke 15:23–24
'And kill the calf we have been fattening. We must celebrate with a feast, for this son of mine was dead and has now returned to life. He was lost, but now he is found.' So the party began.

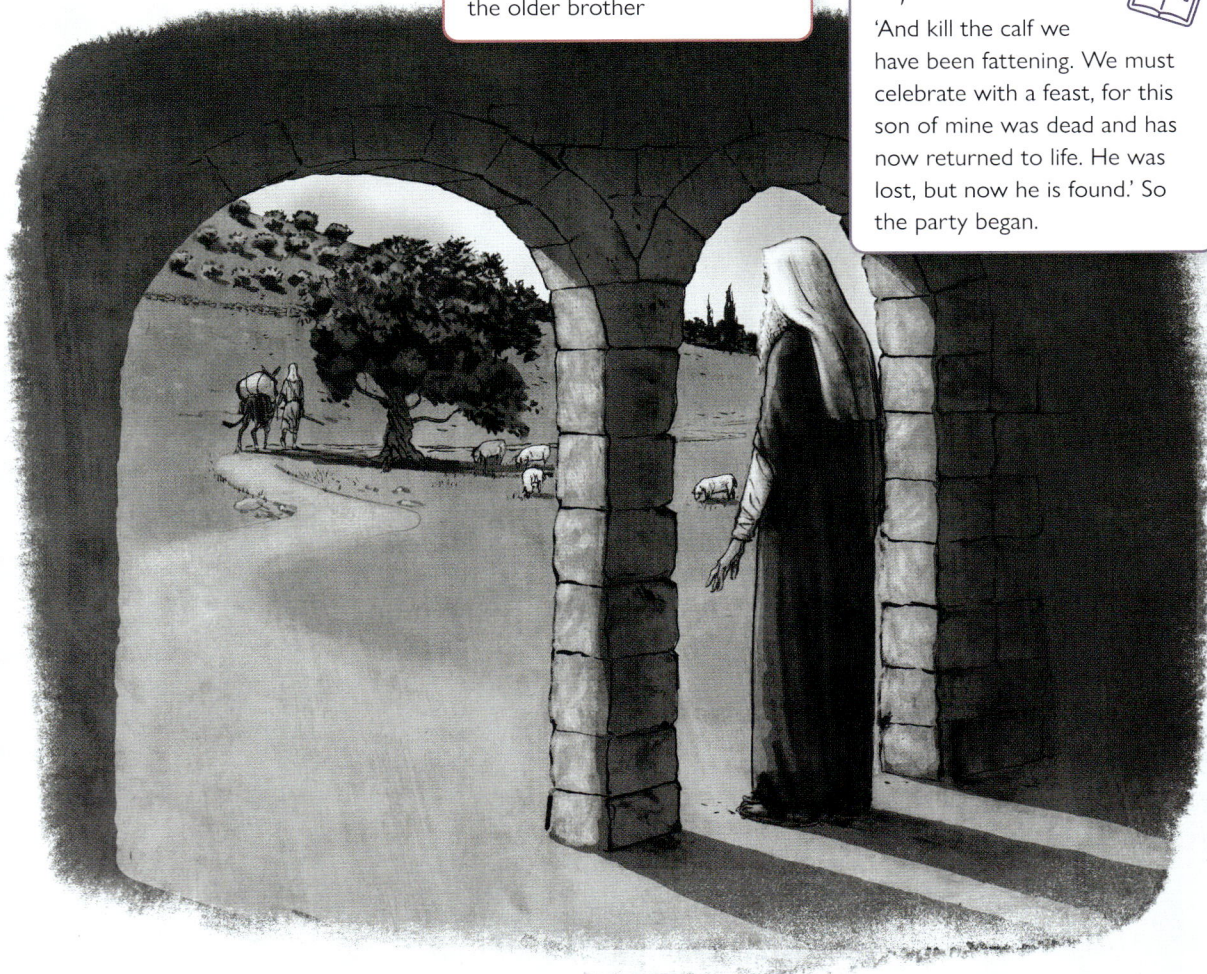

The son leaves the father in the parable of the prodigal son.

# Read the story Luke 15:11–32

[11] To illustrate the point further, Jesus told them this story: 'A man had two sons. [12] The younger son told his father, "I want my share of your estate now before you die." So his father agreed to divide his wealth between his sons.

The son wastes all his money.

[13] 'A few days later this younger son packed all his belongings and moved to a distant land, and there he wasted all his money in wild living. [14] About the time his money ran out, a great famine swept over the land, and he began to starve. [15] He persuaded a local farmer to hire him, and the man sent him into his fields to feed the pigs. [16] The young man became so hungry that even the pods he was feeding the pigs looked good to him. But no one gave him anything.

[17] 'When he finally came to his senses, he said to himself, "At home even the hired servants have food enough to spare, and here I am dying of hunger! [18] I will go home to my father and say, 'Father, I have sinned against both heaven and you, [19] and I am no longer worthy of being called your son. Please take me on as a hired servant.'"

[20] 'So he returned home to his father. And while he was still a long way off, his father saw him coming. Filled with love and compassion,

# Key plot points

**v.11** – Jesus is telling a story about a father who has two sons.

**v.12** – The younger son demands his share of the inheritance.

**v.13** – He goes into a far country and wastes all his money on wild living.

**v.16–19** – The younger son reaches a low point when he is so hungry that he longs to eat pig slop. He decides to return to his father's house as a servant.

**v.20–24** – When he arrives home, the father is so glad to see him that he runs to greet him, clothes him in the best clothes, and throws a great feast of celebration.

The son returns.

v.28–29 – The older brother refuses to come to the feast, so the father goes to speak with him. The older brother is angry about the father celebrating the return of the younger son.

he ran to his son, embraced him, and kissed him. ²¹ His son said to him, "Father, I have sinned against both heaven and you, and I am no longer worthy of being called your son."

²² 'But his father said to the servants, "Quick! Bring the finest robe in the house and put it on him. Get a ring for his finger and sandals for his feet. ²³ And kill the calf we have been fattening. We must celebrate with a feast, ²⁴ for this son of mine was dead and has now returned to life. He was lost, but now he is found." So the party began.

²⁵ 'Meanwhile, the older son was in the fields working. When he returned home, he heard music and dancing in the house, ²⁶ and he asked one of the servants what was going on. ²⁷ "Your brother is back," he was told, "and your father has killed the fattened calf. We are celebrating because of his safe return."

²⁸ 'The older brother was angry and wouldn't go in. His father came out and begged him, ²⁹ but he replied, "All these years I've slaved for you and never once refused to do a single thing you told me to. And in all that time you never gave me even one young goat for a feast with my friends. ³⁰ Yet when this son of yours comes back after squandering your money on prostitutes, you celebrate by killing the fattened calf!"

³¹ 'His father said to him, "Look, dear son, you have always stayed by me, and everything I have is yours. ³² We had to celebrate this happy day. For your brother was dead and has come back to life! He was lost, but now he is found!"'

## Where we end up

The father explains that he has to celebrate because the younger son was dead and has come back to life; that he was lost and has been found.

## My Reflections

# Zaccheus

## 65

Jesus calls to Zacchaeus.

**Main Theme**

Christ came to seek and save the lost.

**Setting**

A road through Jericho and Zacchaeus' house

**Characters**

Zacchaeus, Jesus, and a crowd of people

**Key Verse: Luke 19:9–10**

Jesus responded, 'Salvation has come to this home today, for this man has shown himself to be a true son of Abraham. For the Son of Man came to seek and save those who are lost.'

## Key plot points

**v.1** – Jesus is passing through Jericho.

**v.2** – Zacchaeus is a rich tax collector who is desperate to see Jesus.

**v.3–4** – He is a short man, so he climbs a sycamore tree to see Jesus over the large crowd.

**v.5–6** – Jesus stops and looks up at Zacchaeus. He tells Zacchaeus to come down from the tree so they can go to his house.

**v.7** – Many in the crowd grumble about this because Zacchaeus is a sinner.

**v.8** – Zacchaeus announces that he will give half his possessions to the poor and restore four-fold anything he has stolen.

**v.9** – Jesus proclaims that salvation has come to Zacchaeus' house this day.

## Read the story Luke 19:1–10

¹ Jesus entered Jericho and made his way through the town. ² There was a man there named Zacchaeus. He was the chief tax collector in the region, and he had become very rich. ³ He tried to get a look at Jesus, but he was too short to see over the crowd. ⁴ So he ran ahead and climbed a sycamore-fig tree beside the road, for Jesus was going to pass that way.

⁵ When Jesus came by, he looked up at Zacchaeus and called him by name. 'Zacchaeus!' he said. 'Quick, come down! I must be a guest in your home today.'

⁶ Zacchaeus quickly climbed down and took Jesus to his house in great excitement and joy. ⁷ But the people were displeased. 'He has gone to be the guest of a notorious sinner,' they grumbled.

⁸ Meanwhile, Zacchaeus stood before the Lord and said, 'I will give half my wealth to the poor, Lord, and if I have cheated people on their taxes, I will give them back four times as much!'

⁹ Jesus responded, 'Salvation has come to this home today, for this man has shown himself to be a true son of Abraham. ¹⁰ For the Son of Man came to seek and save those who are lost.'

### Where we end up

Jesus says that seeking and saving the lost sinners like Zacchaeus is the reason he has come.

### My Reflections

# Jesus Journeys to Jerusalem

## 66

**Main Theme**

True greatness in Christ's Kingdom means becoming a servant.

**Setting**

The road from Judea beyond the Jordan up to Jerusalem

**Characters**

Jesus, James, John, and the other disciples

**Key Verse: Mark 10:45**

'For even the Son of Man came not to be served but to serve others and to give his life as a ransom for many.'

Jesus walks along the road going up to Jerusalem.

## Key plot points

**v.32** – The disciples are amazed and afraid as Jesus resolutely walks toward Jerusalem.

**v.33–34** – Jesus once again explains to them that he will be arrested, beaten, and killed in Jerusalem, but that he will rise again.

**v.37** – Two of Jesus' disciples, James and John, approach Jesus and ask to sit at his right and left hand in his Kingdom.

**v.40** – Jesus explains that these positions are not his to grant.

**v.41** – The other disciples get angry with James and John for requesting this honour.

**v.43–44** – Jesus explains that true greatness in his Kingdom is not a matter of high position. Whoever wants to be great in the Kingdom of Christ must become a servant of all.

## Read the story Mark 10:32–45

32 They were now on the way up to Jerusalem, and Jesus was walking ahead of them. The disciples were filled with awe, and the people following behind were overwhelmed with fear. Taking the twelve disciples aside, Jesus once more began to describe ever thing that was about to happen to him. 33 'Listen,' he said, 'we're going up to Jerusalem, where the Son of Man will be betrayed to the leading priests and the teachers of religious law. They will sentence him to die and hand him over to the Romans. 34 They will mock him, spit on him, flog him with a whip, and kill him, but after three days he will rise again.'

35 Then James and John, the sons of Zebedee, came over and spoke to him. 'Teacher,' they said, 'we want you to do us a favour.'

36 'What is your request?' he asked.

37 They replied, 'When you sit on your glorious throne, we want to sit in places of honour next to you, one on your right and the other on your left.'

38 But Jesus said to them, 'You don't know what you are asking! Are you able to drink from the bitter cup of suffering I am about to drink? Are you able to be baptized with the baptism of suffering I must be baptized with?'

39 'Oh yes,' they replied, 'we are able!' Then Jesus told them, 'You will indeed drink from my bitter cup and be baptized with my baptism of suffering. 40 But I have no right to say who will sit on my right or my left. God has prepared those places for the ones he has chosen.'

41 When the ten other disciples heard what James and John had asked, they were indignant. 42 So Jesus called them together and said, 'You know that the rulers in this world lord it over their people, and officials flaunt their authority over those under them. 43 But among you it will be different. Whoever wants to be a leader among you must be your servant, 44 and whoever wants to be first among you must be the slave of everyone else. 45 For even the Son of Man came not to be served but to serve others and to give his life as a ransom for many.'

## Where we end up

Even the Christ, God's Messiah, came to serve and to give his life as a ransom for many.

# The Triumphal Entry

## 67

**Main Theme**

Christ is the Lord's king come to save God's people.

**Setting**

The road from the Mount of Olives into Jerusalem

**Key Verse: Matthew 21:9**

Jesus was in the centre of the procession, and the people all around him were shouting, 'Praise God for the Son of David! Blessings on the one who comes in the name of the LORD! Praise God in highest heaven!'

**Characters**

Jesus, the disciples, and a large crowd

Jesus enters Jerusalem on a donkey.

## Read the story Matthew 21:1–11

[1] As Jesus and the disciples approached Jerusalem, they came to the town of Bethphage on the Mount of Olives. Jesus sent two of them on ahead. [2] 'Go into the village over there,' he said. 'As soon as you enter it, you will see a donkey tied there, with its colt beside it. Untie them and bring them to me. [3] If anyone asks what you are doing, just say,

## Key plot points

**v.1** – Jesus sends two disciples to retrieve a donkey and her colt for him to ride.

**v.2** – He tells them that if anyone asks why they are taking the animals to say, "The Lord needs them."

"The Lord needs them," and he will immediately let you take them.' ⁴ This took place to fulfil the prophecy that said,

⁵ 'Tell the people of Jerusalem,
"Look, your King is coming to you.
He is humble, riding on a donkey –
riding on a donkey's colt."'

⁶ The two disciples did as Jesus commanded. ⁷ They brought the donkey and the colt to him and threw their garments over the colt, and he sat on it.

⁸ Most of the crowd spread their garments on the road ahead of him, and others cut branches from the trees and spread them on the road. ⁹ Jesus was in the centre of the procession, and the people all around him were shouting,

'Praise God for the Son of David!
Blessings on the one who comes in the name of the LORD!
Praise God in highest heaven!'

¹⁰ The entire city of Jerusalem was in an uproar as he entered. 'Who is this?' they asked.

¹¹ And the crowds replied, 'It's Jesus, the prophet from Nazareth in Galilee.'

**v.8** – Jesus rides the donkey from the Mount of Olives into Jerusalem. As he rides a great crowd gathers and spreads their cloaks on the road. They cut palm branches and wave them in celebration.

**v.9** – Everyone is shouting, 'Hosanna to the Son of David!'

## Where we end up

The whole city is stirred up by the news that the prophet from Nazareth has arrived in Jerusalem.

## Old Testament Foundation: The City of the Great King

**The Lord Spoke through the Prophets:** 'Rejoice, O people of Zion! Shout in triumph, O people of Jerusalem! Look, your king is coming to you. He is righteous and victorious, yet he is humble, riding on a donkey – riding on a donkey's colt' (Zechariah 9.9). The Messiah is revealed to the people of God.

# The Last Supper

## 68

## Main Theme

Christ offers the sacrifice of his own body and blood for his followers to remember and reenact his mighty saving deeds.

## Setting

An upper room in a house in or around Jerusalem

## Characters

Jesus, Peter, John, and the disciples

## Key Verse: Luke 22:19–20

He took some bread and gave thanks to God for it. Then he broke it in pieces and gave it to the disciples, saying, 'This is my body, which is given for you. Do this in remembrance of me.' After supper he took another cup of wine and said, 'This cup is the new covenant between God and his people – an agreement confirmed with my blood, which is poured out as a sacrifice for you.'

Jesus shares a final Passover meal with the disciples.

## Key plot points

**v.7–12** – When it comes time to celebrate the Passover, Jesus sends Peter and John to find a man carrying a water jar, who will lead them to the place.

**v.13** – They go and find it just as Jesus has said and prepare the Passover meal.

**v.19** – During the meal Jesus takes bread, and when he had given thanks, he broke it and gave it to them, saying, 'This is my body, which is given for you. Do this in remembrance of me.'

**v.20** – After they had eaten, he took the cup saying, 'This cup is the new covenant between God and his people – an agreement confirmed with my blood, which is poured out as a sacrifice for you.'

## Read the story Luke 22:7–23

[7] Now the Festival of Unleavened Bread arrived, when the Passover lamb is sacrificed. [8] Jesus sent Peter and John ahead and said, 'Go and prepare the Passover meal, so we can eat it together.'

[9] 'Where do you want us to prepare it?' they asked him.

[10] He replied, 'As soon as you enter Jerusalem, a man carrying a jug of water will meet you. Follow him. At the house he enters, [11] say to the owner, "The Teacher asks: Where is the guest room where I can eat the Passover meal with my disciples?" [12] He will take you upstairs to a large room that is already set up. That is where you should prepare our meal.' [13] They went off to the city and found everything just as Jesus had said, and they prepared the Passover meal there.

[14] When the time came, Jesus and the apostles sat down together at the table. [15] Jesus said, 'I have been very eager to eat this Passover meal with you before my suffering begins. [16] For I tell you now that I won't eat this meal again until its meaning is fulfilled in the Kingdom of God.'

[17] Then he took a cup of wine and gave thanks to God for it. Then he said, 'Take this and share it among yourselves. [18] For I will not drink wine again until the Kingdom of God has come.'

[19] He took some bread and gave thanks to God for it. Then he broke it in pieces and gave it to the disciples, saying, 'This is my body, which is given for you. Do this in remembrance of me.'

[20] After supper he took another cup of wine and said, 'This cup is the new covenant between God and his people – an agreement confirmed with my blood, which is poured out as a sacrifice for you.

[21] 'But here at this table, sitting among us as a friend, is the man who will betray me. [22] For it has been determined that the Son of Man must die. But what sorrow awaits the one who betrays him.' [23] The disciples began to ask each other which of them would ever do such a thing.

## Where we end up

Jesus tells the disciples that one of them will betray him. They are disturbed by this news and try to figure out which one of them would do such a thing.

# Jesus Washes the Disciples' Feet

## 69

Jesus washes the disciples' feet.

## Main Theme
Christ cleanses his people from sin by the offering of himself as a suffering servant.

## Setting
An upper room in a house in or around Jerusalem

## Characters
Jesus, Judas, Peter, and the disciples

## Key Verse: John 13:14–15
'And since I, your Lord and Teacher, have washed your feet, you ought to wash each other's feet. I have given you an example to follow. Do as I have done to you.'

## Key plot points

**v.1** – Jesus knows that his hour has come, that Judas is ready to betray him, and that he is about to depart.

**v.4** – At supper, he stands up and strips to his undergarments.

**v.5** – He then proceeds to do the lowly task of washing the feet of the disciples.

**v.6** – When Jesus comes to him, Peter tries to refuse to let the Lord wash his feet.

**v.8** – Jesus tells him that if he will not allow his feet to be washed, Peter will have no share with Christ.

**v.9** – Peter then exclaims that he wants the Lord to bathe his whole body!

**v.10** – Jesus explains that he is already clean, and only needs his feet washed.

## Read the story John 13:1–20

¹ Before the Passover celebration, Jesus knew that his hour had come to leave this world and return to his Father. He had loved his disciples during his ministry on earth, and now he loved them to the very end. ² It was time for supper, and the devil had already prompted Judas, son of Simon Iscariot, to betray Jesus. ³ Jesus knew that the Father had given him authority over everything and that he had come from God and would return to God. ⁴ So he got up from the table, took off his robe, wrapped a towel around his waist, ⁵ and poured water into a basin. Then he began to wash the disciples' feet, drying them with the towel he had around him.

⁶ When Jesus came to Simon Peter, Peter said to him, 'Lord, are you going to wash my feet?'

⁷ Jesus replied, 'You don't understand now what I am doing, but some day you will.'

⁸ 'No,' Peter protested, 'you will never ever wash my feet!'

Jesus replied, 'Unless I wash you, you won't belong to me.'

⁹ Simon Peter exclaimed, 'Then wash my hands and head as well, Lord, not just my feet!'

¹⁰ Jesus replied, 'A person who has bathed all over does not need to wash, except for the feet, to be entirely clean. And you disciples are clean, but not all of you.' ¹¹ For Jesus knew who would betray him. That is what he meant when he said, 'Not all of you are clean.'

¹² After washing their feet, he put on his robe again and sat down and asked, 'Do you understand what I was doing? ¹³ You call me "Teacher" and "Lord", and you are right, because that's what I am. ¹⁴ And since I, your Lord and Teacher, have washed your feet, you ought to wash each other's feet. ¹⁵ I have given you an example to follow. Do as I have done to you. ¹⁶ I tell you the truth, slaves are not greater than their master. Nor is the messenger more important than the one who sends the message. ¹⁷ Now that you know these things, God will bless you for doing them.

¹⁸ 'I am not saying these things to all of you; I know the ones I have chosen. But this fulfils the Scripture that says, "The one who eats my food has turned against me." ¹⁹ I tell you this beforehand, so that when it happens you will believe that I AM the Messiah. ²⁰ I tell

you the truth, anyone who welcomes my messenger is welcoming me, and anyone who welcomes me is welcoming the Father who sent me.'

## Where we end up

Jesus tells the disciples that not all of them are clean. He knew what Judas was about to do.

## My Reflections

# 70    The Passion: Prayer in the Garden

**Main Theme**

Christ submits completely to the will of the Father and his Kingdom purposes.

**Setting**

The Garden of Gethsemane

**Characters**

Jesus, Peter, James, and John

**Key Verse: Matthew 26:39**

He went on a little farther and bowed with his face to the ground, praying, 'My Father! If it is possible, let this cup of suffering be taken away from me. Yet I want your will to be done, not mine.'

Jesus prays in the Garden of Gethsemane.

## Key plot points

**v.36** – Late at night, Jesus takes his disciples to Gethsemane to pray.

**v.37–38** – He takes Peter, James, and John with him and asks them to stay awake with him while he prays.

**v.39** – He goes off alone, falls on his face, and cries out to the Father to let the cup of suffering pass from him. Jesus, however, submits to the will of the Father saying, "Yet I want your will to be done, not mine."

## Read the story Matthew 26:36–46

36 Then Jesus went with them to the olive grove called Gethsemane, and he said, 'Sit here while I go over there to pray.' 37 He took Peter and Zebedee's two sons, James and John, and he became anguished and distressed. 38 He told them, 'My soul is crushed with grief to the point of death. Stay here and keep watch with me.'

39 He went on a little farther and bowed with his face to the ground, praying, 'My Father! If it is possible, let this cup of suffering be taken away from me. Yet I want your will to be done, not mine.'

40 Then he returned to the disciples and found them asleep. He said to Peter, 'Couldn't you watch with me even one hour? 41 Keep watch

and pray, so that you will not give in to temptation. For the spirit is willing, but the body is weak!'

⁴² Then Jesus left them a second time and prayed, 'My Father! If this cup cannot be taken away unless I drink it, your will be done.' ⁴³ When he returned to them again, he found them sleeping, for they couldn't keep their eyes open.

⁴⁴ So he went to pray a third time, saying the same things again. ⁴⁵ Then he came to the disciples and said, 'Go ahead and sleep. Have your rest. But look – the time has come. The Son of Man is betrayed into the hands of sinners. ⁴⁶ Up, let's be going. Look, my betrayer is here!'

**v.40–41** – When he returns to the disciples they are sleeping. He urges them again to stay awake.

**v.42, 44** – He returns and prays in the same way two more times.

### Where we end up

When Jesus finishes, he rouses the disciples. His betrayer is arriving at Gethsemane as he speaks.

### Old Testament Foundation: Types of Christ

**Joseph:** A Picture of Christ (Genesis 37–45) – p. 44. The beloved of his father who was sent to his kinsman, and hated by his brothers, who plotted together to kill him. He was rejected by his brothers the first time and considered dead and sold for 'blood money' (pieces of silver). He was imprisoned with two criminals, one who 'died' and the other who 'lived' but then raised and exalted to a place of authority and power next to the king. He gives all honour to the king and delivers all glory and treasure into the king's hands. He brings his people to repentance and self-knowledge and is acknowledged to be the saviour of his people and their ruler.

### My Reflections

# 71  Betrayal in the Garden

**Main Theme**

Christ submits completely to the will of the Father and his Kingdom purposes.

**Setting**

The Garden of Gethsemane

**Characters**

Jesus, Judas, an armed crowd from the priests and elders, and Peter (the disciple with a sword)

**Key Verse: Matthew 26:53–54**

'Don't you realize that I could ask my Father for thousands of angels to protect us, and he would send them instantly? But if I did, how would the Scriptures be fulfilled that describe what must happen now?'

Judas betrays Jesus with a kiss.

## Key plot points

**v.47** – Judas has betrayed Jesus to the Jewish priests and elders. They give him an armed crowd to go to detain Jesus.

**v.48** – Judas arranges that he will kiss Jesus to identify him for the crowd.

**v.49** – When Judas arrives at Gethsemane, he greets Jesus with a kiss.

## Read the story Matthew 26:47–56

⁴⁷ And even as Jesus said this, Judas, one of the twelve disciples, arrived with a crowd of men armed with swords and clubs. They had been sent by the leading priests and elders of the people. ⁴⁸ The traitor, Judas, had given them a prearranged signal: 'You will know which one to arrest when I greet him with a kiss.' ⁴⁹ So Judas came straight to Jesus. 'Greetings, Rabbi!' he exclaimed and gave him the kiss.

⁵⁰ Jesus said, 'My friend, go ahead and do what you have come for.'

Then the others grabbed Jesus and arrested him. ⁵¹ But one of the men with Jesus pulled out his sword and struck the high priest's slave, slashing off his ear.

⁵² 'Put away your sword,' Jesus told him. 'Those who use the sword will die by the sword. ⁵³ Don't you realize that I could ask my Father for thousands of angels to protect us, and he would send them instantly? ⁵⁴ But if I did, how would the Scriptures be fulfilled that describe what must happen now?'

⁵⁵ Then Jesus said to the crowd, 'Am I some dangerous revolutionary, that you come with swords and clubs to arrest me? Why didn't you arrest me in the Temple? I was there teaching every day. ⁵⁶ But this is all happening to fulfil the words of the prophets as recorded in the Scriptures.' At that point, all the disciples deserted him and fled.

**v.50** – The armed crowd with Judas seizes Jesus.

**v.51** – One of Jesus' disciples (Peter) tries to defend Jesus by cutting off the ear of one of the crowd.

**v.52–54** – Jesus rebukes Peter, telling him that this must take place to fulfil the Scriptures.

## Where we end up

The disciples flee as Jesus is taken away.

## My Reflections

# 72  The Trial before Pilate

**Main Theme**

Christ offers himself as a spotless substitute to be sacrificed for sin.

**Setting**

The governor's headquarters

**Characters**

Jesus, Pilate (the Roman governor), Roman soldiers, and the Jewish religious leaders

**Key Verse: John 18:38**

'What is truth?' Pilate asked. Then he went out again to the people and told them, 'He is not guilty of any crime.'

The Jewish people convince Pilate to have Jesus killed.

## Read the story John 18:28 – 19:16

**18** <sup>28</sup> Jesus' trial before Caiaphas ended in the early hours of the morning. Then he was taken to the headquarters of the Roman governor. His accusers didn't go inside because it would defile them, and they wouldn't be allowed to celebrate the Passover. <sup>29</sup> So Pilate, the governor, went out to them and asked, 'What is your charge against this man?'

<sup>30</sup> 'We wouldn't have handed him over to you if he weren't a criminal!' they retorted.

<sup>31</sup> 'Then take him away and judge him by your own law,' Pilate told them.

'Only the Romans are permitted to execute someone,' the Jewish leaders replied. <sup>32</sup> (This fulfilled Jesus' prediction about the way he would die.)

<sup>33</sup> Then Pilate went back into his headquarters and called for Jesus to be brought to him. 'Are you the king of the Jews?' he asked him.

<sup>34</sup> Jesus replied, 'Is this your own question, or did others tell you about me?'

<sup>35</sup> 'Am I a Jew?' Pilate retorted. 'Your own people and their leading priests brought you to me for trial. Why? What have you done?'

<sup>36</sup> Jesus answered, 'My Kingdom is not an earthly kingdom. If it were, my followers would fight to keep me from being handed over to the Jewish leaders. But my Kingdom is not of this world.'

<sup>37</sup> Pilate said, 'So you are a king?'

Jesus responded, 'You say I am a king. Actually, I was born and came into the world to testify to the truth. All who love the truth recognize that what I say is true.'

<sup>38</sup> 'What is truth?' Pilate asked. Then he went out again to the people and told them, 'He is not guilty of any crime. <sup>39</sup> But you have a custom of asking me to release one prisoner each year at Passover. Would you like me to release this "King of the Jews"?'

<sup>40</sup> But they shouted back, 'No! Not this man. We want Barabbas!' (Barabbas was a revolutionary.)

**19** Then Pilate had Jesus flogged with a lead-tipped whip. <sup>2</sup> The soldiers wove a crown of thorns and put it on his head, and they put a purple robe on him. <sup>3</sup> 'Hail! King of the Jews!' they mocked, as they slapped him across the face.

## Key plot points

**v.28** – After questioning Jesus, the Jewish religious leaders take Jesus to Pilate, the Roman governor.

**v.31** – They request that Jesus be put to death.

**v.33–38** – Pilate questions Jesus but finds no guilt in him worthy of death.

**v.39** – He tries to free Jesus as the customary Passover prisoner release, but the leaders choose Barabbas instead.

**v.1–3** – Pilate has Jesus flogged and mocked.

**v.4–12** – Again Pilate presents Jesus to the people seeking to release Jesus.

[4] Pilate went outside again and said to the people, 'I am going to bring him out to you now, but understand clearly that I find him not guilty.' [5] Then Jesus came out wearing the crown of thorns and the purple robe. And Pilate said, 'Look, here is the man!'

[6] When they saw him, the leading priests and Temple guards began shouting, 'Crucify him! Crucify him!'

'Take him yourselves and crucify him,' Pilate said. 'I find him not guilty.'

[7] The Jewish leaders replied, 'By our law he ought to die because he called himself the Son of God.'

[8] When Pilate heard this, he was more frightened than ever. [9] He took Jesus back into the headquarters again and asked him, 'Where are you from?' But Jesus gave no answer. [10] 'Why don't you talk to me?' Pilate demanded. 'Don't you realize that I have the power to release you or crucify you?'

[11] Then Jesus said, 'You would have no power over me at all unless it were given to you from above. So the one who handed me over to you has the greater sin.'

[12] Then Pilate tried to release him, but the Jewish leaders shouted, 'If you release this man, you are no "friend of Caesar". Anyone who declares himself a king is a rebel against Caesar.'

[13] When they said this, Pilate brought Jesus out to them again. Then Pilate sat down on the judgement seat on the platform that is called the Stone Pavement (in Hebrew, Gabbatha). [14] It was now about noon on the day of preparation for the Passover. And Pilate said to the people, 'Look, here is your king!'

[15] 'Away with him,' they yelled. 'Away with him! Crucify him!'

'What? Crucify your king?' Pilate asked. 'We have no king but Caesar,' the leading priests shouted back.

[16] Then Pilate turned Jesus over to them to be crucified. So they took Jesus away.

## Where we end up

The people reject Jesus as their king and refuse to allow his release so Pilate hands Jesus over to be crucified.

# The Crucifixion: Jesus Carries His Cross

## 73

### Main Theme

Christ offers himself as a spotless substitute to be sacrificed, bearing our sins in his body on the cross.

### Setting

Golgotha (The Place of the Skull)

### Characters

Jesus, Pilate, Roman soldiers, John, Mary, and two other women

### Key Verse: John 19:18

There they nailed him to the cross. Two others were crucified with him, one on either side, with Jesus between them.

Jesus carries his cross to Golgotha.

## Read the story John 19:16–30

**16** Then Pilate turned Jesus over to them to be crucified.

So they took Jesus away. **17** Carrying the cross by himself, he went to the place called Place of the Skull (in Hebrew, Golgotha). **18** There they nailed him to the cross. Two others were crucified with him, one on

## Key plot points

**v.17** – Jesus carries his cross to Golgotha, where he will be crucified.

**v.18** – The Roman soldiers crucify Jesus.

**v.19** – Pilate writes an inscription to put on the cross, 'Jesus of Nazareth, the King of the Jews.'

**v.24** – In fulfilment of Scripture, the soldiers gamble over his tunic.

**v.26–27** – From the cross, Jesus appoints John to care for his mother, Mary.

either side, with Jesus between them. [19] And Pilate posted a sign on the cross that read, 'Jesus of Nazareth, the King of the Jews'. [20] The place where Jesus was crucified was near the city, and the sign was written in Hebrew, Latin, and Greek, so that many people could read it.

[21] Then the leading priests objected and said to Pilate, 'Change it from "The King of the Jews' to "He said, I am King of the Jews."'

[22] Pilate replied, 'No, what I have written, I have written.'

[23] When the soldiers had crucified Jesus, they divided his clothes among the four of them. They also took his robe, but it was seamless, woven in one piece from top to bottom. [24] So they said, 'Rather than tearing it apart, let's throw dice for it.' This fulfilled the Scripture that says, 'They divided my garments among themselves and threw dice for my clothing.' So that is what they did.

[25] Standing near the cross were Jesus' mother, and his mother's sister, Mary (the wife of Clopas), and Mary Magdalene. [26] When Jesus saw his mother standing there beside the disciple he loved, he said to her, 'Dear woman, here is your son.' [27] And he said to this disciple, 'Here is your mother.' And from then on this disciple took her into his home.

[28] Jesus knew that his mission was now finished, and to fulfil Scripture he said, 'I am thirsty.' [29] A jar of sour wine was sitting there, so they soaked a sponge in it, put it on a hyssop branch, and held it up to his lips. [30] When Jesus had tasted it, he said, 'It is finished!' Then he bowed his head and gave up his spirit.

## Where we end up

After receiving a drink of sour wine, Jesus declares, 'It is finished,' and he dies.

## Old Testament Foundation: Jesus' Death Foreshadowed

**The Scapegoat:** 'He will lay both of his hands on the goat's head and confess over it all the wickedness, rebellion, and sins of the people of Israel. In this way, he will transfer the people's sins to the head of the goat. Then a man specially chosen for the task will drive the goat into the wilderness' (Leviticus 16:20–21). As the high priest laid all the sin of Israel on the scapegoat, so all human iniquities (sins) are laid on Christ.

**Abraham Sacrificing Isaac** (Genesis 22:1–19) – p. 41. The Lord stopped Abraham before he killed his beloved son, Isaac, and provided a ram as a substitute. God the Father put forward his own beloved Son as our substitute for all human sin.

# The Crucifixion: Jesus and the Two Criminals

## 74

## Main Theme

Christ offers himself as a spotless substitute to be sacrificed so we can be forgiven.

## Setting

Golgotha, while Jesus is hanging on the cross

## Characters

Jesus and two criminals crucified with him

## Key Verse: Luke 23:42–43

Then he said, 'Jesus, remember me when you come into your Kingdom.' And Jesus replied, 'I assure you, today you will be with me in paradise.'

Jesus is crucified between two criminals.

## Read the story Luke 23:32–43

³² Two others, both criminals, were led out to be executed with him. ³³ When they came to a place called The Skull, they nailed him to the cross. And the criminals were also crucified – one on his right and one on his left.

## Key plot points

**v.33** – Jesus is crucified in the middle of two criminals.

**v.34** – Jesus asks his Father to forgive the soldiers, because they do not understand what they are doing.

**v.36** – The soldiers continue to mock Jesus.

**v.39** – As he is suffering on the cross, one of the criminals begins to mock him as well.

**v.40–41** – The other criminal stops him, saying that Jesus has done nothing wrong to deserve this punishment.

**v.42** – He asks Jesus to remember him when he comes into his Kingdom.

³⁴ Jesus said, 'Father, forgive them, for they don't know what they are doing.' And the soldiers gambled for his clothes by throwing dice.

³⁵ The crowd watched and the leaders scoffed. 'He saved others,' they said, 'let him save himself if he is really God's Messiah, the Chosen One.' ³⁶ The soldiers mocked him, too, by offering him a drink of sour wine. ³⁷ They called out to him, 'If you are the King of the Jews, save yourself!' ³⁸ A sign was fastened above him with these words: 'This is the King of the Jews.'

³⁹ One of the criminals hanging beside him scoffed, 'So you're the Messiah, are you? Prove it by saving yourself – and us, too, while you're at it!'

⁴⁰ But the other criminal protested, 'Don't you fear God even when you have been sentenced to die? ⁴¹ We deserve to die for our crimes, but this man hasn't done anything wrong.' ⁴² Then he said, 'Jesus, remember me when you come into your Kingdom.'

⁴³ And Jesus replied, 'I assure you, today you will be with me in paradise.'

## Where we end up

Jesus tells the repentant criminal that today, he will be with him in paradise.

## Old Testament Foundation: Pictures of Christ's Sacrifice

**The Bronze Serpent:** 'Then the LORD told him (Moses), "Make a replica of a poisonous snake and attach it to a pole. All who are bitten will live if they simply look at it!" So Moses made a snake out of bronze and attached it to a pole. Then anyone who was bitten by a snake could look at the bronze snake and be healed!' (Numbers 21:8–9). As Moses lifted up the bronze serpent in the wilderness, so Jesus was lifted up on the cross for the healing of God's people.

**The Lamb on the Altar:** 'Your Passover sacrifice may be from either the flock or the herd, and it must be sacrificed to the LORD your God at the designated place of worship – the place he chooses for his name to be honoured' (Deuteronomy 16:2).

**The Blood on the Doorposts** (Exodus 12:7–13) – p. 56. As the spotless lamb is slaughtered, and the children of Israel are saved by its blood, so too Christ as the spotless Passover lamb has been slain and his blood redeems humankind from death.

# The Crucifixion: The Onlookers

## 75

## Main Theme

Christ offers himself as a spotless substitute to be sacrificed for the reconciliation of all things to God.

## Setting

Golgotha, while Jesus is hanging on the cross, and the Temple

## Characters

Jesus, a centurion, and the women who had been following Jesus

## Key Verse: Matthew 27:51

At that moment the curtain in the sanctuary of the Temple was torn in two, from top to bottom. The earth shook, rocks split apart.

Darkness covers the land and Jesus' followers look on from a distance.

## Key plot points

**v.45** – As Jesus hangs on the cross, darkness covers the land in the middle of the day.
**v.46** – Jesus cries out, 'My God, my God, why have you abandoned me?'

**v.50** – He submits his spirit to death.

**v.51** – As he dies, the curtain in the Temple that sections off the Holy of Holies rips in two from the top.
**v.51–52** – There is a great earthquake and many dead saints are raised to life.

**v.54** – The centurion who was guarding the cross exclaims in amazement, 'This man truly was the Son of God!'

## Read the story Matthew 27:45–56

[45] At midday, darkness fell across the whole land until three o'clock. [46] At about three o'clock, Jesus called out with a loud voice, 'Eli, Eli, lema sabachthani?' which means 'My God, my God, why have you abandoned me?'

[47] Some of the bystanders misunderstood and thought he was calling for the prophet Elijah. [48] One of them ran and filled a sponge with sour wine, holding it up to him on a reed stick so he could drink. [49] But the rest said, 'Wait! Let's see whether Elijah comes to save him.'

[50] Then Jesus shouted out again, and he released his spirit. [51] At that moment the curtain in the sanctuary of the Temple was torn in two, from top to bottom. The earth shook, rocks split apart, [52] and tombs opened. The bodies of many godly men and women who had died were raised from the dead. [53] They left the cemetery after Jesus' resurrection, went into the holy city of Jerusalem, and appeared to many people.

[54] The Roman officer and the other soldiers at the crucifixion were terrified by the earthquake and all that had happened. They said, 'This man truly was the Son of God!'

[55] And many women who had come from Galilee with Jesus to look after him were watching from a distance. [56] Among them were Mary Magdalene, Mary (the mother of James and Joseph), and the mother of James and John, the sons of Zebedee.

## Where we end up

Many women who had followed Jesus also watch everything unfold from a distance.

# The Burial of Jesus

## 76

**Main Theme**

Christ offers himself as a spotless substitute to be sacrificed and conquer death.

**Setting**

A garden near Golgotha

**Characters**

Joseph of Arimathea, Pilate, and Nicodemus

**Key Verse: John 19:38**

Afterward Joseph of Arimathea, who had been a secret disciple of Jesus (because he feared the Jewish leaders), asked Pilate for permission to take down Jesus' body. When Pilate gave permission, Joseph came and took the body away

Joseph of Arimathea and Nicodemus prepare to put Jesus in a tomb.

## Key plot points

**v.38** — Joseph of Arimathea has been a secret disciple of Jesus out of fear of the Jewish leaders. After the death of Jesus, Joseph asks Pilate if he can take down Jesus' body. Pilate agrees.

**v.39–40** — Nicodemus and Joseph prepare Jesus' body for burial by wrapping him in linen cloth that is rubbed with myrrh and aloes.

## Read the story John 19:38–42

³⁸ Afterwards Joseph of Arimathea, who had been a secret disciple of Jesus (because he feared the Jewish leaders), asked Pilate for permission to take down Jesus' body. When Pilate gave permission, Joseph came and took the body away. ³⁹ With him came Nicodemus, the man who had come to Jesus at night. He brought about thirty-five kilograms of perfumed ointment made from myrrh and aloes. ⁴⁰ Following Jewish burial custom, they wrapped Jesus' body with the spices in long sheets of linen cloth. ⁴¹ The place of crucifixion was near a garden, where there was a new tomb, never used before. ⁴² And so, because it was the day of preparation for the Jewish Passover and since the tomb was close at hand, they laid Jesus there.

### Where we end up

They place Jesus in an empty tomb in a garden near Golgotha.

### My Reflections

# The Guards at the Tomb: Part 1

**Main Theme**

Christ has risen from the dead, victorious over the grave.

**Setting**

Pilate's headquarters and the tomb of Jesus

**Characters**

The chief priests, Pharisees, Pilate, and guards

**Key Verse: Matthew 27:65–66**

Pilate replied, 'Take guards and secure it the best you can.' So they sealed the tomb and posted guards to protect it.

Roman soldiers guard Jesus' tomb.

## Key plot points

**v.62** – The day after Jesus' crucifixion, the chief priests and Pharisees gather before Pilate.

**v.63** – They remind Pilate that Jesus had predicted that he would rise from the dead.

**v.64** – They ask Pilate to make the tomb secure so that Jesus' disciples cannot come steal the body and falsely claim that Jesus has risen from the dead.

## Read the story Matthew 27:62–66

⁶² The next day, on the Sabbath, the leading priests and Pharisees went to see Pilate. ⁶³ They told him, 'Sir, we remember what that deceiver once said while he was still alive: "After three days I will rise from the dead." ⁶⁴ So we request that you seal the tomb until the third day. This will prevent his disciples from coming and stealing his body and then telling everyone he was raised from the dead! If that happens, we'll be worse off than we were at first.'

⁶⁵ Pilate replied, 'Take guards and secure it the best you can.' ⁶⁶ So they sealed the tomb and posted guards to protect it.

### Where we end up

Pilate grants the request, and they make the tomb as secure as they can.

---

### Old Testament Foundation: Pictures of Christ's Sacrifice

**The Captivity** (2 Chronicles 36:15–18 ) – p. 130. As God's people are exiled as captives, so Christ is exiled to the captivity of the grave.

**Jonah** (Jonah 1–4) – p. 125. As Jonah was in the belly of the whale three days and three nights, so Jesus rose on the third day.

---

### My Reflections

# The Guards at the Tomb: Part 2

## Main Theme
Christ has risen from the dead, victorious over death.

## Setting
The tomb of Jesus

## Key Verse: Matthew 28:2
Suddenly there was a great earthquake! For an angel of the Lord came down from heaven, rolled aside the stone, and sat on it.

## Characters
Mary Magdalene, another woman named Mary, an angel of the Lord, and the guards at the tomb

Terrified guards flee the tomb.

## Key plot points

**v.1** – At dawn on the first day of the week, Mary Magdalene and another woman named Mary go to the tomb of Jesus.

**v.2** – There is a great earthquake, and an angel of the Lord comes from heaven and rolls away the stone that covers the entrance to the tomb and sits on it.

## Read the story Matthew 28:1–4

¹ Early on Sunday morning, as the new day was dawning, Mary Magdalene and the other Mary went out to visit the tomb.

² Suddenly there was a great earthquake! For an angel of the Lord came down from heaven, rolled aside the stone, and sat on it. ³ His face shone like lightning, and his clothing was as white as snow. ⁴ The guards shook with fear when they saw him, and they fell into a dead faint.

## Where we end up

The guards that had been stationed by the chief priests and Pharisees faint in terror.

## My Reflections

# The Women at the Tomb

## 79

## Main Theme

Christ has risen from the dead and lives forevermore.

## Setting

The tomb of Jesus

## Characters

Two men in dazzling clothing, three women who had followed Jesus, and Peter

## Key Verse: Luke 24:6–7

'He isn't here! He is risen from the dead! Remember what he told you back in Galilee, that the Son of Man must be betrayed into the hands of sinful men and be crucified, and that he would rise again on the third day.'

Three women come to Jesus' tomb and find it open and empty.

## Key plot points

**v.1** – Three women who had watched where Jesus had been buried came to the tomb. They were wondering how they were going to roll away the stone.

**v.2–3** – When they arrive at the tomb, they are shocked to find the stone rolled away, and the tomb empty.

**v.4–5** – In the confusion, two angelic men appear to them. They ask why the women are seeking Jesus among the dead.

**v.6** – Jesus is not in the tomb. He is risen, just as he promised!

**v.9** – The women return to the disciples to tell them what they had seen and heard.

## Read the story Luke 24:1–12

¹ But very early on Sunday morning the women went to the tomb, taking the spices they had prepared. They found that the stone had been rolled away from the entrance. ³ So they went in, but they didn't find the body of the Lord Jesus. ⁴ As they stood there puzzled, two men suddenly appeared to them, clothed in dazzling robes.

⁵ The women were terrified and bowed with their faces to the ground. Then the men asked, 'Why are you looking among the dead for someone who is alive? ⁶ He isn't here! He is risen from the dead! Remember what he told you back in Galilee, ⁷ that the Son of Man must be betrayed into the hands of sinful men and be crucified, and that he would rise again on the third day.'

⁸ Then they remembered that he had said this. ⁹ So they rushed back from the tomb to tell his eleven disciples – and everyone else – what had happened. ¹⁰ It was Mary Magdalene, Joanna, Mary the mother of James, and several other women who told the apostles what had happened. ¹¹ But the story sounded like nonsense to the men, so they didn't believe it. ¹² However, Peter jumped up and ran to the tomb to look. Stooping, he peered in and saw the empty linen wrappings; then he went home again, wondering what had happened.

### Where we end up

Only Peter is willing to believe the women. He runs to the tomb and finds it empty, just as the women had said.

# Jesus Appears to Mary

## 80

**Main Theme**

Christ has risen from the dead and will wipe away all our tears.

**Setting**

Outside the tomb of Jesus

**Characters**

Mary Magdalene and Jesus

**Key Verse: John 20.16**

'Mary!' Jesus said. She turned to him and cried out, 'Rabboni!' (which is Hebrew for 'Teacher').

Jesus appears to Mary Magdalene.

## Key plot points

**v.11** – Mary Magdalene is weeping outside Jesus' tomb.

**v.12–13** – Two angels ask Mary why she is weeping. She is confused and afraid that someone has stolen Jesus' body.

**v.14** – When Mary turns around she sees another man.

**v.15** – Assuming him to be a gardener, she asks him where Jesus' body has gone.

**v.16** – Jesus speaks her name, 'Mary,' and she recognizes him.

## Read the story John 20:11–18

¹¹ Mary was standing outside the tomb crying, and as she wept, she stooped and looked in. ¹² She saw two white-robed angels, one sitting at the head and the other at the foot of the place where the body of Jesus had been lying. ¹³ 'Dear woman, why are you crying?' the angels asked her.

'Because they have taken away my Lord,' she replied, 'and I don't know where they have put him.'

¹⁴ She turned to leave and saw someone standing there. It was Jesus, but she didn't recognize him. ¹⁵ 'Dear woman, why are you crying?' Jesus asked her. 'Who are you looking for?'

She thought he was the gardener. 'Sir,' she said, 'if you have taken him away, tell me where you have put him, and I will go and get him.'

¹⁶ 'Mary!' Jesus said.

She turned to him and cried out, 'Rabboni!' (which is Hebrew for 'Teacher').

¹⁷ 'Don't cling to me,' Jesus said, 'for I haven't yet ascended to the Father. But go and find my brothers and tell them, "I am ascending to my Father and your Father, to my God and your God."'

¹⁸ Mary Magdalene found the disciples and told them, 'I have seen the Lord!' Then she gave them his message.

### Where we end up

Jesus sends Mary to the disciples to tell them that he is risen from the dead.

### My Reflections

# Jesus Appears to the Disciples

## 81

**Main Theme**

Christ the risen Lord appears to his disciples, fulfilling all the Scriptures.

**Setting**

A house in Jerusalem

**Characters**

The disciples and Jesus

**Key Verse: Luke 24:44**

Then he said, 'When I was with you before, I told you that everything written about me in the law of Moses and the prophets and in the Psalms must be fulfilled.'

After his resurrection, Jesus appears to his disciples.

## Key plot points

**v.36** – The disciples are together talking about Jesus being raised from the dead. Suddenly, Jesus simply appears in their midst.

**v.37** – The disciples are scared and think they are seeing a ghost.

**v.40–43** – He calms the disciples by inviting them to touch his hands and feet. He also eats some fish for them to see.

**v.44–45** – Jesus opens the disciples' minds to understand the Scriptures and to see that he is the one who fulfils all the Law, the Prophets, and the Psalms (the whole Old Testament).

## Read the story Luke 24:36–49

36 And just as they were telling about it, Jesus himself was suddenly standing there among them. 'Peace be with you,' he said. 37 But the whole group was startled and frightened, thinking they were seeing a ghost!

38 'Why are you frightened?' he asked. 'Why are your hearts filled with doubt? 39 Look at my hands. Look at my feet. You can see that it's really me. Touch me and make sure that I am not a ghost, because ghosts don't have bodies, as you see that I do.' 40 As he spoke, he showed them his hands and his feet.

41 Still they stood there in disbelief, filled with joy and wonder. Then he asked them, 'Do you have anything here to eat?' 42 They gave him a piece of broiled fish, 43 and he ate it as they watched.

44 Then he said, 'When I was with you before, I told you that everything written about me in the law of Moses and the prophets and in the Psalms must be fulfilled.' 45 Then he opened their minds to understand the Scriptures. 46 And he said, 'Yes, it was written long ago that the Messiah would suffer and die and rise from the dead on the third day. 47 It was also written that this message would be proclaimed in the authority of his name to all the nations, beginning in Jerusalem: "There is forgiveness of sins for all who repent." 48 You are witnesses of all these things.

49 'And now I will send the Holy Spirit, just as my Father promised. But stay here in the city until the Holy Spirit comes and fills you with power from heaven.'

## Where we end up

Jesus commissions his disciples as witnesses to proclaim Christ to all nations and he promises to clothe them with power from on high.

# The Great Commission

## 82

**Main Theme**

Christ the risen Lord sends his disciples to gather all nations into his Kingdom.

**Setting**

A mountain in Galilee

**Characters**

Jesus and the eleven disciples

**Key Verse: Matthew 28:19**

'Therefore, go and make disciples of all the nations, baptizing them in the name of the Father and the Son and the Holy Spirit.'

'Therefore, go and make disciples of all nations …'

## Key plot points

**v.16** – The disciples travel to a mountain in Galilee where Jesus has directed them.

**v.17** – When Jesus comes they worship him, but some doubt.

**v.18** – Jesus declares that all authority in heaven and on earth has been given to him.

**v.19–20** – Jesus commissions his disciples to go and make disciples of all nations, baptizing them in the name of the Father and of the Son and of the Holy Spirit, and to teach them to observe all that he had commanded.

## Read the story Matthew 28:16–20

[16] Then the eleven disciples left for Galilee, going to the mountain where Jesus had told them to go. [17] When they saw him, they worshipped him – but some of them doubted!

[18] Jesus came and told his disciples, 'I have been given all authority in heaven and on earth. [19] Therefore, go and make disciples of all the nations, baptizing them in the name of the Father and the Son and the Holy Spirit. [20] Teach these new disciples to obey all the commands I have given you. And be sure of this: I am with you always, even to the end of the age.'

### Where we end up

Jesus promises that he is with them always, to the end of the age.

## My Reflections

# The Ascension of Christ

## 83

### Main Theme

Christ ascends to the right hand of the Father where he reigns until all his enemies are put under his feet.

### Setting

The Mount of Olives

### Characters

Jesus, the disciples, and two angelic men

### Key Verse: Acts 1:8

'But you will receive power when the Holy Spirit comes upon you. And you will be my witnesses, telling people about me everywhere – in Jerusalem, throughout Judea, in Samaria, and to the ends of the earth.'

Jesus ascends to the right hand of the Father.

## Key plot points

**v.6** – Jesus is talking with his disciples on the Mount of Olives. They ask him if it is time for him to restore the kingdom to Israel.

**v.7** – Jesus explains that only the Father knows the times for these things.

**v.8** – He promises to send the Holy Spirit to empower them to be his witnesses to the whole world.

**v.9** – As he is speaking, he lifts off the ground and ascends into the sky until the clouds hide him.

**v.10** – The disciples are left staring into the sky.

## Read the story Acts 1.6–11

⁶ So when the apostles were with Jesus, they kept asking him, 'Lord, has the time come for you to free Israel and restore our kingdom?'

⁷ He replied, 'The Father alone has the authority to set those dates and times, and they are not for you to know. ⁸ But you will receive power when the Holy Spirit comes upon you. And you will be my witnesses, telling people about me everywhere – in Jerusalem, throughout Judea, in Samaria, and to the ends of the earth.'

⁹ After saying this, he was taken up into a cloud while they were watching, and they could no longer see him. ¹⁰ As they strained to see him rising into heaven, two white-robed men suddenly stood among them. ¹¹ 'Men of Galilee,' they said, 'why are you standing here staring into heaven? Jesus has been taken from you into heaven, but some day he will return from heaven in the same way you saw him go!'

### Where we end up

Two angelic men appear and ask the disciples what they are doing. They tell the disciples that Jesus has ascended to heaven and remind them that Jesus promised to return in the same way.

### Old Testament Foundation: The Triumph of the Son of Man

**Elijah Taken into Heaven:** 'As they were walking along and talking, suddenly a chariot of fire appeared, drawn by horses of fire. It drove between the two men, separating them, and Elijah was carried by a whirlwind into heaven' (2 Kings 2:11). As Elijah was taken up into heaven never to taste death, so the risen Lord is taken up into heaven and eternal life.

**Melchizedek** (Genesis 14:17–24) – p. 36. The Lord Jesus ascends to the right hand of the Father where he waits for his enemies to be made a footstool for his feet, where he is both king and priest forever after the order of Melchizedek.

# The Coming of the Holy Spirit

## 84

### Main Theme
The Lord sends his Holy Spirit, personally dwelling among his people to empower and guide us.

### Setting
A house in Jerusalem

### Characters
Many followers of Jesus and a diverse international crowd of Jews

### Key Verse: Acts 2:3–4
Then, what looked like flames or tongues of fire appeared and settled on each of them. And everyone present was filled with the Holy Spirit and began speaking in other languages, as the Holy Spirit gave them this ability.

The Holy Spirit comes on the believers at Pentecost.

## Read the story Acts 2:1–47

¹ On the day of Pentecost all the believers were meeting together in one place. ² Suddenly, there was a sound from heaven like the roaring of a mighty windstorm, and it filled the house where they were sitting. ³ Then, what looked like flames or tongues of fire appeared and settled on each of them. ⁴ And everyone present was filled with the Holy

## Key plot points

**v.1** – A large group of Jesus' followers are gathered in Jerusalem during the Jewish festival of Pentecost. Pentecost celebrated the first fruits of the wheat harvest.

**v.2** – Suddenly there is a sound like a mighty rushing wind.

**v.3–4** — The Holy Spirit descends in the form of 'tongues of fire' that enable the believers to proclaim the Gospel in foreign languages.

**v.5–6** — People had come from all over the world for the festival. Each of them heard the Gospel in their own language.

**v.14, 17** — Peter, the leader of the apostles, stood up in the crowd and declared boldly that the arrival of the Holy Spirit marks the dawn of 'the last days.'

Spirit and began speaking in other languages, as the Holy Spirit gave them this ability.

⁵ At that time there were devout Jews from every nation living in Jerusalem. ⁶ When they heard the loud noise, everyone came running, and they were bewildered to hear their own languages being spoken by the believers.

⁷ They were completely amazed. 'How can this be?' they exclaimed. 'These people are all from Galilee, ⁸ and yet we hear them speaking in our own native languages! ⁹ Here we are – Parthians, Medes, Elamites, people from Mesopotamia, Judea, Cappadocia, Pontus, the province of Asia, ¹⁰ Phrygia, Pamphylia, Egypt, and the areas of Libya around Cyrene, visitors from Rome ¹¹ (both Jews and converts to Judaism), Cretans, and Arabs. And we all hear these people speaking in our own languages about the wonderful things God has done!' ¹² They stood there amazed and perplexed. 'What can this mean?' they asked each other.

¹³ But others in the crowd ridiculed them, saying, 'They're just drunk, that's all!'

¹⁴ Then Peter stepped forward with the eleven other apostles and shouted to the crowd, 'Listen carefully, all of you, fellow Jews and residents of Jerusalem! Make no mistake about this. ¹⁵ These people are not drunk, as some of you are assuming. Nine o'clock in the morning is much too early for that. ¹⁶ No, what you see was predicted long ago by the prophet Joel:

¹⁷ "In the last days", God says,
　　"I will pour out my Spirit upon all people.
　Your sons and daughters will prophesy.
　　Your young men will see visions,
　　and your old men will dream dreams.
¹⁸ In those days I will pour out my Spirit
　　even on my servants – men and women alike –
　　and they will prophesy.
¹⁹ And I will cause wonders in the heavens above
　　and signs on the earth below –
　　blood and fire and clouds of smoke.
²⁰ The sun will become dark,
　　and the moon will turn blood red
　　before that great and glorious day of the LORD arrives.

²¹ But everyone who calls on the name of the Lord
    will be saved."

²² 'People of Israel, listen! God publicly endorsed Jesus the Nazarene by doing powerful miracles, wonders, and signs through him, as you well know. ²³ But God knew what would happen, and his prearranged plan was carried out when Jesus was betrayed. With the help of lawless Gentiles, you nailed him to a cross and killed him. ²⁴ But God released him from the horrors of death and raised him back to life, for death could not keep him in its grip. ²⁵ King David said this about him:

"I see that the Lord is always with me.
    I will not be shaken, for he is right beside me.
²⁶ No wonder my heart is glad,
    and my tongue shouts his praises!
    My body rests in hope.
²⁷ For you will not leave my soul among the dead
    or allow your Holy One to rot in the grave.
²⁸ You have shown me the way of life,
    and you will fill me with the joy of your presence."

²⁹ 'Dear brothers, think about this! You can be sure that the patriarch David wasn't referring to himself, for he died and was buried, and his tomb is still here among us. ³⁰ But he was a prophet, and he knew God had promised with an oath that one of David's own descendants would sit on his throne. ³¹ David was looking into the future and speaking of the Messiah's resurrection. He was saying that God would not leave him among the dead or allow his body to rot in the grave.

³² 'God raised Jesus from the dead, and we are all witnesses of this. ³³ Now he is exalted to the place of highest honour in heaven, at God's right hand. And the Father, as he had promised, gave him the Holy Spirit to pour out upon us, just as you see and hear today. ³⁴ For David himself never ascended into heaven, yet he said,

"The Lord said to my Lord,
    'Sit in the place of honour at my right hand
³⁵ until I humble your enemies,
    making them a footstool under your feet.'"

**v.36** – According to Peter, the arrival of the Holy Spirit at Pentecost is the sign that 'God has made this Jesus, whom you crucified, to be both Lord and Messiah!'

**v.41** – After he preaches, the listeners repent and receive baptism as a sign of their faith in Jesus as the Christ, sent from God.

³⁶ 'So let everyone in Israel know for certain that God has made this Jesus, whom you crucified, to be both Lord and Messiah!'

³⁷ Peter's words pierced their hearts, and they said to him and to the other apostles, 'Brothers, what should we do?'

³⁸ Peter replied, 'Each of you must repent of your sins and turn to God, and be baptized in the name of Jesus Christ for the forgiveness of your sins. Then you will receive the gift of the Holy Spirit. ³⁹ This promise is to you, to your children, and to those far away – all who have been called by the Lord our God.' ⁴⁰ Then Peter continued preaching for a long time, strongly urging all his listeners, 'Save yourselves from this crooked generation!'

⁴¹ Those who believed what Peter said were baptized and added to the church that day – about 3,000 in all.

⁴² All the believers devoted themselves to the apostles' teaching, and to fellowship, and to sharing in meals (including the Lord's Supper), and to prayer.

⁴³ A deep sense of awe came over them all, and the apostles performed many miraculous signs and wonders. ⁴⁴ And all the believers met together in one place and shared everything they had. ⁴⁵ They sold their property and possessions and shared the money with those in need. ⁴⁶ They worshipped together at the Temple each day, met in homes for the Lord's Supper, and shared their meals with great joy and generosity – ⁴⁷ all the while praising God and enjoying the goodwill of all the people. And each day the Lord added to their fellowship those who were being saved.

## Where we end up

The early Church shares everything in common, listening to the apostles' teachings, sharing meals, praying, and praising God.

## Old Testament Foundation: Dry Bones Can Live Again

**The Valley of Dry Bones** (Ezekiel 37:1–14) – p. 133. The Lord fulfils his vision to Ezekiel when he sends forth his Spirit and gives eternal life to his people.

**The Spirit Spoke through the Prophets:** 'Then, after doing all those things, I will pour out my Spirit upon all people. Your sons and daughters will prophesy. Your old men will dream dreams, and your young men will see visions.' (Joel 2:28) – p. 161. The Spirit of God that spoke by the prophets is poured out on the Church, signalling the beginning of the last days.

# Paul's Missionary Journeys

## Main Theme

As ambassadors of the Kingdom, the Church proclaims Jesus as Lord.

## Setting

The Temple in Jerusalem

## Characters

Paul, a crowd of Jews, and Roman soldiers

## Key Verse: Acts 22:7–8

'I fell to the ground and heard a voice saying to me, "Saul, Saul, why are you persecuting me?" "Who are you, lord?" I asked. And the voice replied, "I am Jesus the Nazarene, the one you are persecuting."'

Paul shares the testimony (story) of his conversion and calling.

## Key plot points

**Introduction** – Paul has been attacked by a crowd in the Temple in Jerusalem, and Roman soldiers have detained him for questioning. Paul asks if he can address the crowd.

**v.3–4** – Paul tells the crowd that he also once hated and persecuted the followers of Jesus.

**v.6–10** – However, one day on the way to persecute believers in Damascus, the Lord appeared to him.

**v.11–13** – After three days of blindness, Paul was baptized by Ananias.

**v.17–18** – Paul then escaped from harm in Jerusalem, having been warned in a vision.

## Read the story Acts 22:1–21

[1] Paul said, 'Listen to me as I offer my defence.' [2] When they heard him speaking in their own language, the silence was even greater.

[3] Then Paul said, 'I am a Jew, born in Tarsus, a city in Cilicia, and I was brought up and educated here in Jerusalem under Gamaliel. As his student, I was carefully trained in our Jewish laws and customs. I became very zealous to honour God in everything I did, just like all of you today. [4] And I persecuted the followers of the Way, hounding some to death, arresting both men and women and throwing them in prison. [5] The high priest and the whole council of elders can testify that this is so. For I received letters from them to our Jewish brothers in Damascus, authorizing me to bring the followers of the Way from there to Jerusalem, in chains, to be punished.

[6] 'As I was on the road, approaching Damascus about midday, a very bright light from heaven suddenly shone down around me. [7] I fell to the ground and heard a voice saying to me, "Saul, Saul, why are you persecuting me?"

[8] '"Who are you, lord?" I asked.

'And the voice replied, "I am Jesus the Nazarene, the one you are persecuting." [9] The people with me saw the light but didn't understand the voice speaking to me.

[10] 'I asked, "What should I do, Lord?"

'And the Lord told me, "Get up and go into Damascus, and there you will be told everything you are to do."

[11] 'I was blinded by the intense light and had to be led by the hand to Damascus by my companions. [12] A man named Ananias lived there. He was a godly man, deeply devoted to the law, and well regarded by all the Jews of Damascus. [13] He came and stood beside me and said, "Brother Saul, regain your sight." And that very moment I could see him!

[14] 'Then he told me, "The God of our ancestors has chosen you to know his will and to see the Righteous One and hear him speak. [15] For you are to be his witness, telling everyone what you have seen and heard. [16] What are you waiting for? Get up and be baptized. Have your sins washed away by calling on the name of the Lord."

[17] 'After I returned to Jerusalem, I was praying in the Temple and fell into a trance. [18] I saw a vision of Jesus saying to me, "Hurry! Leave Jerusalem, for the people here won't accept your testimony about me."

**19** "'But Lord,' I argued, "they certainly know that in every synagogue I imprisoned and beat those who believed in you. **20** And I was in complete agreement when your witness Stephen was killed. I stood by and kept the coats they took off when they stoned him."

**21** 'But the Lord said to me, "Go, for I will send you far away to the Gentiles!"'

## Where we end up
The Lord sent Paul to the Gentiles (non-Jews) to proclaim the Gospel.

## My Reflections

# 86 Paul, Ambassador in Chains

The apostle Paul is imprisoned for his Gospel testimony.

## Main Theme

As ambassadors of God's Kingdom, the Church suffers with Christ in order to be glorified with him.

## Setting

Philippi

## Characters

Paul, Silas (Paul's travelling partner), Lydia (a merchant), and a jailer

## Key Verse: Acts 16:30–31

Then he brought them out and asked, 'Sirs, what must I do to be saved?' They replied, 'Believe in the Lord Jesus and you will be saved, along with everyone in your household.'

## Key plot points

**Introduction** – Paul and Silas preach the Gospel in Philippi. Lydia, a merchant, hears the message and believes. She is baptized along with her whole household.

**v.16–23** – While in Philippi, Paul and Silas are imprisoned for casting the demon out of a young girl.

## Read the story Acts 16:16–34

16 One day as we were going down to the place of prayer, we met a slave girl who had a spirit that enabled her to tell the future. She earned a lot of money for her masters by telling fortunes. 17 She followed Paul and the rest of us, shouting, 'These men are servants of the Most High God, and they have come to tell you how to be saved.'

18 This went on day after day until Paul got so exasperated that he turned and said to the demon within her, 'I command you in the name of Jesus Christ to come out of her.' And instantly it left her.

¹⁹ Her masters' hopes of wealth were now shattered, so they grabbed Paul and Silas and dragged them before the authorities at the market-place. ²⁰ 'The whole city is in an uproar because of these Jews!' they shouted to the city officials. ²¹ 'They are teaching customs that are illegal for us Romans to practise.'

²² A mob quickly formed against Paul and Silas, and the city officials ordered them stripped and beaten with wooden rods. ²³ They were severely beaten, and then they were thrown into prison. The jailer was ordered to make sure they didn't escape. ²⁴ So the jailer put them into the inner dungeon and clamped their feet in the stocks.

²⁵ Around midnight Paul and Silas were praying and singing hymns to God, and the other prisoners were listening. ²⁶ Suddenly, there was a massive earthquake, and the prison was shaken to its foundations. All the doors immediately flew open, and the chains of every prisoner fell off! ²⁷ The jailer woke up to see the prison doors wide open. He assumed the prisoners had escaped, so he drew his sword to kill himself. ²⁸ But Paul shouted to him, 'Stop! Don't kill yourself! We are all here!'

²⁹ The jailer called for lights and ran to the dungeon and fell down trembling before Paul and Silas. ³⁰ Then he brought them out and asked, 'Sirs, what must I do to be saved?'

³¹ They replied, 'Believe in the Lord Jesus and you will be saved, along with everyone in your household.' ³² And they shared the word of the Lord with him and with all who lived in his household. ³³ Even at that hour of the night, the jailer cared for them and washed their wounds. Then he and everyone in his household were immediately baptized. ³⁴ He brought them into his house and set a meal before them, and he and his entire household rejoiced because they all believed in God.

**v.25** – In prison, Paul and Silas sing and praise the Lord.

**v.26** – Suddenly, all the doors of the prison open and the prisoners' chains fall off.

**v.27–28** – Paul stops the jailer from killing himself, telling him that no one has escaped.

**v.29–30** – The jailer is amazed and asks how he can be saved. Paul tells him, 'Believe in the Lord Jesus and you will be saved, along with everyone in your household.'

## Where we end up

The jailer and his whole household believe and are baptized. He brings Paul and Silas to his house for a joyful feast.

## Old Testament Foundation: The Lord Delivers

**Daniel in the Lions' Den** (Daniel 6) – p. 139. As the Lord delivered Daniel from the mouths of the lions, so the Lord delivered Paul from terrible opposition and threats as he preached the Gospel (2 Timothy 4:16).

# 87 Salvation to the World

## Main Theme

By his own grace, God has invited everyone everywhere into his Kingdom through faith in Jesus Christ.

## Setting

The whole earth

## Characters

The Holy Spirit, the apostles, and the Church

## Key Verse: Acts 10:42–43

'And he ordered us to preach everywhere and to testify that Jesus is the one appointed by God to be the judge of all – the living and the dead. He is the one all the prophets testified about, saying that everyone who believes in him will have their sins forgiven through his name.'

Repentance and forgiveness of sins in the name of Jesus is proclaimed to all nations.

# Read the story Acts 10:34–43

³⁴ Then Peter replied, 'I see very clearly that God shows no favouritism. ³⁵ In every nation he accepts those who fear him and do what is right. ³⁶ This is the message of Good News for the people of Israel – that there is peace with God through Jesus Christ, who is Lord of all. ³⁷ You know what happened throughout Judea, beginning in Galilee, after John began preaching his message of baptism. ³⁸ And you know that God anointed Jesus of Nazareth with the Holy Spirit and with power. Then Jesus went around doing good and healing all who were oppressed by the devil, for God was with him.

³⁹ 'And we apostles are witnesses of all he did throughout Judea and in Jerusalem. They put him to death by hanging him on a cross, ⁴⁰ but God raised him to life on the third day. Then God allowed him to appear, ⁴¹ not to the general public, but to us whom God had chosen in advance to be his witnesses. We were those who ate and drank with him after he rose from the dead. ⁴² And he ordered us to preach everywhere and to testify that Jesus is the one appointed by God to be the judge of all – the living and the dead. ⁴³ He is the one all the prophets testified about, saying that everyone who believes in him will have their sins forgiven through his name.'

# Key plot points

**Introduction** – The apostles gave witness to Christ the risen Lord.

**v.34–35** – The apostles proclaimed that in Jesus, God had made a way for men and women, boys and girls of every nation, culture, class, and station to have salvation and eternal life in his Kingdom.

**v.42–43** – They entrusted the Gospel to the Church as the words of eternal life.

## Where we end up

Generations of Christians have proclaimed the Gospel of Christ in every nation. One day the Lord will return and gather his people from the whole earth to be with him forever.

## My Reflections

# 88 The Communion of Saints in Church History

**Main Theme**

The Church continues to expand God's Kingdom into every tribe and language and people and nation until he returns.

**Setting**

Multiple, including heaven

**Characters**

John (the one seeing the vision), the Lord, the Church, and the saints of the Lord

**Key Verse: Revelation 5:9–10**

And they sang a new song with these words: 'You are worthy to take the scroll and break its seals and open it. For you were slaughtered, and your blood has ransomed people for God from every tribe and language and people and nation. And you have caused them to become a Kingdom of priests for our God. And they will reign on the earth.'

Christ has paid the price for God's saints from every tribe, language, people, and nation.

# Read the story Revelation 5

[1] Then I saw a scroll in the right hand of the one who was sitting on the throne. There was writing on the inside and the outside of the scroll, and it was sealed with seven seals. [2] And I saw a strong angel, who shouted with a loud voice: 'Who is worthy to break the seals on this scroll and open it?' [3] But no one in heaven or on earth or under the earth was able to open the scroll and read it.

[4] Then I began to weep bitterly because no one was found worthy to open the scroll and read it. [5] But one of the twenty-four elders said to me, 'Stop weeping! Look, the Lion of the tribe of Judah, the heir to David's throne, has won the victory. He is worthy to open the scroll and its seven seals.'

[6] Then I saw a Lamb that looked as if it had been slaughtered, but it was now standing between the throne and the four living beings and among the twenty-four elders. He had seven horns and seven eyes, which represent the sevenfold Spirit of God that is sent out into every part of the earth. [7] He stepped forward and took the scroll from the right hand of the one sitting on the throne. [8] And when he took the scroll, the four living beings and the twenty-four elders fell down before the Lamb. Each one had a harp, and they held gold bowls filled with incense, which are the prayers of God's people. [9] And they sang a new song with these words:

'You are worthy to take the scroll
　　and break its seals and open it.
For you were slaughtered, and your blood has ransomed people
　　　for God
　　from every tribe and language and people and nation.
[10] And you have caused them to become
　　a Kingdom of priests for our God.
　　And they will reign on the earth.'

[11] Then I looked again, and I heard the voices of thousands and millions of angels around the throne and of the living beings and the elders. [12] And they sang in a mighty chorus:

**v.1** – The apostle John has a vision of heaven. God sits on the throne, holding a scroll. The scroll has seven seals and is the will of God.

**v.3** – No one is worthy of opening the scroll.

**v.5** – Jesus, the heir to David's throne, is worthy because of his victory.

**v.7** – Jesus, as the sacrificial lamb, takes the scroll.

**v.9** – Immediately the elders sing, honouring Jesus for paying the price for everyone.

**v.11** – All the angels sing, praising Jesus.

'Worthy is the Lamb who was slaughtered –
  to receive power and riches
and wisdom and strength
  and honour and glory and blessing.'

**v.13** – Every living thing sings, worshipping God.

¹³ And then I heard every creature in heaven and on earth and under the earth and in the sea. They sang:
'Blessing and honour and glory and power
belong to the one sitting on the throne
and to the Lamb for ever and ever.'
¹⁴ And the four living beings said, 'Amen!' And the twenty-four elders fell down and worshipped the Lamb.

## Where we end up

Through the victory of Jesus Christ, the people of God's Kingdom on earth (the Church) proclaim the good news of the Gospel.

## Christian Martyrs (Rome, first to fourth centuries)

'I want to know Christ and experience the mighty power that raised him from the dead. I want to suffer with him, sharing in his death' (Philippians 3:10). Early Christians faced persecution and death at the hands of the Roman Empire. Even being fed to lions could not stop the Church from proclaiming Christ!

## Augustine of Hippo (North Africa, fourth to fifth century)

'Don't copy the behaviour and customs of this world, but let God transform you into a new person by changing the way you think. Then you will learn to know God's will for you, which is good and pleasing and perfect' (Romans 12:2).

Augustine fought for the truth of the Gospel in the face of many false teachers. The enemy has always tried to twist the Scriptures, but the Church has faithfully held to the teachings of the apostles.

## Saint Francis of Assisi (Italy, twelfth to thirteenth century)

'And then he told them, "Go into all the world and preach the Good News to everyone"' (Mark 16:15).

Saint Francis rejected a comfortable life and embraced suffering and difficulty for the sake of the Gospel. Men and women across history have accepted the calling of God to a life of prayer and prophetic witness to the world.

## Martin Luther (Germany, fifteenth to sixteenth century)

'For I am not ashamed of this Good News about Christ. It is the power of God at work, saving everyone who believes – the Jew first and also the Gentile' (Romans 1:16).

Martin Luther stood against Church leaders who abandoned the Gospel in favour of money and power. Reformers have always called the Church back to the Lord.

## Martin Luther King, Jr (United States of America, twentieth century)

'Instead, I want to see a mighty flood of justice, an endless river of righteous living' (Amos 5:24).

Martin Luther King, Jr led oppressed and impoverished people in a fight for justice and equality. He was assassinated for his work. Across history, saints of the Lord have given their lives in pursuit of Christ and his Kingdom.

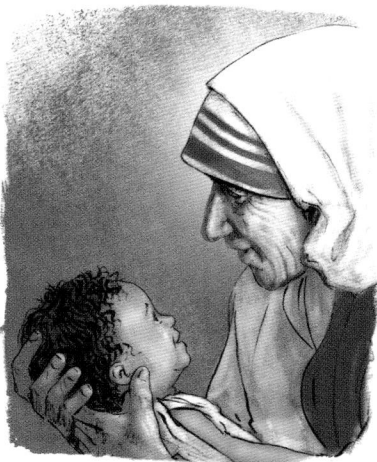

## Mother Teresa of Calcutta (India, twentieth century)

'And the King will say, "I tell you the truth, when you did it to one of the least of these my brothers and sisters, you were doing it to me!"' (Matthew 25:40)

Mother Teresa founded a missionary society that ministers to the needs of some of the sickest, poorest, most broken people in the world. The Church has always sought to minister to the lowest and least in the world with the compassion and love of Jesus.

# The Return of Christ

### Main Theme

Christ is the Saviour who will destroy the devil and deliver humanity from sin and death forever.

### Characters

John (the one seeing the vision), Jesus (a conquering warrior on a white horse), the beast, and the false prophet (enemies of God)

### Key Verse: Revelation 19:11

Then I saw heaven opened, and a white horse was standing there. Its rider was named Faithful and True, for he judges fairly and wages a righteous war.

### Setting

John's vision of the final battle

Christ will come again and destroy death and the evil one forever.

## Read the story Revelation 19

¹ After this, I heard what sounded like a vast crowd in heaven shouting,

'Praise the LORD!
Salvation and glory and power belong to our God.

## Key plot points

**v.1** – A great multitude of people praise the Lord.

² His judgements are true and just.

He has punished the great prostitute
who corrupted the earth with her immorality.
He has avenged the murder of his servants.'

³ And again their voices rang out:

'Praise the LORD!
The smoke from that city ascends for ever and ever!'

⁴ Then the twenty-four elders and the four living beings fell down and worshipped God, who was sitting on the throne. They cried out, 'Amen! Praise the LORD!'
⁵ And from the throne came a voice that said,

'Praise our God,
all his servants,
all who fear him,
from the least to the greatest.'

**v.6–8** – They cry out, 'Praise the Lord!' for the great wedding supper of the Lamb has arrived, and his Bride is ready.

⁶ Then I heard again what sounded like the shout of a vast crowd or the roar of mighty ocean waves or the crash of loud thunder:

'Praise the LORD!
For the Lord our God, the Almighty, reigns.
⁷ Let us be glad and rejoice,
and let us give honour to him.
For the time has come for the wedding feast of the Lamb,
and his bride has prepared herself.
⁸ She has been given the finest of pure white linen to wear.'
For the fine linen represents the good deeds of God's holy
people.

⁹ And the angel said to me, 'Write this: Blessed are those who are invited to the wedding feast of the Lamb.' And he added, 'These are true words that come from God.'
¹⁰ Then I fell down at his feet to worship him, but he said, 'No, don't worship me. I am a servant of God, just like you and your brothers and

sisters who testify about their faith in Jesus. Worship only God. For the essence of prophecy is to give a clear witness for Jesus.'

[11] Then I saw heaven opened, and a white horse was standing there. Its rider was named Faithful and True, for he judges fairly and wages a righteous war. [12] His eyes were like flames of fire, and on his head were many crowns. A name was written on him that no one understood except himself. [13] He wore a robe dipped in blood, and his title was the Word of God. [14] The armies of heaven, dressed in the finest of pure white linen, followed him on white horses. [15] From his mouth came a sharp sword to strike down the nations. He will rule them with an iron rod. He will release the fierce wrath of God, the Almighty, like juice flowing from a winepress. [16] On his robe at his thigh was written this title: King of all kings and Lord of all lords.

[17] Then I saw an angel standing in the sun, shouting to the vultures flying high in the sky: 'Come! Gather together for the great banquet God has prepared. [18] Come and eat the flesh of kings, generals, and strong warriors; of horses and their riders; and of all humanity, both free and slave, small and great.'

[19] Then I saw the beast and the kings of the world and their armies gathered together to fight against the one sitting on the horse and his army. [20] And the beast was captured, and with him the false prophet who did mighty miracles on behalf of the beast – miracles that deceived all who had accepted the mark of the beast and who worshipped his statue. Both the beast and his false prophet were thrown alive into the fiery lake of burning sulphur. [21] Their entire army was killed by the sharp sword that came from the mouth of the one riding the white horse. And the vultures all gorged themselves on the dead bodies.

**v.11, 16** – Jesus comes as a warrior on a white horse to do battle against evil. He is called Faithful and True, the Word of God, and King of all kings and Lord of all lords.

**v.17–18** – An angel announces the destruction of the wicked before the battle even begins.

**v.19** – Under the leadership of the beast, the forces of wickedness draw up battle lines against the Lord.

## Where we end up

Christ's victory is decisive and swift. He conquers God's enemies and throws them into the lake of fire.

## Old Testament Foundation: The Completion and Fulfilment of the Promise

**The Protoevangelium** (Genesis 3:15) – p. 20. With the Second Coming of Jesus Christ to restore all things under the rule of God, the original promise that was given in Genesis after the Fall, was fulfilled. God's promise to overcome evil and destroy the evil one comes to its completion in Christ's final victory.

# 90 The New Heaven and New Earth

**Main Theme**

God brings his Kingdom blessing to all creation forever.

**Setting**

John's vision of a new heaven and a new earth

**Characters**

John (the one seeing the vision), God on his throne, and John's angelic guide

**Key Verse: Revelation 21:3–4**

I heard a loud shout from the throne, saying, 'Look, God's home is now among his people! He will live with them, and they will be his people. God himself will be with them. He will wipe every tear from their eyes, and there will be no more death or sorrow or crying or pain. All these things are gone forever.'

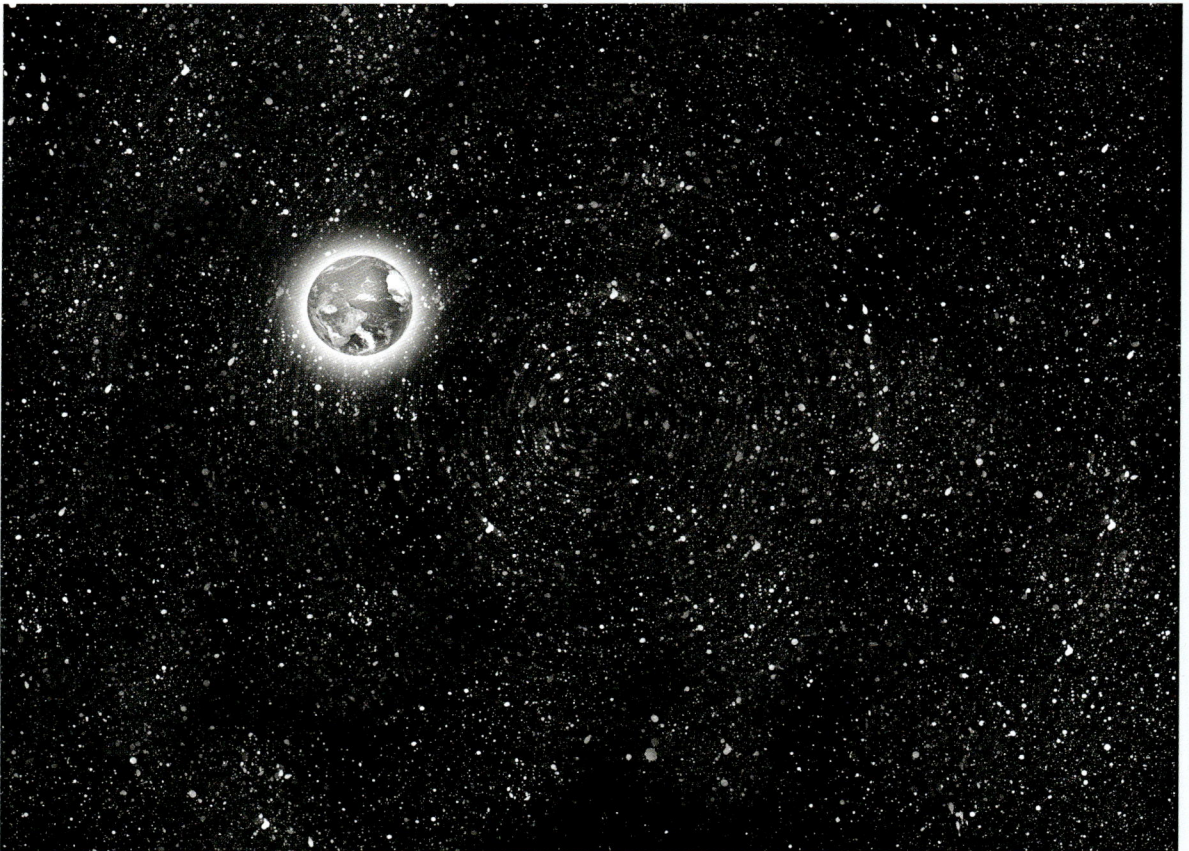

John sees a new heaven and a new earth.

# Read the story Revelation 21:1–7, 22:1–6

## Key plot points

**21** Then I saw a new heaven and a new earth, for the old heaven and the old earth had disappeared. And the sea was also gone. ² And I saw the holy city, the new Jerusalem, coming down from God out of heaven like a bride beautifully dressed for her husband.

³ I heard a loud shout from the throne, saying, 'Look, God's home is now among his people! He will live with them, and they will be his people. God himself will be with them. ⁴ He will wipe every tear from their eyes, and there will be no more death or sorrow or crying or pain. All these things are gone for ever.'

⁵ And the one sitting on the throne said, 'Look, I am making everything new!' And then he said to me, 'Write this down, for what I tell you is trustworthy and true.' ⁶ And he also said, 'It is finished! I am the Alpha and the Omega – the Beginning and the End. To all who are thirsty I will give freely from the springs of the water of life. ⁷ All who are victorious will inherit all these blessings, and I will be their God, and they will be my children.'

…

**22** Then the angel showed me a river with the water of life, clear as crystal, flowing from the throne of God and of the Lamb. ² It flowed down the centre of the main street. On each side of the river grew a tree of life, bearing twelve crops of fruit, with a fresh crop each month. The leaves were used for medicine to heal the nations.

³ No longer will there be a curse upon anything. For the throne of God and of the Lamb will be there, and his servants will worship him. ⁴ And they will see his face, and his name will be written on their foreheads. ⁵ And there will be no night there – no need for lamps or sun – for the Lord God will shine on them. And they will reign for ever and ever.

⁶ Then the angel said to me, 'Everything you have heard and seen is trustworthy and true. The Lord God, who inspires his prophets, has sent his angel to tell his servants what will happen soon.'

**v.1** – John sees a new heaven and a new earth.

**v.2** – The holy city, the New Jerusalem descends from the heaven to the earth.

**v.3** – The voice of God declares from the throne that his eternal dwelling place is among his people.

**v.4** – All signs of sin, the curse, evil, and death are wiped away. God is making all things new.

**v.1** – John sees a river of the water of life flowing from the throne of God and of the Lamb. The water feeds the tree of life that is for the healing of the nations.

**v.4–5** – The servants of God will live forever in his presence, seeing him face to face. The Lord will be their light forever.

## Where we end up

The angel leaves John with the promise of the trustworthiness of his word, and of the imminent return of Christ.

. . . and the story will never end . . .

# The Plotline of the Church Year

Christians developed the Church year as a cycle of retelling and reenacting the Gospel story — the story of Christ and his Kingdom.

**Advent** joyously affirms the First and Second Comings of the Lord, and the sure promise of God that the Deliverer will come and ransom captive Israel and the world. Through the prophets, God foretold the Messiah's appearing to his people, Israel. Through the angels, he announced his birth to Zechariah, Mary, and the shepherds.

**Christmas** celebrates the birth of the Messiah, Jesus, who is the incarnation of the Son of God, Mary's child. He is the word made flesh, the conqueror who enters this fallen world to reveal the Father's love, to destroy the devil's work, and to redeem his people from their sins.

**Epiphany** commemorates the coming of the magi, the wise men from the East who followed the star in search of the Christ child. This season emphasizes Christ's mission to and for the world. The light of God's salvation is revealed to all peoples in the person of Jesus, the Son of God.

**Lent** is a forty-day period starting on Ash Wednesday and ending on Holy Saturday of Holy Week. This season is a time of reflection on Jesus' suffering, crucifixion, and death. Disciples of Christ, embracing his lowliness and humility, seek to share the mind of him who was obedient to death, even death on a cross.

**Kingdomtide**, the season after Pentecost, is a season of Christ's headship, harvest, and hope. As Christus Victor, Jesus is exalted at God's right hand. He is the head of the body, the Church, and he is Lord of the harvest, empowering his people to bear witness to his saving grace in the world and gather the harvest of people. This is a season of the blessed hope, looking toward Christ's return to complete God's salvation for the world.

At **Pentecost** the descent of the Holy Spirit to earth on Christ's believers is remembered, his infilling of the people of God, the Church. Through him, the third person of the Trinity, Jesus our Lord is now present with his people. The Spirit is the guarantee of the promised inheritance to come. The fullness and mystery of God's person and work is celebrated on **Trinity Sunday**.

On **Easter Sunday** the bodily resurrection of Jesus is celebrated. The same lowly Nazarene – he who was betrayed by his own disciple, who suffered under Pilate's cruel gaze, who was crucified on a Roman cross, and who was buried in a borrowed tomb – the same Lord rose triumphantly on the third day. Jesus has risen from death to life through the power of God.

**Ascension** For forty days after his resurrection, Jesus revealed himself alive to his disciples. On the fortieth day, he ascended to heaven to take his place as Lord and Christ at God's right hand. Ten days after this, on the fiftieth day after his resurrection, he would send the promise of the Father – the Holy Spirit.

**Holy Week** recalls the events of our Lord's suffering and death: his triumphant entry into Jerusalem on Palm Sunday, his giving of the commandments on Maundy Thursday, his crucifixion and burial on Good Friday, and the solemn vigil of Saturday night before Easter Sunday.

**Holy Bible**
New Living Translation
Anglicized edition

NLT

**Holy Bible**

ANGLICIZED EDITION

NLT

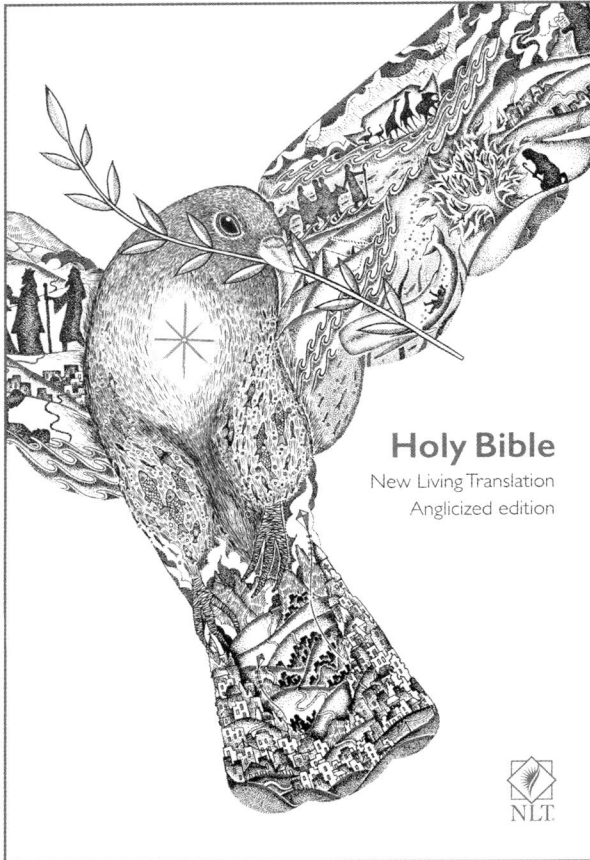

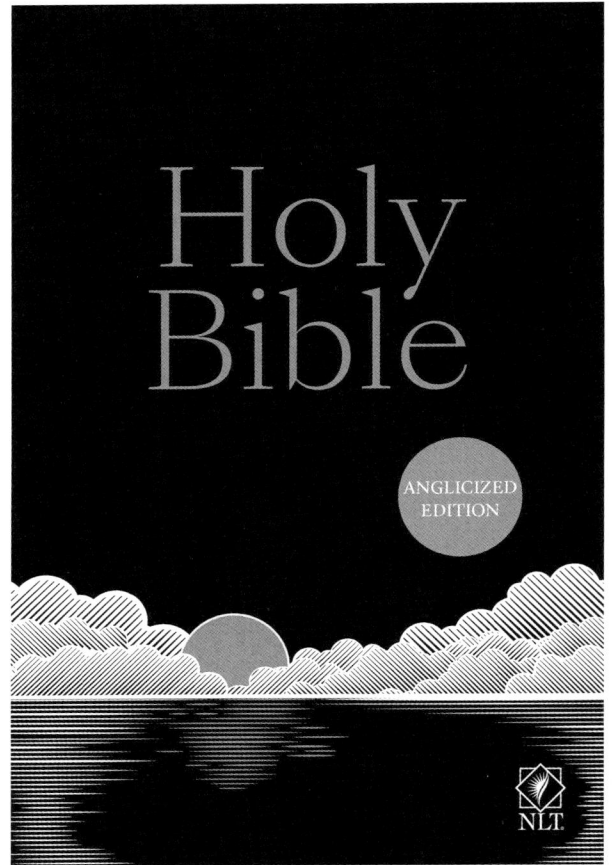

Also available are these complete NLT Holy Bible (anglicized) editions
Flexibound ISBN 9780281079544
Hardback ISBN 9780281079537